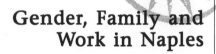

Gender, Family and
Work in Naples

Mediterranea Series

GENERAL EDITOR: Jackie Waldren, *Lecturer at Oxford Brookes University; Research Associate CCCRW, Queen Elizabeth House, Oxford; and Field Co-ordinator, Deya Archaeological Museum and Research Centre, Spain.*

This is a new series which will feature ethnographic monographs and collected works on theoretical approaches to aspects of life and culture in the areas bordering the Mediterranean. Rather than presenting a unified concept of 'the Mediterranean', the aim of the series is to reveal the background and differences in the cultural constructions of social space and its part in patterning social relations among the peoples of this fascinating geographical area.

ISSN: 1354-358X

Other titles in the series:

Gender, Family and Work in Naples

WITHDRAWN

V.A. Goddard

BERG

Oxford • Washington, D.C.

First published in 1996 by
Berg
Editorial offices:
150 Cowley Road, Oxford, OX4 1JJ, UK
13950 Park Center Road, Herndon, VA 22071, USA

Berg is the imprint of Oxford International Publishers Ltd.

Library of Congress Cataloging-in-Publication Data

A catalogue record for this book is available from the Library of
Congress.

British Library Cataloguing-in-Publication Data

A catalogue record for this book is available from the British
Library.

ISBN 1 85973 034 5 (Cloth)
       1 85973 039 6 (Paper)

Printed in the United Kingdom by WBC Bookbinders, Bridgend,
Mid Glamorgan.

To Mary, Joseph and Joaquin

Contents

Acknowledgements

Many people have shown an interest in my research and have shaped and encouraged my work over the years, and I remember them all with gratitude. However, there are a number of people whom I wish to single out. In particular, my gratitude goes to Nunzia Casale for her invaluable help and her equally invaluable friendship. I also wish to thank Enrico Bercioux, Michele Gargiullo, Domenico Liccardo, Domenico Baiano, Lia Santacroce, Franco Capasso, Mario De Rosa, Maria Giuliano, Anna Maria D'Angelo, and all other colleagues and friends at the Naples FILTEA, the Federbracciante and the FLM. I am very grateful to Mr and Mrs Casale, their children and grand-children, to Mr and Mrs Bercioux and family, and to my neighbours in Pianura and Rione Traiano, for their warmth and hospitality. I am also indebted to all those men and women in Naples who were so generous with their time. In Rome, Giuseppina Vittone and Nella Marcellino helped me on my way to Naples. I would also like to thank staff and students of the University of Naples, and at the Centro di Ricerche e Specializzazione per il Mezzogiorno, and the staff at the ISTAT office in Naples.

I owe a great debt of gratitude to Sally Humphries and Rosemary Harris for their invaluable guidance, and to Nigel Colclough and Sandra Wallman for their comments and suggestions as to how I might convert my thesis into a book. Pat Caplan and Luciano Li Causi read extensive sections of the manuscript and made useful criticisms and comments – many of which I have, unfortunately, been unable to address in the final text. Saundra Satterlee made helpful suggestions regarding the introduction. I am also grateful to Jackie Waldren for her contagious enthusiasm and to David Phelps for his patience and his interesting and erudite comments. My friends and colleagues at Goldsmiths College have been unfaltering in their support, and students have been a constant source of inspiration. I would mention, especially, Josep Llobera, Olivia Harris, Brian Morris, Stephen Nugent, Nici Nelson, Cris Shore, Sophie Day and Jean Besson. Jenny Gault, Marilyn Stead and Tabitha Springhall provided invaluable support. I am grateful to the Social Science Research Council, the University of London and Goldsmiths College for financing different stages of this work. Finally, my thanks go to Joaquin, Guillem and Ignasi for their considerable patience during the final stages of preparation of this text.

Part I

Life and Work in the City of Naples

Introduction

Having grown up in Argentina, a peripheral country which had placed its hopes for development on attracting migrants from the impoverished regions of Europe, I found my childhood environment dotted with landmarks which spoke of distant places. None seemed closer than Naples. References to Capri, to Vesuvius, to Napoli were an integral part of the urban landscape. Images of these places filtered through the neighbourhood, the music and the food of daily life. Naples was also the place from which so many people had come or from where their grandparents had set sail to build a new life in the then prosperous Americas.

Much later, I was impressed by M.T. Macciocchi's account of her impressions of Naples (1973). I was particularly interested in her description of the women who for generations had worked from their homes, linked to the world market yet never leaving their own neighbourhood. I had been thinking about the relationship between gender, family and work for some time, and was looking for a way to explore the relationships between these, and it was Macciocchi's account which made me settle for outwork as the focus of my doctoral research.

On reaching Italy in the mid-1970s I discovered that outwork and subcontracting were at the centre of debates involving many academics, politicians and trade unionists. Several research projects had attempted to quantify the extent of the phenomenon of subcontracting (Frey 1973) and more localized studies had described the mechanisms through which subcontracting operated (Brusco 1975; Botta *et al.*, n.d.; Crespi *et al.* 1975; Cutrufelli 1975; De Marco and Talamo 1976). These works confirmed my initial hypothesis that subcontracting and outwork responded to contemporary conditions of both local and global markets as well as systems of production, rather than being survivals from earlier stages of development. They also indicated that family and gender were important dimensions here, in that they contributed to the creation of specific pockets of workers.

In Rome I was warmly welcomed and encouraged by members of

3

the trade union to pursue my research on outwork. I accepted their invitation to visit Naples – which included a tour of the old city, where indeed, just as Macciocchi had described, women sat at their sewing machines, occasionally looking out on to the narrow streets from their doorways – and this convinced me that Naples should be my first port of call. My original intention had been to look into two different localities and so compare the organization and impact of subcontracting in two different contexts. However, as time passed, I found it difficult to leave Naples. Personal commitments persuaded me to stay for longer than I had intended, and to postpone indefinitely any plans to research another city.

Part of the original attraction of Naples was that, in spite of its unfamiliar setting, it was still quite familiar because the Neapolitan diaspora had shaped the environment in which I grew up in Latin America. A more practical consideration was that Naples appeared to be an accessible environment. In particular the outworkers, whom I had expected to be relatively invisible, were here almost literally on the streets. This seemed to be an initial advantage of considerable importance. I was not mistaken. I found Neapolitans to be extremely welcoming and friendly, willing to talk and put their views forward on almost any subject that might be broached. Furthermore, those outworkers who lived in the *bassi*[1] were the most accessible members of a very inaccessible category and they were generally quite willing to grant interviews.

This does not mean that there were no problems in the research. Anthropological research in a city involves dealing with quite specific conditions. These make for difficulties in defining a relevant unit of study, in gaining access to informants as well as in defining oneself within the research setting. One possible solution to these problems is to concentrate on one area or neighbourhood of a city and treat this as a kind of village or community.[2] I decided not to follow this path, given that the questions I was interested in could not be contained within a neighbourhood study. On the other hand, by concentrating on outworkers I created some fiction of an 'object of analysis' which kept me (albeit loosely) focused for much of the time and allowed me to legitimize my inquiries in the eyes of the people of the city.

Given the interest and support of the trade union and their concern to set up links with outworkers and organize them, I thought it best to find informants through them. Furthermore, very early on I had made some acquaintances whose contacts with outworkers would putatively enable them to arrange meetings, interviews and so on. But as the days and then the weeks passed, I realized that the only way ahead was to contact these workers on my own. So, ignoring the warnings proffered by concerned friends against venturing on my own into the old city, I set out to find an outworker who would be willing to talk to me. The first success was followed by many days of walking through the narrow streets or *vicoli*, peering as discreetly as I could into the doorways in search of workers or listening out for the hum of the sewing machine, often following the sound along passages and up stairs to its source. Of course, many of these expeditions were unsuccessful.

Often, the women I approached refused me an interview on the grounds that they were too busy or that they would risk their jobs by talking to me. I found these to be absolutely valid and convincing reasons for not talking to me, yet I still surprised myself when, as time went by and I had clocked up many miles of *vicolo* walking, I found myself reacting with a certain amount of indignation when my request for an interview was turned down. It was as though I felt I had achieved the right to be there, knocking on the doors of complete strangers! But the outright refusals were few and far between and they were completely overshadowed by the hospitality, time and patience offered to me by the majority of women and men who did agree to talk to me. Their generosity and hospitality made my stay in Naples an enjoyable and engrossing experience.

Much of the information I wanted at the time was about how much people produced, how much they were paid, what were the mechanisms behind the system into which they were locked. It therefore seemed opportune to devise a questionnaire. The first version of this questionnaire covered everything from how many units each worker produced to whether they were baptized. After one week I replaced this questionnaire with a shortened version. I noticed, however, that my constant scribbling puzzled people, as did my frequent referral to the questions on the form. Furthermore, the questions were perceived as something of a strait-jacket. So after a further week or two the questionnaire was abandoned completely and I limited my scribbles to noting figures or other such details. After each interview, I went home and typed up the day's events. This meant that I was unable to carry out more than one interview a day, but the advantages were many. Having obtained a minimum amount of structured information, I encouraged the interviewees to speak for themselves. Each had a story to tell, and in retrospect it was this story that I have found to be the most interesting.

One of the difficulties of urban research of this kind is that every day meant starting anew. There were some families and contacts with whom a relationship was established and where a dynamic was set up independent of myself. But my continuing interest in outworkers and then small enterprises meant that I was forced to search for new informants and to knock on the door of strangers day after day, hoping that I would not be refused. Apart from these emotional and physical demands, there was also the problem of setting up and justifying second and third visits, let alone maintaining contacts over a long period of time.

Scouting around the streets of the old city was one strategy I pursued to obtain interviews. A second one was to use the personal networks of friends and trade union colleagues, which started to open up to me after a number of months. These networks gave me access to outworkers I could never find on my own, who lived in the suburbs, in flats, or who lived and worked behind closed doors, invisible to the outsider. Sometimes the quality of these interviews was different from the street contacts I made on my own because they were set up by mutual friends and the occasion could double as a social meeting. Many of these people became friends. Contact with them was complex because we were involved in the same networks, and information regarding both themselves and myself flowed in several directions, and was not restricted to the immediate and direct exchanges which took place between us.

The content of the interviews therefore varied considerably. Whereas some were only able to grant a short interview, others took advantage of the presence of an interested audience to expound on a number of topics and give a detailed account of their lives. Interviews with women generally went better when there were no men present. This was partly because, in the absence of husbands and fathers in particular, women were less inhibited, and partly because the majority of men found it hard to accept that they were not expected to take centre stage.[3]

One of the problems of researching activities in the informal sector is that, because of legal invisibility, people are sensitive to the risks involved in giving information. In any case there was a clear awareness of the links between information and power, and by divulging certain details about work or private lives, they might be placing themselves in a vulnerable position. But where illegal activities are involved, this awareness is far more acute and the risks are graver. The case of outworkers was not helped by the threats of many entrepreneurs to take retaliatory action against any worker who did give away information that they felt could be damaging to their interests. This meant that informants frequently avoided giving certain information; and it is also probable that they might give me incorrect information. However, a number of close friendships with men and women who were experienced in this area helped to clarify these matters and provided parameters of plausibility against which I could assess informants' statements. Judging from their comments, it is likely that many people had their own agenda when providing information and accounts about themselves. Some may have exaggerated the burden of their work and the drudgery of their lives or dwelt on particular issues they felt were relevant to themselves. Not infrequently, people assumed or hoped that I could intervene in their favour to help a relative get a job in the *comune* or local government, in spite of my attempts to explain the powerlessness of my status. This might have skewed our conversation towards issues to do with employment, health and so on. But on the whole the majority of accounts were plausible portraits of working people living in the difficult circumstances of a city such as Naples.

The focus on data concerning rates of production, incomes, and hours of work provided some sense of solidity and allowed for some comparisons and generalizations. However, over time there were other issues which seemed as central as the questions concerning production volumes, or credit facilities. These concerned more personal aspects of people's biography, their attitudes and feelings toward the family and marriage, sexuality or procreation. These areas are difficult to research and generally only surfaced in conversations with particular individuals and under specific circumstances. Although questions of sexuality, for example, gained importance in my work, they were not pursued as systematically as other areas of research. Insights, explanations and reactions generally came from closer friends and were more deeply explored with women than with men. The outcomes of these discussions cannot be generalized and are clearly not representative of all Neapolitan men and women. Instead, the statements of informants and friends, the accounts of their experiences, their reactions to the experience of others including my own, have been dealt with in an exploratory way and analysed in the light of the findings of others who have specialized in the field of psychosexual relations (see Chapter 10).

But the shift in interest away from what appeared to be the safe and more tangible data on production and incomes towards issues of subjectivity raised a difficult emotional and ethical problem. Most of the data were obtained on the relatively clearly negotiated basis of an interview where the interviewees were briefed about the purposes of the research and their contribution to it. In a few cases life histories were recorded on tape. These frequently referred to different aspects of the intimate experiences of the individuals concerned. But much of the material concerning more personal issues, particularly in the areas of courtship, marriage and sexuality, emerged from conversations held in non-formalized circumstances. Within such circumstances those who provided the information were acting as friends rather than informants. It was difficult to neglect this information; yet it was equally difficult to see it as 'data'. The problem seems to originate with the fact that at the time of conducting the research, even I did not perceive those situations as 'research-defined '. Unavoidably, these insights would inform my understanding of Neapolitan men and women and their relationships to each other. But blurred distinctions between participant-observation, participation and mere observation were unclear and unstated at the time of research, and were to cause some difficulties at the time of writing up.

Some Observations Regarding the Anthropology of the Mediterranean

For many anthropologists Naples would be unproblematically located within the Mediterranean ethnographic area. In spite of an early characterization of the area as highly urbanized (Kenny 1963; Pitkin 1963), it is also an area of research which, as Kenny and Kertzer pointed out in 1983, has produced few urban ethnographies. The situation has not altered substantially. The paucity of urban research has meant that generalizations concerning 'the Mediterranean' have been based on studies of small rural communities. This has meant that much of what has been claimed by anthropologists as typifying the area has little resonance in studies of urban situations. The first and most obvious issue is the emphasis on 'communities'. This concept referred to small-scale populations characterized by face-to-face relations which putatively had their own specific socio-cultural characteristics. The use of 'community' is problematic, not least for studies of the city. But interestingly, the concept has been central not only within anthropology but also within political discourse, moulding legislation and public opinion. It therefore remains a central idea within this work, although this is a community in the 'imagined' sense rather than an unproblematic and clearly bounded entity (Anderson 1983).

The second area which is problematic within Mediterranean anthropology relates quite directly to the contents of this book. Mediterranean anthropology has long rested on the assumption of the generalized and shared values of honour and shame. These values were seen as important factors in the negotiation of status in face-to-face communities. An emphasis on values has all too often resulted in simplistic accounts of social phenomena. In the specific case of Naples, it fails to grasp the complexity of urban forms and the contradictory nature of social values and social behaviour. Thus much of what I found to hold in Naples was at odds with what the literature on honour and shame claimed as characteristic for the area.

A related aspect here is the question of cultural homogeneity and consensus. Although Pitt-Rivers (1974) and Davis (1973) recognized the impact of class position on the performance and implications of the honour code, the general thrust of the honour and shame literature has been towards the assumption of universally held values. This was of course compatible with the consensus model of society which dominated structural functionalist anthropology. In Italy, on the other hand, the influence of Gramsci informed the work of folklorists and ethnologists such as De Martino, who were acutely aware of the cultural discontinuities and of the power relations that underpin social relations. De Martino's approach was critical of the equilibrium model promoted by Malinowski's school of anthropology and instead concerned itself with the analysis of the culture of 'subaltern groups' (De Martino 1949).

The concept of 'subaltern groups' is derived from Gramsci's work and recognizes the complex relationship that exists between dominant and dominated, whereby the dominated exercise a degree of cultural autonomy while at the same time undergoing the shaping influence of the culture of the dominant groups. Because the history of subaltern groups is intertwined with the history of civil society and of the State, neither can these groups be studied in isolation from wider economic and political processes, nor can we assume homogeneity and continuity between these groups and the wider society. Instead, there are contradictory trends to take into account: the assimilation of the cultural and political formations of the State and civil society on the one hand and the tendency towards rejecting these formations; the experience of encapsulation and the struggle for autonomy (Gramsci 1973: 52–3).

It is important to bear these observations in mind when considering the anthropology of the Mediterranean, given that these are class societies of great complexity and which furthermore display significant regional discontinuities. In the case of Italy, regional differences are pertinent to any analysis of social processes; and in the case of Naples there are the specificities of the social structure and the history of the South to take into account. History impinges on people's lives and informs the ways people construct meaning concerning their experiences and their society.

Gender, Work and the Family

In Gramsci's work the question of power and inequality was not restricted to classes or groups. He also stressed the importance of gender for the creation of a new civil order. Gramsci considered that it was just as important for women to acquire a new sense of self and a new way of conceiving their role in sexual relations as it was for them to be materially autonomous from men. In spite of Gramsci's influence on the Italian left and progressive academic and political circles, this early observation was not fully addressed until the late 1960s, when Italian feminists made the exploration of the subjective construction of gender identities through consciousness-raising the centre-piece of their political project.

Women's movements in Italy have a much longer history of course, as do interventions regarding 'the woman question' in Italian political culture (Togliatti 1973; Seroni 1977). But these tended to focus on the emancipatory aspects of the question, fighting for equality in the law and at work. What Italian women came to argue was that although they had achieved victories concerning their legal rights and their political status, they continued to be oppressed (Kemp and Bono 1993: 5).[4] Whilst not denying the significance of legal equality, many feminists argued that the question of subjectivity was central for understanding, and changing, the relations between men and women. They also stressed that women had to play the key role in this transformation of themselves and their society; they had to become the subjects rather than the objects of 'the woman question' (Kemp and Bono 1993: 6). This dual perspective on gender has been adopted in this book. Whilst considering the material conditions that encompass the actions and choices of men and women, I have also explored some of the subjective conditions which reproduce and/or subvert dominant views of gender.

Work has been a central concern and an important measure of the 'emancipation' of women, a common index being the relative presence of women in the labour-market. In the 1970s Italian debates regarding the labour-market revolved largely around the question of the 'fragmentation' of the labour-market (Paci 1973, 1982). In particular the question of women and the labour-market was frequently linked to the progress or otherwise of the informal sector (Frey *et al.* 1976; May 1977).

At that time, women's presence in the labour-market was declining. There were, broadly, two ways of explaining this: either the women were not coming forward as workers or they were not being offered employment. For some, women had voluntarily withdrawn from the market because rising incomes had diminished the need for additional sources of income (De Meo 1970). This had meant that the old could retire earlier, the young could continue studying for longer, and women could return to the home. A problem with this was that women were not withdrawing at a greater rate where incomes were higher, but rather where incomes were lower, in the underdeveloped South. Another hypothesis was that changes in productivity had made some categories of worker redundant while the labour-market privileged the 'strong' or 'central' labour of adult males with experience and relatively high educational qualifications (De Cecco 1972). The 'discouraged' workers (women, the old, the very young, the unqualified) withdrew from the labour-market, many of them finding alternative employment in the informal sector, where their participation in the economy remained invisible (La Malfa and Vinci 1970). The weakness of women workers was attributed to cultural definitions of gender roles and the role of women within the family, which limited their choices and impinged on their working lives (Paci 1980). It was also the case that women tended to be concentrated in certain industries such as textiles and garments, which had suffered particularly from changing markets and changing conditions of production.[5]

Since the early 1970s the negative trend in women's presence in the labour-market has been reversed. But the increase recorded for women's employment has been paralleled by a rise in their unemployment relative to men. Another contradictory trend has been the decline in the prevalence of young women in the labour-market, matched by a greater presence of married women. Bettio attributes both these phenomena to what she sees as 'a fundamental development affecting the economy of the family' (1988: 195). The intervention of the State has been important here because it has restricted the use of child labour through legislation and the extension of education, and has provided welfare support and health care. Because families have become less dependent on the contributions of children and more reliant on parental earnings, there has been a shift of emphasis from women's reproductive role in the household towards their employment.

Bettio, like Paci, sees women's participation in the labour-market as intrinsically linked to their role within the family. Changes in family organization and family strategies are associated with greater involvement of women in work. On the other hand, continuities in the domestic responsibilities of women predispose them to work in the informal sector. As Bettio points out, changes in the role of children are also important here, although by concentrating on the material aspects of the parent–child relationship Bettio underestimates the ideological and emotional significance of having children. These subjective factors are crucially important in Naples. However, the emotional value of children does not mean that reproductive behaviour in Naples has been impervious to change. But it does mean that changes have to be understood in terms of a number of factors, including changing expectations regarding children's own future achievements and happiness. In other words, many 'reproductive' decisions and behaviours are less instrumental than Bettio's analysis allows for.

However Bettio's claim that the employment of women, and especially married women, in informal activities is a consequence of what she calls 'distinctive family patterns', is generally borne out. In fact, in some areas of Italy, notably the Centre and North, family forms have been identified as the basis of an extensive informal economy which relies on small enterprises (Paci 1980). Over time, the distinction between the official economy, where workers have legal rights and where there are mechanisms to protect these rights, and the informal economy, where these rights are irrelevant, has become sharper. The burden caused by the shortage of jobs and the inadequacy of State support is borne by individual families. Pooling what income is available is one strategy for coping with this situation and Bettio estimates that in Italy 72–88 per cent of families in poorer social groups pool their incomes, providing a safety net for the unemployed and their dependants. But the price to pay is the continuing or indeed increasing pressure on women to uphold the family and maintain these networks and relationships.[6]

In the background of Bettio's analysis lurks a historical model of transformation of the family from forms associated with pre-capitalist agrarian societies, where it is frequently a productive unit, towards forms which are compatible with a market economy. These changes from a family to a wage-labour system have meant that institutions outside the family, such as the State and the market, have progressively taken over the family's role of coordinating production and reproduction. The view that the family loses important functions to the market or the State is compatible with Polanyi's classification of economic systems and with Talcott-Parsons' approach to the analysis of the family in industrial societies, both of which have been influential in shaping academic and political views of the family and the economy in industrial societies. These views were also dominant within Italian debates during the 1960s, but were subsequently revised during the 1970s and 1980s.

The revision responded to clear indications in the statistical record that development and change in Italy had not deprived the family of its economic functions. On the contrary, at certain times such functions have been encouraged by both economic and political conditions. For example, Fascism accentuated the economic role of the family by encouraging subsistence practices and supporting small family-based enterprises in industry, agriculture and services. In the post-war period, land reform increased the number of small family-based agricultural units from 47.4 per cent of all cultivated land in 1949 to 57.4 per cent in 1970 (Vicarelli 1987: 136). The recession which affected Italy during the 1970s further reinforced the importance of family and kin-based enterprises. The State played a significant role, for it allowed or even fomented the creation of spaces for the expansion of small units in the informal sector, by maintaining a lax approach to irregularities in the fiscal contributions of companies, and to the illegal employment of workers as well as the employment of illegal categories of workers such as children. Whereas in the Centre and North-east there is evidence that informalization has declined, and with it a heavy reliance on family labour, because of an economic take-off based on small enterprises (Vicarelli 1987; Capecchi 1989), in other parts of the country the family continues to be an important focus for survival strategies (cf. Mingione 1983) as well as for the mobilization of political influence and resources (Gribaudi 1980). In the early 1990s 13.2 per cent of Italian families are involved in some way in the ownership and operation of an enterprise, and these are defined by some as 'entrepreneurial families'.[7]

Fascism imposed a predominantly reproductive role on women. Much later, in the second half of the 1960s, a combination of circumstances again reinforced the role of women as wives and mothers. The declining efficiency of public services was one of the factors that led to the withdrawal of women from the labour-market. This was a result of their attempt to maintain the standard of living of their families, which had improved during the 1950s boom, by investing more time and energy in domestic work and self-provisioning. It was during this period that women's identity as housewives was consolidated and this was furthermore ideologically denied any productive content. A separation of production and reproduction entailed a view of the family as separate from society and as a refuge from the economy (Bimbi 1985). Such a view strengthened cultural perceptions of women as mothers and housewives, which were simultaneously being challenged by new definitions of womanhood, by women's demands for emancipatory policies and legislation, and the new possibilities opened up for women by a more developed and more effective educational system (Vicarelli 1987: 140, 142).

The privileging of motherhood and domesticity predisposed women towards engaging in informalized work such as outwork because it allowed them to strike a compromise between economic needs and their primary obligations as housewives. At the same time, this contributed to the creation of an important pool of labour for small or large firms to draw upon.

But the subsequent re-entry of women into the labour-market did not displace the ideals of women as mothers and carers. On the contrary, research indicates that housewives and women wage-earners spend a comparable number of hours on housework

(Vicarelli 1987: 143).

In the Neapolitan case the centrality of ideas concerning the family and the mobilization of solidarity through kinship was true of many households and indeed groups of households who might be linked through exchange networks aimed at providing assistance to those in need. In this book I suggest that the household is an important focus for strategies which are perceived as deriving from natural duties and reciprocal obligations. This does not imply that households are in fact based on natural and reciprocal arrangements and that reciprocity is unproblematic here. On the contrary, the examples discussed in this book exemplify the unequal distribution of time and resources between household members, and the differential impact that household strategies have on household members.[8] The creation of a small enterprise, which for many was an attractive alternative to other forms of employment or underemployment, relied on family relationships and ideologies. These were particularly important for the mobilization of labour, contacts and support. In spite of the apparent autonomy of small enterprises and of the sense of independence expressed by many entrepreneurs, they were frequently linked into subcontracting chains which rendered them vulnerable and dependent. To compete and survive, many entrepreneurs took advantage of the flexible nature of family and kin relations in addition to handing out work to outworkers, most of whom were women. But although family and kinship relations provided the networks and the concrete elements such as labour or capital for outwork and micro-enterprises, there were other aspects of kinship which should not be neglected. These were to do with ideologies regarding the nature of the family and the qualities attaching to gender identities. A fuller understanding of individual and household strategies requires a consideration of the ideas and sentiments as well as the goals and material calculations which direct and inform them.[9]

Gender and the Construction of Identities

To approach the issues of gender identity and subjectivity I started by looking at the Mediterranean literature on honour and shame to find some guidelines for exploring the place of gender ideals within social relations. Although here again the emphasis has all too often been on consensus and cultural homogeneity, discussions of honour and shame raised important questions regarding the role of sexuality and gender within social relations. What was important in this literature was that it placed gender, and female sexuality in particular, at the centre of the analysis. This was because they were identified as central elements in the construction and negotiation of reputations, not only of women but also of men and of entire groups. The early work on honour and shame in particular is disappointing in that the emphasis is on codes of behaviour and values, which are almost exclusively male. Whereas Davis (1973) recognized that honourable behaviour for men and women differed, most of the literature collapsed the issues of honour and male reputation. This relegated women to a passive role, which was seen as a burden for men, for 'once the responsibility (of women) in this matter has been delegated, the woman remains with her own responsibility alleviated' (Pitt-Rivers 1974). Women's honour or reputation was therefore a resource which was controlled and manipulated by men. There was little space then in this type of analysis for an analysis of women in society other than as passive and subordinate. Understanding of men was also limited by reducing male behaviour to the pursuit of honour, which provided scant opportunity to consider male subjectivity and actions as complex and dynamic rather than as a mere code-sponsored response.

Whether or not a concern with honour and shame is generalized within the Mediterranean area or whether it is restricted to this area alone are both contentious questions. Manifestations of ideologies of group honour which rely on a symbolic privileging of women's chastity are widespread. In many cases these concerns have been seen as an integral aspect of the creation and reproduction of hierarchies (Yalman 1967; Martinez-Alier 1972). In the Mediterranean on the other hand, emphasis has been on competition for and protection of resources and patrimony in a more egalitarian context (Schneider 1971; Blok 1981).[10] A concern with honour was seen as originating from the uncertainties of pastoralist society, which persisted in the face of a State which was unable or unwilling to fully incorporate these groups and regions. But the regions under scrutiny have long been part of larger political and economic systems, a fact that is acknowledged and explored in J. and P. Schneider's work (1976), which in fact sees the code of honour as a reactive cultural mechanism to defend communities against encroachment.

But these analyses beg the question of why women should be the focus of cultural elaborations which often are to do with male hierarchies. Schneider addressed this when she proposed that 'men not only want to control the sexuality of women; women are for them a convenient focus, the most likely symbol around which to organise solidary groups . . .' (Schneider 1971: 22). More recent work has developed aspects of her argument. Giovannini (1981), for example, argues that women are used in symbolic elaboration because of their physical characteristics. She identifies six female figures, some of which have positive while others carry negative meaning. The 'virgin' in particular offers a kind of 'cognitive map' for the family by representing its boundaries and internal unity. There are a number of limitations in Giovannini's analysis, not least the direct link she draws between women's bodies and the content of the symbols which are derived from them. Although women's bodies are undoubtedly material entities, they are also symbolically constructed.

Nevertheless, there is an interesting connection here between the work of the Schneiders, of Giovannini and others working in the Mediterranean and the insights offered by the work of Mary Douglas (1966), for whom bodies, and especially female bodies, can be used as a model for the unity and distinctiveness of social groups. Concerns about the limits of the body and therefore anxieties regarding incursions into the body, such as that involved in sexual intercourse, reflect concerns and anxieties regarding the limits of the social unit. The body can thus become a symbol for and a means of conceptualizing social and cultural boundaries.

On the other hand, there is also a potential link here with recent work on ethnicity and nationalism, where gender and family are important in the symbolic construction of boundaries. Here again, it is women and women's bodies that tend to provide symbols and images which speak of social and cultural identities. This book explores some of the ways in which ideas of womanhood become entwined with group identities and the impact of this on the material realities of individual men and women. Taking my cue from the emphasis on gender and sexuality in the Mediterranean literature as well as from the statements of informants and my own observations of life in Naples, questions of sexuality and subjectivity are examined in order to offer a contribution to the understanding of these important links between women and social identities.

Chapter Overview

While the contributions of Mediterranean anthropology have provided a stimulus to the exploration of a number of issues within the Neapolitan context, the limitations of this literature have also had to be tackled. In particular, the neglect of wider economic and political processes and the relative paucity of historical analysis have seriously limited the contribution of anthropologists in the area.[11] In the first section of this book, some aspects of these processes have been examined. Chapter 2 examines some of the economic factors that have contributed to Italy's particular development trajectory, and especially the regional differentiation which characterizes the country to this day. These chapters also aim at locating and contextualizing the interview material which is presented in subsequent chapters. This is vital, because the bulk of interviews were carried out during the late 1970s, so that it is particularly important to understand them as part of a historical process. In retrospect, the period covered by the interviews appears as a particularly significant one, since these were simultaneously years of economic crisis which, also, paradoxically, marked the initiation of a process of development which during the 1980s placed Italy amongst the top-ranking industrial powers of the world.

The question of underdevelopment is central when discussing southern Europe, southern Italy or Naples. Studies of underdevelopment have included political issues as well as the economic mechanisms which generate regional differentiation. In particular cultural orientations or political cultures have been the focus of some explanations or accounts of underdevelopment. This was the case of many studies inspired by a modernization perspective, such as Foster's work in Yucatan (1965) or, for Italy, Banfield's study of Montegrano (1958). A more rigorous approach was suggested in the debates concerning 'marginality', principally evolved in the context of Latin American underdevelopment. Chapter 3 introduces the Neapolitan context through a discussion of attitudes towards 'the political', which challenges assumptions regarding the political ideologies of those excluded from formal employment and who live in conditions of economic underprivilege. In particular the chapter rejects claims that such sectors of the population are by nature passive and incapable of contesting government and power.

In Chapter 4 the urban context is seen as providing different kinds of space which in turn offer different opportunities for and impose specific limits on household strategies. It is important to emphasize that in spite of continuities there are also significant discontinuities in the characteristics of different areas of the city. These are considered by focusing on a sample of households that reside in different areas of the city.

Outwork and petty entrepreneurship are considered in Chapters 5 and 6 as outcomes both of individual initiative and of household strategy. The working histories of outworkers are discussed in Chapter 5 by looking at individual cases of outworkers in a number of trades. This material raises a number of issues relating to household structure, gender ideals and the importance of kinship in shaping the lives of women. An in-depth study of cultural attitudes and individual strategies focuses on an examination of small enterprises. This considers the biography of petty entrepreneurs and the history of a sample of small enterprises. The interrelationships between cultural orientations, individual aspirations, social context and economic possibilities are exemplified through these cases. The pursuit of autonomy appears to be as important a motivation for starting an independent enterprise as the material considerations concerning the scarcity of employment opportunities in Naples. Women too might aspire to greater economic autonomy; but a combination of factors creates very different opportunities for men and women within the economic domain.

Having set out the material context within which men and women in Naples are active, Part II explores the more subjective aspects of gender and sexuality, which nonetheless impinge on the performance of men and women in a material context. In Chapter 7 consideration is given to the effects of courtship, marriage and sexuality on individual choices and opportunities. The question of women's sexuality is one that is frequently referred to in connection with the sphere of work and in the definition of appropriate spheres of action for both men and women. The exploration of ethnographic material in this chapter suggests that the situation of women alters according to the different stages of the life-cycle. It also shows that in Naples at least the situation is far more fluid and contradictory than we are led to expect by the literature on honour and shame.

The family is explored both as a set of relationships within which gendered subjects are produced and as an important locus for the elaboration of wider identities, in this case Neapolitan identity. Motherhood is identified both as an important symbol of group identity, as a dominant figure within the family and as a symbolic parameter in the construction of male and female subjectivities. Thus, the chapters which constitute Part II discuss the question of gender and identity from somewhat different perspectives while emphasizing the importance of family and kinship. This discussion is aimed at exploring the subjective conditions which impinge on individuals in their complex interaction with the material circumstances of their environment.

In Chapter 8 familism is considered as an important element within local social relations. At the same time this chapter recognizes the important changes which have taken place in attitudes to family, childhood and marriage, and that these changes respond to a number of factors. Familism may result from the material and symbolic importance of the family at a local level; but it is also constructed by State legislation and the ideological interventions of the Church. However, the privileged position of the family within both local and hegemonic discourses replicates its importance as a focus for individual and group identity. This is examined in connection with the emphasis on the hospitality and reciprocity which are seen as characteristic of family relationships and are significantly embodied in the preparation, in the offering and in the consumption of food.

While the family may be central to a number of individual and household strategies and constitute the material and/or ideological basis of many economic activities, it is also central to forging the subjectivities of the men and women who people and transform the city. Chapter 9 discusses ethnographic material in relation to the important work of Anne Parsons, who carried out research in Naples in the 1950s. Her work confirms the importance of motherhood within the family in the construction of male and female identities. The practical importance of mothers is matched by their ideological significance. The issue of wider identities is discussed again in Chapter 10, drawing on anthropological work which considers the role of kinship in generating and perpetuating social memory and group identity. It concludes that both ideological and material aspects must be seen as integral to the construction of identities and to the various ways in which Neapolitan men and women negotiate their relationships with their social reality.

Notes

1. *Bassi* are street-level dwellings which frequently have a single door with glass panes. Furthermore, the doors are often the only opening to the street, so that they are often left open. This makes for a great deal of visibility of the home and for little distance between the home and the street.
2. See T. Belmonte's study of a Neapolitan neighbourhood (1979).
3. Around 100 semi-structured interviews were held, out of which 60 were used in systematic comparisons regarding outworkers, independent workers and factory workers. The remaining interviews, along with conversations, group discussions and material gained through participant observation fed into these comparisons or expanded the observations derived from them. In about 10% of interviews, some form of follow-up was possible.
4. It is worth pointing out however that there has been a striking continuity in legislation from the Fascist period to the liberal republic which was hardly favourable to women. See Caldwell (1978).
5. Distribution of women in industry: see Padoa-Scioppa (1977).
6. See the work of E. Mingione (1983, 1985), who analyses the strategies of the poor in the South, and the consequences of these for individuals, families and the State. See also Pugliese and Pinnarò (1985) for a discussion of resistance to informalization in Naples.
7. A study carried out for the Banca d'Italia by Giovanni D'Alessio on 'The diffusion of enterprise ownership' also indicated the regional differences in family enterprise distribution. The majority of entrepreneurs live in the North (21.8%); 16.4% live in the Centre, whereas only 14.9% live in the

South (quoted in R. Petrini, 'Diciotto famiglie su 100 con le mani nelle imprese', *la Repubblica*, 18 January 1995: 38).

8. See O. Harris (1981).

9. The literature on gender and development has been particularly sensitive to the interplay of material relations and ideological constructs. See for example D. Elson and R. Pearson (1981, 1988); IDS Bulletin (1981); Mitter (1994). For outwork see in particular L. Beneria and M. Roldán (1991).

10. The control of women's sexuality (and the code of honour is one derivative of this concern) can be seen as a means of controlling marriage and through this, access to property. A high value placed on virginity is likely to be associated with societies with 'diverging devolution', i.e. societies where women inherit property as well as men (Goody and Tambiah 1973).

Although the control of property is no doubt an important consideration, it is worth noting that Pitt-Rivers argues that the local Andalusian aristocracy, the propertied class *par excellence,* was relatively free from the constraints on sexuality that prevailed for the lower classes. For the aristocracy honour was a birthright and its permanent existence was guaranteed.

11. However, the work of J. and P. Schneider is exceptional on both counts.

two

Italian Economic Development and the Problem of the South

In the 1990s Italy stands as the fifth largest industrial power in the world. Yet Italy's history as a world economic power has been a chequered one. In many respects this history has followed the same trends as other European countries and has certainly been subjected to the same influences, yet Italy's position in the world system and its responses to different pressures have been somewhat unique.

The Roots of Regional Differentiation

Italy was a latecomer to the economic transformations which so dramatically changed the face of European societies in the nineteenth century. Unlike the countries which assumed the leadership of the European system, a unified Italian state was formed very late. Furthermore, the new Italian state that emerged in 1861 faced a constant struggle to achieve core status within the international division of labour. Italy's position here has typically remained a somewhat fragile one, not helped by a heavy reliance on the international market for raw materials and technological inputs and the resulting pressure to safeguard exports. Perhaps the most persistent and significant element in Italy's struggle has been the ability of entrepreneurs to benefit from relatively abundant supplies of cheap labour power (D'Antonio 1973). This possibility derives from the marked internal differentiation which is one of the central features of the Italian system. Regional differences have meant uneven development and the possibility this offers enterprises for moving factors of production between regions to maximum advantage. During periods of expansion of the world market, the internal differences, particularly those between the Centre–North and the South of the country, have been functional attributes of Italy's competitiveness and development. However, in periods of recession these differences and

21

inequalities have exacerbated negative trends, and have proved to be an obstacle to recovery (Boccella 1987).

The internal differences which characterize Italy are consequent upon the time and mode of the creation of a united Italy, and the policies pursued by subsequent governments. Prior to unification there were already striking differences between the political units that would come together in 1861, and these differences were to determine the outcome of unification and of Italy's particular economic and political history. The major issue to emerge from these inequalities, and one which has dominated Italian political discourse and policy, is 'the Southern Question'. The Southern territories, wrestled by Garibaldi from the Bourbons, appeared to Northerners, at the time of Unification and since, as contradictory. On the one hand the area was seen as poor and backward, a place where a pauperized and servile peasantry eked a meagre existence out of barren land. At the same time, images of 'Etrurian fields', of an area of great natural abundance, with a particularly benign climate and great natural beauty, were also commonplace. In fact both of these characterizations were correct. Much of the rural landscape of the South represented a daunting challenge for any agricultural project. The hills of the interior had for centuries sustained semi-nomadic pastoralists, but seemed to offer few opportunities for more intensive exploitation. Along the coasts olive groves and vineyards have been cultivated since the time of Greek colonization. Less craggy terrain has again, for many centuries, specialized in the production of grain. Yet other areas along the coastal plains have been extremely fertile, supporting dense populations and producing an abundance of crops, particularly fruit and vegetables. Some areas were cultivated only at enormous cost, as in the rice fields of the Maremma, where the malarial mosquito took its toll amongst those who had little option but to work there. Massive state investments in drainage and land recovery programmes were necessary before these areas could become fully inhabitable and productive.

But natural landscape is not the only consideration here. Feudal lords were able to maintain their privileges in the South, and did so ruthlessly. The discontent of the peasantry erupted regularly and brutal suppressions followed. Emigration to the cities or brigandage seemed to many to be the only alternative. Large latifundia worked by impoverished and terrorized peasants, mountainous terrain where relative autonomy was coupled with a very meagre subsistence and where banditry was common, and small but often very productive landholdings generally cultivated by tenants, formed the mosaic of the Southern countryside. This contrasted significantly with other areas of the peninsula, in particular the North, where energetic transformations and improvements had increased agricultural productivity dramatically, and where agriculture and industry had developed in a more integrated way than elsewhere.

Indeed, the North-west was the site of the major developments in manufacturing. The South was not without an industrial sector, but this was concentrated in the larger cities, notably Naples as the capital of the Bourbon kingdom. The Bourbons had fomented industrial activity and supported some large-scale units and artisan producers, largely through the implementation of protectionist measures. The nature of these interventions did not prepare Southern industries for the massive competition they would face from their Northern counterparts after 1861. In addition, the South had been especially vulnerable to speculative operations by foreign capital and in fact had been an arena for aggressive competition between French and English capital. Northern industry was better able to regulate and accommodate foreign capital without this posing a threat to local production. Similarly, Northern producers were largely successful in withstanding the impact of free-trade policies, whereas Southern artisans and cottage industries were catastrophically affected by the onslaught of cheaper goods from abroad when Cavourian Piedmont, the political leader of Unification, extended free-trade policies to the rest of the peninsula (Romeo 1961).

The unification of different economic and political units offered opportunities for economic expansion which would not have been available to an autonomous Piedmont.[1] But it also posed a number of problems which were to shape the evolution of Italian society and politics. One of the first problems encountered was the lack of contact and of complementarity between the South, the Centre and the North, and this would prove to be a critical factor in the subsequent development of a 'dual economy' from 1861 onwards (Caracciolo 1973). But an especially persistent problem was the achievement and consolidation of national integrity.

The need to consolidate a single Italian state in spite of differences and discontinuities appeared urgent if Italy was to succeed as a key player in the world system. Italy was under considerable pressure, since at the time of Unification it was very uncertain whether she would be able to catch up with the economically advanced countries of Europe or whether she would instead be relegated to peripherality. This pressure encouraged Crispi, who was Prime Minister on several occasions between 1876 and 1896, to shift from his position as a separatist in his native Sicily to being a determined unionist who acted energetically against any murmurs of dissent and has left behind a record of brutal repression of peasant uprisings in his native land.

According to Gramsci (1973) Crispi subordinated the South to the needs of Northern industry, which was privileged as the spearhead of Italy's success. Instead of tackling the problems of the South, Crispi entered an alliance with the latifundists, who were willing to shift their allegiance from the Bourbons to the Union led by Piedmont, in exchange for guarantees concerning control of the disgruntled Southern peasantry. To preserve the privileges of the landowners a solution other than the redistribution of land was necessary. Colonialism seemed to offer just such a solution. Crispi's colonial aspirations and exploits, and those of other Italian governments, including that of Mussolini, were linked to the promise of land to the desperate peasants: if they could not have land in their own country, they would have it abroad.

In spite of Crispi's energetic unionism, which was consolidated by subsequent governments, the Italian state has been plagued by the danger of secessionism. In the late nineteenth century it was rumoured (and some suggest that Crispi himself fomented these rumours to justify his hard-line policies) that the Sicilian peasant *fasci*[2] had entered an alliance with the English to bring about the secession of the island. In the 1920s it was the turn of the Sicilian aristocracy to proclaim their opposition to 'the government of Rome'. For long after unification, many Sicilian aristocrats clung to Spanish nationality and maintained close ties with Madrid. Much later, during the Second World War, local élites linked to the mafia supported the Allied invasion with a view to gaining support for Sicilian secession after the conflict. In Naples the Scarfoglio brothers, who ran *Il Mattino*, at the time the most widely read and influential newspaper in the South, unceasingly expressed support for Maria Sophia, the last Bourbon queen, who from exile continued to plan the restoration of the Bourbon throne. From their position of influence they argued that the South had joined the Union on a contractual basis and, if the terms of that contract were altered, the South was entitled to reconsider its membership. The tension surrounding this issue exploded on two occasions: in 1919–20 because of changes which responded to the threat of social revolution and in 1924–5 with the changes brought about by the consolidation of Fascism. Other regions of the South, notably Sardinia, also experienced autonomist movements in the early twentieth century, but so did Lombardy in the North, where the upper classes, in a move which Gramsci defined as 'a temporary policy of blackmail toward the government', threatened to secede under the leadership of a revived Duchy of Milan (Gramsci 1973: 69).

On the other hand, the first twenty years of life of the new state were blessed by an international conjuncture which brought high prices for grain and fruit. This meant that the free-trade policies of the early governments were very favourable to the agricultural sector, and the country's position on the international market improved. However, the true beneficiaries of free-trade policies were the powerful economies of England and France, and for Italy the overall effect of free trade was a confirmation of its subordination to the core countries of Europe as a supplier of agricultural goods. An expression of this subordination is the fact that both public and private finance was for long under the control of foreign companies. When the economic crisis of 1873 encouraged a resumption of protectionism and a reassessment of the role of the State within the economy by Germany, France, Russia, Austro-Hungary and England, Italy followed suit. As the weaker countries came to the realization that their process of development was the more difficult for occurring at such a late stage, they perceived the State as having a particularly important role in countering this disadvantage. But State intervention, which took the form of protectionist policies and new credit institutions, had uneven effects. Along the lines of the model of development that had inspired Crispi, these policies favoured industry, particularly heavy industry, while agriculture declined as it lost capital, which was redirected towards urban centres and industrial production.

Conditions in the agricultural sector forced many off the land. The Northern agricultural wage labourers and small cultivators were the first of a long line of Italians to emigrate overseas. But the South soon took over as the major exporter of Italian labour power. From 1886–90 the average number of emigrants to leave each year was approximately 222,000 (Procacci 1968). The collapse of small landholdings and the continuing decline in agricultural wages also forced emigration to the cities, increasing the supplies of labour-power available for the industrial sector.

The first decade of the twentieth century (generally referred to as the 'Giolitti period' after the Prime Minister who dominated the political scene until the First World War) is recognized as the first important period of real expansion of Italian industry. This was assisted by a world-wide cycle of high prices and economic expansion and by the fact that Italy's balanced trade accounts placed her in a good position to take full advantage of these conditions. This positive state of affairs was largely the consequence of emigration, which continued to increase during the first decades of the century. From 1901 to 1910 the annual average number of emigrants was equal to 600,000 increasing in 1909–13 to an average of 873,000. Migrants' remittances and savings were an invaluable source of foreign currency. From 1901 to 1913, against a commercial deficit of 10,230 million lire, 'invisible items' show a credit of 12,291 million lire, and over one-third of these invisible items is attributed to tourism and one-half to emigrants' remittances (Cafagna 1973; Castronovo 1973). An added advantage was that, in spite of its continuing decline, the agricultural sector was able to maintain a balance between imports and exports.

The opening of a railway through the St Gothard pass in 1882, and the development of an important engineering industry in Piedmont took the region to a position of economic leadership and established Turin as the most important industrial centre. So was born the 'industrial triangle', linking Milan in Lombardy, Genoa in Liguria and Turin in Piedmont. The growing economic importance of the area further consolidated its political weight, and with it that of Northern cities, entrepreneurs and workers. Cafagna (ibid.) suggests that although to some extent the North-west operated as an autonomous entity, the fact that it was part of a larger whole greatly increased its growth potential. Its links to the North-east, Centre and South provided an extended tax base which increased the public funds available to provide an impulse to industrialization. Furthermore, although the domestic market for manufactured consumer goods was mainly localized in the wealthier centres of the North, at least the urban centres of the rest of Italy provided a market for Northern manufactured goods and, as has been mentioned, the remittances sent home by migrants, who by now originated mainly from the South of the country, favourably affected the balance of payments. 'Thus one of the characteristic features of Italian dualism – the extreme poverty of the South – played a part as an organic component in the structure of the development process that went on between 1896 and 1913' (Cafagna ibid., p.325).

Economic progress was difficult and partial, but progress there was. Italy managed to maintain its position on the fringes of the 'central' industrial nations. However, development was uneven and territorially restricted. According to the 1911 census, 58.06 per cent of workers in industries with more than 10 employees were in the North-west, which accounted for only 21.6 per cent of the total population. In addition, the area utilized 48.89 per cent of all mechanized horsepower. The First World War accentuated these internal differences, as it gave a boost to Northern heavy industry and directed more funds and investments towards this sector. During the years of conflict taxation transferred resources from agriculture to industry and from small and medium enterprises to large-scale concerns. Poor areas also suffered from the interruption of transoceanic emigration, which wiped out an important source of income. Population growth and high levels of unemployment in rural areas further benefited industry by creating a surplus of cheap labour (Castronovo, ibid.).

The First World War also had important political repercussions, notably on the process of 'Italianization'. Procacci (1968) suggested that it was only with this war that a 'national' public opinion emerged. For many, this constituted a negative view of the nation and the State. As Procacci says: 'Humble, provincial Italy, the Italy of those whose main problem was to survive, and who left their village and parish pump only to go to America, was hurled into war, and its poor sons learned that they were citizens only when they found themselves in military uniforms and were sent to fight in the trenches' (ibid.: 406). For other sectors of society, notably the petty-bourgeoisie, nationhood and war were also conceptually linked; but here this identification took on triumphalistic overtones.

This triumphalism was supported by changes in the international distribution of power. The dissolution of the Austro-Hungarian Empire, the fall of Czarist Russia and the defeat of Germany created a vacuum within which Italy appeared to become a true international power. This encouraged some sectors of the population to harbour expansionist ambitions quite out of proportion with Italy's real political and diplomatic power. In fact, Europe as a whole was seriously weakened by the war and economic renewal relied heavily on the assistance and support of the United States of America, which was already beginning to overshadow European powers and emerge as the new leader of the international market and the world political arena. United States exports to Europe increased dramatically; for Italy the war had meant a shift from reliance on German industry and finance towards reliance on the USA, and the level of Italian imports of US products rose from 13 per cent to 15 per cent before the war, to 40 per cent of its total imports after the war.

The Rise of Fascism

The disaffection felt by large sectors of the population, the difficult economic situation of the immediate post-war years and the example of the Soviet Revolution encouraged revolutionary restlessness. The period between 1919 and 1920 is known as the *Biennio Rosso* or the Red Biennium. Trade union membership increased, as did the number of strikes; peasants organized and in areas of the South mass occupations of the large estates took place. Expressions of popular discontent were widespread and profound and the general feeling was that change was imminent. Although the war had consolidated authoritarian trends within the government, this remained weak and suffered from an increasing credibility crisis and a growing sense of alienation from the people (Carocci 1975). But although revolution was in the air, divisions within the Socialist Party,[3] and between the Socialists and other political and Catholic organizations which were strong in many rural areas, added to the growing unemployment caused by the deepening post-war crisis, meant that peasants and workers lacked the unified leadership needed to make a bid for power. However, other sectors of society were galvanized by the crisis, and especially in the 'Red' areas (the Po valley, Emilia, Tuscany) a strong reaction against this popular unrest emerged, which came to be channelled through Benito Mussolini's Fascist Party. In fact, at the end of 1920 Fascism was preponderantly a rural phenomenon, but by the end of 1921 Fascist trade unions had also taken over and displaced the socialist movement (Carocci ibid.). The Fascist movement was seized upon by a weak and hesitant government as a means of solving the problems of social order, and in 1922, after Fascist squads marched on Rome from a rally in Naples, Mussolini was invited by the King to form a new government.

A favourable surge in the European economies helped to consolidate Fascism. In the period from 1922 to 1929, production in Italy increased by 50 per cent. However, the symptoms of the 1930s depression affecting the USA and Europe caught up with Italy as well. In Italy, as elsewhere, this meant a collapse in prices and shares and a significant decline in the production of cars, steel and cotton. Average incomes fell rapidly and unemployment rose from a total of 300,000 unemployed in 1929 to 1,019,000 in 1933. The crisis put pressure on all advanced capitalist countries, and arguments in favour of a new and more energetic role for the State gained ground in the industrialized world.

In Italy, this trend was reflected in the interventions of the Fascist State in the economy, the most significant measures being the creation of State-controlled bodies such as the IMI and IRI,[4] intended as a salvaging operation for ailing industries. This expansion of State intervention made Italy's State sector the largest of any capitalist country of the time. Italian corporativism also imposed strong controls over labour: wages were cut, the movement of people within and out of the country was restricted and monitored, and Fascist labour and management unions were expected to collaborate with the mediating interventions of the State. The position of women workers in particular was restricted, while emphasis was placed on their reproductive role. To reduce unemployment, work was distributed by cutting the working week from 48 to 40 hours in 1934, and after 1927 employers were forced to take on more workers than they wanted. Although entrepreneurs were bullied as well as the workers, Fascism ultimately helped to preserve private capitalism (Clough 1964: 238).

The problem of the South and of the peasantry was yet again to be solved through colonialism, and Mussolini's rhetoric made much of the heritage of the Roman Empire, which he found ways of emulating, not least through colonial adventures in North Africa. Although Italian Fascism was a unique response to the world crisis and although some of Mussolini's exploits provoked the indignation of other countries, Fascism was not out of step with the mood that prevailed in other capitalist countries, as is witnessed by the sympathy with which Mussolini's economic policy was viewed by some politicians and economists, such as Schumpeter (Harvey 1989: 129).

Fascism also determined the entry of Italy into the Second World War. The war aggravated the weaknesses in the Italian economy, causing a decline in agriculture and industry. The war changed the distribution of wealth, it upset foreign commerce, concentrated industry on weapons rather than on means of production and sucked up national savings. It also caused enormous physical destruction. Italy participated in the war for five years and was a battlefield for two of these. In the war of attrition between the Allies and the Germans, about one-third of Italian national wealth was destroyed. National income fell by more than one-half from 1938 to 1945, and did not again surpass its pre-war level until 1949. Some 444,523 persons, of whom 291,376 were military personnel, were killed or lost, and many more were wounded.

The damaging experience of war was for Italians, and especially for the working people, a cause for disenchantment and growing distrust towards the State rather than a source of patriotic enthusiasm. Although in the inter-war period the Fascist regime had attempted to overcome the entrenched popular distrust towards the State by incorporating the working people into its organizations, corporativism in all its guises failed to promote a true sense of participation and inclusion. The government's reckless entry into the Second World War and the afflictions it brought upon the people increased this long-standing distance between the Italian people and the Italian State.[5] But in spite of the losses and the disillusionment of many, the end of the Second World War was also a time of hope for change and renewal. Some, like Clough (1964), argue that the country's recovery was positive and rapid. Others, such as Procacci (1968) and Boccella (1987), detect in the immediate post-war years the seeds of many of the political and economic problems that would plague the country for the next half century.

The Post-War Period

Between 1945 and 1950 Italy adjusted to the new configuration of forces in the international arena, now characterized by a severely weakened Europe and by a clearly dominant position for the USA within the international political and financial systems. The end of the war laid the ground for US hegemony and the victory of Fordism, which were to be the basis for the long post-war boom. US influence was consolidated and a new world order was crafted at the Bretton Woods Agreement and through the creation of the IMF and of the GATT.[6] These institutions aimed at securing a world economy open to trade and investment and at curbing autarky and devaluatory competitive strategies. The US Dollar became the central currency against which all others were pegged, providing unity and some degree of stability, as well as reinforcing US economic power. Through the Marshall Plan and direct investment from the US, the model of mass production for mass consumption was exported to Europe and further afield. The package included not only an emphasis on standardized products turned out by the assembly line under the control of rationalized and bureaucratized corporations, but also sought to devise mechanisms to guarantee mass consumption for the products of industry. Here the State was to play a central role in the management of the economy.

The problems that had already emerged in the 1930s concerning the role of the State now seemed to find a general solution. Keynesianism and Fordism were seen as compatible and complementary partners. Different countries developed different variants of the solution, depending on their particular economic and political histories (see Lash and Urry 1987), but there was generally an emphasis on State interventions through public investment, an attempt to maintain relatively full employment, and to provide support through investment in education, health and housing. At the same time, a tense but generally balanced relationship was sought between corporate capital and organized labour. The relations between capitalist and worker were not easy, but improved standards of living, State provision of key services, and the backdrop of uncertainty fomented by the Cold War contributed to maintain order and a relatively high level of consensus.

However the model generated its own contradictions, which resulted in ever greater disenchantment and ultimately in opposition. According to the dominant model, the key sectors of the economy were to be heavy industry: cars, steel, transport, petrochemicals, but also electric consumer goods for the mass market. One of the effects of heavy investment in such key areas and of the emphasis on negotiated agreements between capital and organized labour was the emergence of dualisms in the economic system, as the rift widened between those employed in key industries, or the monopoly sector, where workers were relatively well paid, and those excluded from these sectors and relegated to the low-pay competitive sector (Harvey 1990).

The post-war reconstruction of Europe was built with US credit and financial assistance. This had profound implications for the shape that economic and political developments were to take in this period. US funds generated recovery and growth, but also placed the US in a position to influence the economic and political models that prevailed in Europe at the time. The political climate had a decisive impact on developments in Italy, perhaps more so than in other European countries. The Cold War and the suspicion aroused by communism and socialism had resulted in the removal of the PCI and PSI from the coalition government of the immediate post-war period and the hegemonic position conferred thereafter on the Christian Democrat party. This was to be decisive, for it resulted in a very particular configuration of administrative, political and ideological characteristics. The new Christian Democrat government, with Einaudi as Minister of Finance, was, to an extent, faithful to the Fordist model and identified the 'good of the country' with the good of large-scale industry.[7] But unemployment was a growing problem, not only because of its implications for domestic policy but because of pressures from the US, which was uneasy about the possible consequences of widespread unemployment. The US was also worried by the poor performance of Italian industry and demanded a more radical use of the funds loaned under the Marshall plan towards increased productivity, which was to be achieved through the application of Fordist principles. As a result of these pressures State intervention was resumed through a number of measures such as the Fanfani Plan (1949) to build workers' houses, the La Malfa Plan (1951) to deal with the reorganization of enterprises with State participation, and the creation of ENI (Ente Nazionale Idrocarburi) to exploit the country's fuel resources. There was a subsequent period of growth led by the 'key' industries identified by the model. But while Italy had built its recovery in accordance with its status as a satellite of the USA, it was not the US market that Italian exporters had targeted. Instead, European markets were to be the goal of Italian industry, which in fact specialized in the manufacture of consumer goods for the wealthier European countries. The effect of this strategy was to reinforce the status of the 'industrial triangle' and to exacerbate the differences between the regions.

The Problem of Development in the South

The reconstruction of Italy after the war neglected the South and concentrated its efforts on the industries of the North-west, which were identified as the leaders of national recovery. If anything, the immediate post-war period saw a dramatic decline in the South. To the damages inflicted on Southern agriculture, which under Fascism had been frozen as a source of labour and which later had been drained of workers by the war, were added the blows of the closure of the ILVA plant in Torre Annunziata, the Navalmeccanica plant in Baia, the Ansaldo, and the Manifatturiere Cotoniere, as well as the shipyards of Naples, Taranto and Palermo. Furthermore, the payment of compensation for war damages was received much later in the South than in the North, in spite of the devastation caused by war and occupation in the South. In the 1950s, however, the Southern problem was recognized as a political priority, and targeted via the creation of the *Cassa per il Mezzogiorno* in 1950 to aid the development of the South. Later schemes were intended to direct capital to the South so as to kick-start development there, such as the 1957 law obliging the IRI (Istituto per la Ricostruzione Industriale) to direct 40 per cent of its investments to the South, 60 per cent of which had to be invested in industry. Owing to effective controls on investments, these were concentrated in high-return sectors only, and generally had little impact on the economy or the employment profile of the South. The 'pole of development' projects established large-scale industries in the South, expecting a trickle-down effect to promote development. But the impact was limited, given the tendency of large-scale, capital-intensive industries to absorb relatively small quantities of labour. Subsequently, more labour-intensive industries within what was seen as the leading sector of industry were established, as for example with the Alfa Sud car factory in Pomigliano D'Arco, on the outskirts of Naples.

In rural areas of the South, particularly in Puglia under Di Vittorio but also in Sicily and to a lesser extent in Campania as well, peasant unrest was led by the Communist Party. The PCI had placed the Southern Question and the proposal of agrarian reform at the centre of its manifesto. The 1948 elections had indicated that the left was gaining support. As a response to this the left wing of the Christian Democrat party pushed through special laws for land improvement programmes, founded a union of small and medium peasants, and put through a land reform. This reform was met with strong criticism on account of the limited extent of the redistributions and the size of the holdings. It has been suggested that the main aim of the reform was to quell peasant protest, weaken left-wing support in the area, and create a rural petty-bourgeoisie. It was not long before many units ended in ruin, causing further exodus from the land (Castronovo 1973: 394). In spite of these shortcomings, the government's policies for the South were seen to support the claims of the Christian Democrat party as the defender of 'community' values and as the party which represented the interests of the South (Gribaudi 1980). The pursuit of political hegemony by the Christian Democrats is a crucial dimension of the 'Southern question' after the Second World War. The party produced a number of theoreticians concerned with the development of the South, many of whom worked within the SVIMEZ, a research entity aimed at analysing Southern problems and devising policies. Gribaudi (1980) argues that initially government policies were aimed at preserving Southern society and inhibiting or preventing a process of proletarianization from taking place. This was achieved first by governing through local notaries and later through the creation of a class of 'mediator–entrepreneurs' (Gribaudi 1980) who acted as a link between local communities and the State. However, this preservation of 'community' and its 'values' was to contradict the other central tenet of the Christian Democrat vision: the promotion of capitalism, of industrialization and the development of a mass market.

A number of changes resulted from these commitments. Firstly there were significant modifications in the mode of operation of the Christian Democrat party, which shifted from operating a system of patronage through notables towards a system of party patronage. Political entrepreneurs filled the crucial space between locality and State and exchanged funds and concessions for votes in favour of the Christian Democrat party. The second was the acceleration of investments in the South, not only in relation to large capital-intensive units like the steel plant built in Taranto at the end of the 1950s, but also for more labour-intensive operations involving private capital, such as Alfa-Sud.

Christian Democrat theoreticians such as Della Porta recognized that development in the South would cause disruption, but argued that the negative effects would be offset by the benefits. The State had to play an important role here in coordinating this process and in rectifying the distortions within the Italian development process (Gribaudi 1980). And indeed the State played a central role in the South, embodied in the figures of the Christian Democrat mediators. But interventions did little to alleviate the problems of unemployment and in fact exacerbated the problem by disrupting local production. The expansion of the mass market increased dependence on imports and displaced locally produced goods and, of course, their producers. The nexus between public funds and party power, achieved through clientelistic politics, tended to reinforce and reproduce the problems and the strategies that had caused them, and provided ample opportunities for manipulation, speculation and corruption, which in fact came to engulf the entire Italian system.

Similarly, it was expected that entry into the European Common Market would have a modernizing impact on the country; but on the other hand it was also seen as posing serious dangers to Southern agriculture. The development of a Southern industry, producing for export rather than for the weak Southern market, was intended to provide opportunities for growth without endangering Northern interests. All these investments, and the management of the *Cassa per il Mezzogiorno*, provided the means for the consolidation of a mediating élite and their clientelistic networks, and therefore for the hegemony of the CD (Gribaudi 1980). In fact, entry into the EEC[8] consolidated the role of the South as a supplier of cheap labour – now aimed not only at Northern Italian industry but at North-western European centres as well.

The Italian Boom and New Models of Accumulation

In spite of many problems, Italy participated in the 1950s boom, as the influx of US loans and assistance to Europe, the spin-off effects from the cycle of expansion of the US economy, the devaluation of currencies with respect to the dollar, the renewal of plants and technical processes, new and cheaper sources of energy and the diffusion of new mass consumer goods fostered a period of economic growth. Western Europe, especially Italy and Germany, together with Japan, had benefited from a favourable international market and the availability of large amounts of cheap labour resulting from the displacement of working people caused by the war (cf. D'Antonio 1973 and Mandel 1975).

In fact, Italy boasted one of the highest rates of economic growth in Europe. Here, as in the earlier Giolitti period of expansion, the Southern labour force was a crucial factor, as were the remittances of migrants which, as in the past, positively affected the balance of payments alongside tourism. So whereas France, England and other countries suffered periodically from inflation and balance of payments crises, Italian industry expanded within the context of a positive balance of payments and no inflation. At the same time, during the period of the 'economic miracle' productivity outstripped wage levels and investments increased. Italy's competitive edge increased, but, in spite of migration, unemployment levels rose. Weakened by this situation, the unions were unable to resist further manipulations by management, which had a positive impact on costs.

However, Italian expansion was limited by its exclusion from African and Latin American markets, which were controlled by Anglo-French and/or US interests. Italy's dependence on Europe was as important as ever, and a reaffirmation and expansion of European markets became crucial. In 1953 Italy entered the European Community to trade coal and steel, and established an almost complete liberalization of trade with OECD countries. Entry into the EEC in 1958 encouraged Italy to tailor production even further in response to the requirements of the European market and in favour of consumer goods such as cars, television sets, refrigerators, typewriters and synthetic fibres. This enhanced earlier imbalances between different industrial sectors and between agriculture and industry, and further widened the gap between the North and the South. In spite of generally low wage levels, wages in the export-oriented industries were higher and therefore widened the gap between higher and lower income groups even further.[9]

The export sector (which gradually also came to include some small and medium-sized units in the garments and shoe industries) became increasingly differentiated from other sectors such as textiles and food, in terms of capital input, efficiency and wage levels. The export sector was encouraged to invest in new technology, increasing productivity levels rather than expanding employment, so that greater output was not paralleled by a growth in the demand for labour-power. The absorption of the unemployed was therefore left to the less advanced and less labour-efficient sectors, or to commerce or public employment. At the same time, the internal market had grown. In industry incomes in 1961 were 200,000 lire higher than at the beginning of the 'miracle'. Even the provincial petty-bourgeoisie and some sections of the urban proletariat and the peasantry acquired televisions, cars and refrigerators.

Towards the end of the 1950s and in the early 1960s the boom declined as the US increased its exports to Europe, displacing less competitive producers. In the early 1960s competition from Western European and Japanese producers also became more aggressive. At the same time working-class organizations in Italy had recovered from the experiences of war, Fascism, high unemployment and pauperization. Membership of the trade unions increased, as did their levels of combativeness. Attempts by the government to incorporate sectors of the working class and gain consensus failed, and as a result of working-class pressure wages started showing an upward trend from 1962. This threatened Italian industry with the loss of its already declining competitive edge on the international market (Castronovo 1973).

To control an impending crisis caused by inflation, expansion of imports and the dangers of an unfavourable balance of payments (which resulted in the securing of a US loan), credit restrictions were introduced in 1963. This slowed down production and employment fell. The ensuing growth in unemployment enabled Northern industry to increase profits once again. Expansion of profits was achieved through employing cheaper labour and by reorganizing labour, increasing rhythms of production, and resorting to overtime, rather than by improving productivity through capital investment. As smaller units collapsed because of the credit squeeze, they were absorbed by larger units, resulting in a greater concentration of industry.

The conflict of interest between workers and industry exploded in the autumn of 1968, with widespread working-class militancy demanding improvements in working and living conditions. Given the difficult competitive conditions which faced industry abroad and the rigidity of the labour force at home, many industries resorted to the strategy of decentralized production. This relied on subcontracting to small firms and outworkers. This way output was maintained while investments could be allowed to decline. There were also important implications for the workforce: between 1961 and 1966 levels of production in manufacturing industries rose by 58 per cent, whereas official employment figures only showed a rise of 1.6 per cent. Women in particular seemed to disappear from labour-force statistics.

The 1970s and the Decline of Fordism

Whereas the Fordist–Keynesian model proposed the intervention of the State to maintain an equilibrium between supply and demand in the mass market in advanced industrial economies, it also guaranteed the stability of the system by expanding capital operations to a global level. Vast areas of the world were brought ever closer into the capitalist world market. Cheap raw materials fed the boom, new markets were opened up, and capital was invested in plants abroad, taking advantage of the cheap labour available in peripheral countries and opening up markets there. The result was a dynamic world economy characterized by a massive flow of goods. But investment abroad resulted in competition for core countries such as that faced by the USA with respect to the European industries it had helped rebuild, prompting the implementation of 'tied aid' to guarantee a place for US goods, and later confronted both the USA and Europe with the cheap imports from newly industrialized countries.

Within this dynamic world market Italian exports increased, and almost 90 per cent of these were manufactured goods: Italy was no longer a mere supplier of raw materials. But the Italian economy had specialized in 'secondary' spaces of the market, such as garments, textiles and shoes, food products and electrical appliances. In these sectors changes in the structure of demand can be met rapidly with little technological innovation. But here competition from the newly industrialized countries (NICs) was strong and came early.

The 1970s posed other challenges which complicated the issue of competitiveness. The oil crises of 1973 and 1979 increased the cost of raw materials and had long-term repercussions on the world market. Fiscal measures were taken in 1973 to salvage Italy's position in the international market, but had little impact. In fact 1973 marks the beginning of a long period of economic stagnation. The joint effects of the problems of the agricultural sector, the North–South divide, working-class militancy and unfavourable international conjunctures accelerated the decline. Italy's entrance into the European Monetary System in 1979 did little to alter these trends. What it would come to mean was a weakened capacity to manoeuvre through fiscal measures such as devaluations and a definitive shift towards the German currency and away from the hegemonic position of the US dollar.

The middle and early 1970s have been identified as a breaking point in the dominant Fordist–Keynesian regime of balanced forces, not only in Italy but in other European countries and in the USA.

Qualitative changes in the organization of capitalism were noted by
Offe (1985), who discusses the emergence of 'disorganized capitalism'
bringing with it a challenge to the concept of work itself. Lash and
Urry (1987) also speak of the dispersal and disorganization of
industrial relations and the fragmentation of working-class identity.
Harvey (1990) agrees that a major transformation has and is taking
place – but not in the direction of disorganization. On the contrary,
capitalism is becoming more organized, but is doing so through
dispersal, mobility and flexibility.

The consequences of the changes in world capitalism for any single
economy are dramatic. As the crisis of Fordism has encouraged a
strategy of expansion through the establishment of 'peripheral
Fordism' (Harvey 1990: 186), core industries have been subsequently
displaced as their functions are relocated in areas with lower costs.
Deindustrialization in traditional industrial centres follows, with
consequent unemployment and informalization. Revolutions in
information technology have allowed the acceleration of global
processes and generated new global networks as well as new patterns
of production. So deindustrialization and tertiarization are the
hallmarks of advanced capitalist countries. The decline of industry
in advanced capitalism has been marked by growth in the service
sector, with a new area of services which has strategic significance:
information technology, expertise and knowledge, access to
information networks, and control of the means of communication
has assumed an unprecedented importance within the global
economy.

The trajectory followed by Italy is parallel to that of other European
countries, but here again the Italian social formation reveals its unique
character. In the early 1970s, as a response to the recession and to
counter working-class militancy and the rigidity of labour within the
core 'monopoly' sector, entrepreneurs in many sectors of production
reduced the size of their factories or avoided further expansion.
Instead, specific phases of production were subcontracted out to
smaller, semi-autonomous firms and outworkers in what was
sometimes a dense network of interrelated enterprises. This allowed
enterprises to circumvent taxation, health and safety regulations, trade
union activities and the application of minimum wages and national
contracts. It allowed for expansion without increasing direct
investment, and it furthermore allowed for a reduction in output
without incurring losses because either workers and/or machinery are
left idle. Overheads could be reduced while allowing the parent firm
a great deal of flexibility both in terms of meeting market demand
and cutting costs.

By the late 1970s it became clear that this strategy of
decentralization was very widespread within Italian industry, and that

the face of the country had altered significantly. During the 1970s the work of Luigi Frey and his associates revealed that, contrary to expectations derived from dominant orthodoxies, whereby large-scale industry would be both indicative of and follow from growth, small-scale enterprises were not only holding their own in the modernized Italy, but were actually growing in number. This to many was indicative of the distorted nature of Italian capitalist development. Frey pointed out, however, that these small units were not generally representative of pre- or non-capitalist artisans who might have survived outside the process of capitalist growth. On the contrary, research indicated that a very high percentage of these small enterprises were not autonomous, and were in fact dependent on larger parent-firms for their operations. This was no simple dichotomy between traditional and modern sectors – this was a strategy aimed at maintaining a competitive edge by keeping costs low. Frey linked these findings to two other characteristics of the Italian economy: the apparent decline in women's participation in the economy and the growth of the service sector. So he argued that, in particular, in those sectors of work where women were predominant, factory work had been replaced by decentralized production. Women were thus still an active part of the labour force, but invisibly present, since many of these enterprises fell outside the formal, official and tax-paying sector. Official statistics therefore were misleading.

In 1977 Bagnasco made what was to be a very significant contribution to the analysis of the Italian economy and society. To the old problematic of the North–South divide he added the question of the 'third Italy'. He argued that North, South and Central Italy had different social structures which translated into different economic patterns. Their characteristics had to be understood historically and in the context of the relationships that had evolved between the different regions. But the economic profiles and socio-cultural character of the three areas were clearly distinct, and Bagnasco stressed that these differences are related to the connections which exist between economic and social characteristics. The North, in particular the 'industrial triangle', was the site for large-scale industries and large concentrations of industrial workers with relatively low levels of employment in agriculture. Many indexes showed that the South diverged significantly from the North in terms of output, efficiency and the productivity of labour, the ratio of agriculture to industry, levels of export and ratio of small to large enterprises. But there were some indications of trends towards convergence between the two areas, as government interventions had an impact on the Southern economy through the creation of large establishments. There was also a decline in the South of the percentage of small units and the population involved in agriculture. In the Centre–North-east the percentage of enterprises with fewer than 250 workers averaged between a low of 61.2 per cent for Friuli-Venezia Giulia and 86.3 per cent in the Marche, and indicated a tendency towards the increase of small and medium firms. The area differed significantly from the South by the absence of very large units and the relatively lower level of very small units (<10 workers), and by its higher share of Italian exports.

By the late 1980s and early 1990s the configuration of the Three Italies had become consolidated into three markedly distinct types, which underwent different processes of transformation and were differentially affected by the changing circumstances of the world economy. In the North-west a process of deindustrialization has been taking place, as rising costs and international pressures undermine large-scale industries. Large firms like Fiat had begun streamlining production in the mid-seventies with the 'robotization' of the production line, thus shrinking demand for labour. Large firms might also opt for decentralizing production. In the North-east and Centre of the country a well-defined model emerges, which successfully survives the vicissitudes of the recession, and which is based primarily on small enterprises. In the South, on the other hand, an unhappy combination of forms survives. The area was adversely affected by the decline of large industries, such as the steelworks in Bagnoli, which had been built at the turn of the century as a spearhead of Southern development, and were closed down as part of the Italian steel industry's rationalization programme. Around 18,000 workers lost their jobs and were either retired or placed on *Cassa Integrazione*,[10] thus adding to the burden of public expenditure in the area. The impact of the closure went further than the 18,000 workers laid off, since a number of satellite workshops depended on the plant for their survival. At the same time, petty entrepreneurship has been unable to take a leading role as it has done in the Centre.[11]

The decline of large-scale industry in the North cancelled the need for supplies of cheap labour from the South, so that the exodus of workers from the South that had fuelled Italian industry's moments of expansion became dysfunctional. The aim of policy therefore shifted more clearly towards fixing populations locally and sustaining them in their place of origin through State subsidies (Graziani 1989). Mass unemployment and widespread informalization, whether through decentralized production or other informal practices, have serious fiscal consequences, since they mean an increase in public expenditure and a loss of income through taxation. Given the historic relationship between North and South, the latter has become the major consumer of public funding in the form of pensions, unemployment benefits, invalidity payments, and payments to non-active workers through the *Cassa Integrazione*. This is due at least in part to the absence of a sufficiently dense network of small businesses or because of a higher percentage of these being in the informal sector, while larger units have been unable – and are increasingly so – to make a sufficiently large impact on the labour market.

In both the North and the South the decline of large-scale industry and its strategies of rationalization have resulted in growing unemployment. To some extent the unemployed were absorbed by small units, self-employment and informal activities, which appear to involve women disproportionately. Graziani (1989) argues that unemployment patterns in Italy differ from those of other European countries: here there has been an increase in both unemployment and employment, with unemployment concentrated in the young, women, and the South. Rates of unemployment in the South are higher for the vulnerable categories mentioned, that is women and young persons, but are also significantly higher for adult men.

The burden of these processes on fiscal resources is enormous. In the 1990s tax evasion has been identified as the Achilles' heel of Italy's claim to being a world power. Tax evasion is not only a problem confined to the petty entrepreneur or the outworker, and pressure on fiscal resources does not come exclusively from unemployment and state subsidies. The non-payment of full taxes and contributions is a widespread phenomenon. As a member of the European Community, the country is under pressure to conform to the financial standards required for economic unification, and as full European integration looms ever nearer, the Italian political arena has turned its attention to the basic contradiction of successful production and export strategies on the one hand, and the country's financial ruin on the other. There has been pressure from US banks, reluctant to extend credit to the country because of what they called the 'Italy risk' factor. Again Italy struggles to maintain its place in the heart of Europe; yet again in 1994 the United Nations Economic Commission expressed concern at the extent of the problems of public sector debt and mass unemployment, which could endanger Italy's full participation in the international community.[12] But the years of intervention, of boom and change have had an impact, and Italy is much altered for this. Graziani (n.d.) for one argues that we cannot today speak of real misery in the South. The years of special policies geared to improving conditions in the South have brought about quite dramatic improvements in the standard of living of Southerners. But the disparity between them and their fellow-countrymen in the North and Centre persists.[13] Much of the improvement in living standards is due to a policy of state subsidies via benefits and grants rather than to local economic activities, so that the South is dependent on income generated in other regions of Italy and abroad. This is one of the elements that fuels anti-Southern arguments and sentiments as articulated by the separatist leagues in the North, such as the Lega Nord. At the same time, although private consumption levels may have improved, Southern regions face deteriorating public services across the board, from education and health to the provision of water. The dramatic lack of employment opportunities for the young in the towns, cities and villages of the South has provided human material for the growth of illegal trades, such as the distribution and consumption of narcotics. It is estimated that the drug trade has all but taken over entire villages and the poor neighbourhoods of cities like Naples.

At the same time, many observers world-wide have turned to the 'Italian model' as the limits of Taylorism are felt increasingly, and as technological revolutions, particularly in the area of information technology, and growing competition from newly industrialized countries forces the search for alternatives (Piore and Sabel 1984). The prevalence of small enterprises, once seen as an index of Italy's backwardness relative to other European economies, has been hailed as the key to Italy's continued growth. Having pointed out that Italy's rate of growth in the 1970s and 1980s was consistently above the average for the OECD and the EEC, Nanetti (1988) suggests that this is a result of the success of small and medium enterprises. In fact, as we have seen, the success of the small enterprise model is somewhat restricted to the centre of the country, or what is often now referred to as the 'Third Italy'. However, Nanetti argues that the model has spread from here Southwards along the Adriatic coast to areas which heretofore have been considered markedly 'underdeveloped', such as Molise, Abruzzi, and Basilicata.

The case of Emilia in particular has been hailed as an example of 'flexible accumulation', a model presaged by many to represent an effective capitalist alternative in the face of recent changes in the world economic system which render Taylorism and large-scale production unviable for European economies. However, spontaneous entrepreneurship is in itself insufficient to explain or promote the Emilian 'capillary' model of production. Success depends not only on the presence of petty entrepreneurship, but also on political and ideological factors that support the entrepreneurial effort. Nanetti in particular emphasizes the role of local government and the decentralization of local government which has taken place since the early 1970s and which parallels and supports the decentralization of production. Trigilia (1987) adds to this the existence of specific sub-cultures. In the Centre there is a long history of support for the Socialists and later the Communists. Rather than being restricted to certain classes or groups, this support cuts across the class structure. In the North-east there is a long-standing tradition of Catholicism as a source of identity and solidarity. One of the effects of these sub-cultures, he argues, is the presence of a strong sense of community, a close interaction between localities and their governments and limited class polarization.

The Emilian case has been the most widely discussed, and Capecchi's study (1989) is a useful illustration of the intersection of entrepreneurship and local social and political relations. Emilia was characterized until recently by a predominantly agricultural economy, although cities such as Bologna had long and well-established manufacturing and artisan traditions, and even in rural areas different groups of peasants were involved in non-agricultural production. The small category of owner-cultivators (18 per cent in 1901) were especially well-placed to invest in some machinery and become involved in cottage industries. From 1913 cooperatives and leagues were widespread under Socialist leadership, and the anti-Fascist effort consolidated a strong Communist and Socialist affiliation in the area. From the 1950s to the 1970s the agricultural workforce declined and the percentage of those involved in industrial work increased. These workers were concentrated within a network of small and medium units producing capital goods and consumer goods. Grass-roots entrepreneurial efforts were supported by local government, which provided credit, equipment and efficient social services. Local government also invested in education, including child-care for very young children. These units were characteristically linked within interdependent networks, unlike the classical decentralization model which has a core enterprise and a number of secondary, dependent units. Production was flexible not only in relation to volume but also in relation to product, and goods were made to the order of clients. Whereas the majority of these units were in the textile and mechanical industries, in the 1970s and 1980s a new brand of small enterprise emerged, providing personal services, especially tourism and business services, particularly in relation to product research and development.

The sustained growth of the region and its success in terms of exports suggests that this is indeed an exemplary case. A number of points are worth emphasizing. In the first place, these enterprises appear to be related less by competition than by complementarity. Indeed, Capecchi argues that they tend to support each other through the provision of goods and services. Also, they cluster locally, so that different districts specialize in different products. There is a history of informal activities in the region, and although Capecchi argues that the majority of enterprises are not informal, they nevertheless tend to be supported by informal inputs, particularly and especially from women. This suggests that while informal activities may be important in promoting small enterprises, under appropriate circumstances a semi-formalized or a totally formalized profile can be achieved. But perhaps the most significant point here for our purposes is the role of local government. In spite of tensions and difficulties between a Christian Democrat central government and a Communist regional government, local government was able to provide the services necessary to assist entrepreneurs from different class backgrounds in setting up a business and administering it successfully. Capecchi stresses the open channels of communication that prevailed between local government and residents, so that local policies and initiatives were directly informed by local needs. But an important element here seems to be what Capecchi refers to as a 'community' culture, supported by strong communist ideologies (paralleled by strong Catholic ideologies in Friuli-Venezia Giulia). This suggests that having as a point of reference a strong associationist ideology contributes to both a collaborative relationship between government and population and between entrepreneurs linked through these capillary networks.

At the same time, it is worth bearing in mind research carried out in the region of Emilia during the 1970s amongst outworkers. It is clear from this research that the success or at least the operation of small enterprises has been largely dependent on outworkers who are in their majority women. For most of them outwork was their major activity. Women also constituted a high percentage of those employed in the small enterprises, and the description of this work experience does not coincide with the sense of community and solidarity which has been identified as an important basis for the success of the Emilian model (Trigilia 1987). Trigilia agrees that the family and kinship networks are central to the operation of small enterprises, although research in Tuscany and in the Veneto region during the 1980s suggests that the significance of family involvement dwindles as the enterprises and the system becomes consolidated (Vicarelli 1987). But it is important not to minimize the potential for exploitation in family firms and small enterprises in general (Centro Studi Federlibro 1974). On the one hand, it is important to recognize that authority relations derived from kinship statuses lend themselves to unequal treatment in the workplace, and on the other, that the informal nature of many of these enterprises allows for particular forms of abuse of workers such as the use of child labour, the neglect of health and safety and the superexploitation of illegal immigrants. These conditions have had tragic consequences on many occasions, such as the case in Ravenna in 1987 described by Ginsborg, when seventeen men lost their lives (1990: 416).

In any case, the system that has evolved in the Centre–North-east is fairly unique. Indeed, the characteristics of small enterprises and the relationships between enterprises vary within and between regions. In Milan for example, they are typically linked to larger units. In Emilia-Romagna and the Veneto region they have a greater degree of autonomy. In the South, on the other hand, the supportive structures described by Capecchi for Emilia are quite absent. The extension of the ancillary model from the Centre–North-east into some areas of the South seems so far to be producing a somewhat different economic structure from that of the Centre. In the Southern regions in 1984, 55 per cent of medium-sized enterprises, employing 70 per cent of workers employed in this category, were owned by persons or companies from outside the area; for smaller enterprises of 50 to 99 workers, 30 per cent were 'foreign' owned, and for enterprises with less than 50 workers, 15 per cent (Giannola n.d.). Entrepreneurs in the South are, with significant exceptions, placed in a disadvantageous position given the absence of infrastructures and the clientelistic web of local political relationships, so frequently intertwined with the interests of *camorra, 'ndrangheta* or *mafia*. Southern entrepreneurs and Southern industry generally has also been starved of investment, which has suffered a steady decline here since 1973. The system of government subsidies operated by the *Cassa per il Mezzogiorno* all too often result in 'phantom enterprises', or fake businesses with false names intended merely to gain funds but never actually function, and 'mushroom enterprises', those who use the funds to set up a business under precarious conditions and close down to re-open elsewhere as soon as there is a threat of workers demanding their rights or bringing in the trade union to represent them. The effect is of course to increase the malfunctioning of the economy and the precariousness of work.

Conclusion

The dwindling demand for Southern labour in the North and the virtual impossibility of migrating abroad, coupled with the decline of large-scale and small-scale enterprises in the South raises serious problems for Southern regions. Added to this is the growing pressure of return migrants, as their work opportunities abroad also disappear. The rate of population growth is higher by far in the South than in the Centre–North.[14] The provinces of Naples and Caserta and the entire region of Puglia have the highest rates of demographic growth in the country (Imbruglia n.d.). These figures, when set against statistics for industry, employment and services, suggest that the problems that lie ahead may be graver than the problems already confronted so far. The implications are that the government's switch from investment in the South towards a supported economy will be forbiddingly expensive to maintain. A continuation of this approach can only provoke a widening gap between the different regions of Italy, ultimately to the detriment of all, and accelerate a moment of deep crisis in the Italian economic and political system. The South may well have been brought into mass consumer society, but the resources to sustain participation in this society are precarious and conditions for local development remain extremely unfavourable.

Notes

1. It was the potential for growth which unification offered Piedmont that worried the French, who, seeing a possible rival in united Italy, were opposed to unification.

2. The Sicilian *fasci* were a peasant movement.

3. The Socialist Party, which was founded in the early 1890s, split at the Party's National Congress in Livorno in 1921, giving rise to the Italian Communist Party (PCI).

4. IRI stands for the *Istituto di Ricostruzione Industriale* and IMI for the *Istituto Mobiliare Italiano*.

5. The Italian state proved unable to meet the challenge of war, and towards the end of the conflict the people were left without leadership when the King and Badoglio, appointed head of government since 1943, abandoned Rome following the Allied landings in the South.

6. The Bretton Woods meeting set up the International Monetary Fund, aimed at providing funds for recovery and growth, and initiated the General Agreement on Trade and Tariffs, which was to promote global trade.

7. But other aspects of the 'American' package were not embraced. The government followed a policy directed towards re-establishing private enterprise, and away from public intervention and from experiments involving collaboration between industry and workers. There was a marked deterioration in working conditions, but a degree of collaboration from the unions was secured as the left agreed on the urgency of combatting inflation as a priority, thus postponing challenges to government policies.

8. The EEC was at the time the name of the European Common Market.

9. But overall labour was cheap: in 1956 wages were 50% lower than in England and one-third of the cost of labour in Germany and Belgium.

10. *Cassa Integrazione* is a scheme for the disbursement of a percentage of a workers' wage when s/he is suspended from work.

11. The Italsider plant has subsequently been purchased and is being dismantled and prepared for shipment to India. Many ex-Italsider workers are currently employed by the Indian purchasers to carry out the dismantling operation. It is rumoured that the site, which as a matter of fact overlooks a beautiful bay, will eventually be redeveloped as a tourist complex. Some see these plans as offering job prospects in the future, whereas others are pessimistic about the impact such a development would have on the job market.

12. See Ascoli (1987) regarding the subsidies provided to the middle classes, artisans, etc. from the late 1950s and early 1960s, which related to the party political support system.

13. Average income in the South has fluctuated between 55% and 60% of Northern incomes from the 1950s to the present day.

14. Not taking into account the effects of migration, the rate of population growth in the Centre–North is equal to 1.1 per thousand. In the South this rate is of 8.8 per thousand.

Marginality and Political Culture in Naples

Since the 1950s, research in a number of Third World cities has pointed to the presence of groups who are not absorbed by the limited industrial and commercial sectors characteristic of many peripheral cities and who appear to survive on the margins of modern industrial society. These groups and their survival strategies have been described under a variety of labels, ranging from the traditional as opposed to the modern sector, to Geertz's distinction between the bazaar and the firm economies (Geertz 1963), and to the informal (as opposed to the formal) sector (Hart 1973). Underlying much of the discussion regarding these groups was the assumption that capitalist growth meant expansion and that this would eventually result in the incorporation of ever-larger sectors of the population in some form of regular employment. This was seen as already having taken place in the core economies of Europe, where changes in agriculture, with consequently lower levels of employment in that sector, were matched by growth of employment opportunities in manufacturing and services. The European example suggested to some a model of an integrated economy with full employment, although others had for long argued that an unemployed sector was integral – and indeed functional – to a capitalist system.[1] This full-employment model was in contrast with the problems of a fragmented – and in some analyses immature – economy with high unemployment and under-employment which prevailed in much of the Third World and the less developed areas of Europe.

One of the central concepts used to analyse these phenomena was 'marginality', which was transposed from its origins in the study of US cities with large immigrant populations (mainly through the work of Park) and adapted to the Third World, particularly Latin America. Underdeveloped regions of the world were thus understood to generate large sectors of the population who were excluded from the economy, politics and culture of mainstream 'modern' society. 'Marginality' was thus not merely an economic status: marginals

47

tended to live in slums and shanty towns, to display unreliable patterns of political behaviour, and disrupted and disruptive social relationships. Another influential concept was Oscar Lewis's 'culture of poverty', which referred to a pathological cultural orientation which was generated by poverty and social exclusion. However, for Lewis this world-view was not exclusive to the Third World city; his study of New York (albeit amongst immigrant populations there) confirmed the existence of these attitudes in areas of the core as well (Lewis 1968).

Marginality as a structural feature was seen as resulting from an incomplete transition from a traditional to a modern society (Germani 1962) or as a consequence of the specific strategies pursued by capital in dependent economies. Marginal sectors of the population were sometimes seen as permanently excluded, and/or as living literally on the margins of society. Critics of this work (see Perlman 1976; Roberts 1978) pointed to the strong evidence for the existence of links and continuities between the residential patterns, economic activities and political ideologies of those employed in the formal economy and those excluded from it.

Similarly, the concepts of informal and formal sectors, first used by Keith Hart in 1973 in connection with his research in Accra, Ghana became widely used, principally in the context of peripheral countries. Empirical studies and critiques pointed out that although the formal sector may be characterized as the visible, official and regulated economy and the informal sector – which as Caroline Moser (1978) has pointed out is a rag-bag of a category – as unregulated, unofficial, invisible and illegal economic activities, the two are closely interrelated. Far from constituting separate areas as dualist models proposed, these activities were integrated in a number of ways, so that formal activities and businesses benefited from informalization.

At the same time, the influence of Wallerstein's world systems theory added to the recent trends in the world economy have made social scientists and policy-makers increasingly aware of a convergence in economic trends in core, periphery and semi-periphery countries, and of the complexity of the relationships governing the system. The category 'Third World', which has had the advantage of focusing attention on global inequalities, has at the same time misled many into a view of the 'other' countries as constituting a homogeneous group. The term 'Third World' has forced together in a single category economies as disparate as those of India, Cameroon, and Brazil. These disparities and the over-simplifications inherent in the category of Third World are more obvious now, with the enormous growth of heretofore peripheral economies such as South Korea, Taiwan, Malaysia, Singapore and Hong Kong. Feagin and Smith (1987) suggest that the leading underdeveloped countries (adding to the above Brazil, India and Mexico) produce an estimated three-quarters of all manufactured goods. South Korea, for example, has developed its own multi-national corporation (MNC), Hyundai.

Transnational corporations play a far more important role in the world economy than they did twenty years ago. Whereas transnational corporations (TNCs) had generally invested in peripheral areas to supply local markets, since the 1970s capital investments here have targeted the production of goods for markets in core countries. The threat of competition from peripheral and semi-peripheral producers has been felt increasingly by manufacturers in core areas. The links between regions have therefore intensified, as has the dependence of all areas on TNC strategies. The global movement of capital is such that pockets of affluence in core cities are matched by low-pay wage work and informalization in these same cities. Uneven development is now a feature of core cities (Feagin and Smith 1987). Deindustrialization of some old manufacturing centres of the core has led to unemployment, and the poor have been increasingly obliged to define strategies based on informal work. At the same time, formal enterprises in the core resort to subcontracting to sweatshops and firms in the informal sector. As new centres emerge in core and periphery, there are significant shifts in the distribution of capital, wealth, jobs and resources within cities, between the cities of a single country, between regions and between nation-states.

The changes that have taken place in the global world economy over the last twenty years have therefore had profound effects in different regions of the world, including areas in the core. The movement of capital has meant job losses and unemployment for heretofore well-established sectors of the working class. As capital relocation and industrial restructuring generate greater unemployment, the problem comes to be seen as a long-term one and the illusions of a full-employment economy increasingly fade from view. The political problems posed by mass unemployment and the financial burden it involves for the State are seen as the most pressing political issue of the developed world in the 1990s. European countries in particular suffer from high rates of long-term unemployment and a low rate of growth of jobs, and these are in any case concentrated in the public sector. The question posed by European governments is how to dismantle the welfare state and render European industries competitive on the world market, without causing even further unemployment and increasing the risk of political disruption. Just as Third World populism and nationalism were seen by some as resulting from the exclusion of marginal groups from the benefits of modern society and government, so in Europe today many point to growing unemployment as a potential source of racism, xenophobia and right-wing political orientations.

The case of Naples is of special interest here, since while Naples is a large city within one of the wealthiest countries in the world, the problems of unemployment and underemployment are hardly new there. On the contrary, it has a long, uninterrupted history of poverty and urban decay.[2] The city has for long been seen as exceptional within Europe for its 'Third World' problems and 'Third World' charm. Already in the eighteenth and nineteenth centuries visitors to the city described the *lazzaroni*, the urban poor who lived by wits and stealth and became famous world-wide as the classical embodiment of the urban lumpen-proletarian. The poverty of Naples thus has a long history, one that shocked Maria Antonietta Macciocchi when she was 'parachuted' into Naples as the electoral candidate for the Communist Party in 1968. In a letter to Althusser she wrote:

> If Naples had Argus's hundred eyes, her poverty would make her cry out of every one of them. The city is more decadent and diseased than it was twenty years ago. Capitalism, you see, has no interest in 'saving' her . . . Since the city is not really productive, it could just as well be petrified like Pompeii. The capitalist equilibrium here in Italy, in fact, is based on an organic interrelationship between growth and backwardness: poverty here is functional to well-being elsewhere. (Macciocchi 1973: 12,13)

The long-term problems of urban poverty and deprivation are reflected in a number of cultural practices and ideas. There is a 'folklore' of poverty and unemployment, of living by one's wits, of surviving somehow or other, of '*l'arte dell'arrangiarsi*' or the art of managing, of making do. A popular Neapolitan song expresses this:

Aiere ssera a Piazza Dante
'O stommaco mie era vacante
Si nun era pe' contrabando
Mo' ci stevo 'o Campusanto.

· · · · · · · · · · · · · · · · · · · ·

Last night in Piazza Dante
My stomach was empty
Had it not been for contraband
By now I'd be under Holy Ground.

As the song indicates, contraband has been an important feature of economic activity in the city. Neapolitans often joked that if the authorities ever did close down contraband operations the entire city would collapse. In fact, contraband (and more recently the drug trade) is one of the several illegal activities which can keep individuals and households alive, and a wide range of persons are involved in its different phases, from obtaining the goods to distributing and selling them. Alternatively, women and older men might take advantage of a ground-floor window to improvise a small shop, generally selling sweets and chocolates. Others invent jobs for themselves, such as becoming a self-appointed car-park attendant where, in the absence of a car park, a man might carve out a protected area on a given stretch of road, perhaps near a restaurant, where he can, for a small fee, guarantee that the diners will find their car intact once their meal is over. Car windscreen cleaners ensure they have a market for their services by taking the precaution of rapidly passing a dirty rag over the windscreen when the traffic lights turn red. Small boys might stand at the traffic lights near the cemetery selling roses which, it is said, have been stolen from the graves. *Scippatori* or muggers act at lightning speed, often from a Vespa motorbike, quickly disappearing into the crowded streets.

But in addition to these improvised income-generating activities there are also those which, although they too have been included under the rubric of the 'informal sector', show clearer signs of being linked to the mainstream economy: these are small artisan units, sweatshops which often produce for large local, national or international companies, and individual workers sewing bags, shoes or gloves which may end up in an expensive shop in New York or Milan.

The economy of much of Naples has been described as '*l'economia del vicolo*' (Allum 1975). This concept of the 'economy of the alley' attempts to describe the survival of a fairly large number of people on perhaps a single 'income' which is redistributed within the immediate neighbourhood. Allum points to the duality of Neapolitan social life: in the old city or what he, along with many Neapolitans and other Italians refers to as the 'casbah', it is characterized by relations and ideals based in the *Gemeinschaft*. In the newer districts, in which status and income bracket are more clearly aligned, the residential areas of the middle classes and the proletarian housing districts represent the germs of a *Gesellschaft* society. The economy reflects this dualism, and the economic activities of the alley represent the closed character of *Gemeinschaft*.

Allum's approach fails to bring out the links between the alley and wider economic processes, for the inhabitants of the alley were not producing only for local consumption but rather for wider markets. On the other hand, it indicates that there were a number of arrangements and exchanges between kin and neighbours. These exchanges, and the growing informalization of activities as individuals and households withdraw from the monetary economy in response to unemployment and underemployment, have been studied in a variety of contexts (Pahl 1984). As Mingione (1985) points out for Southern Italy, whereas informalization solves a number of economic and political problems by offering survival opportunities for those excluded from full and proper employment, it generates a new set of problems, in particular the acceleration of the fiscal crisis of the State, since it deprives the State of an increasingly significant taxation source.

Naples and the 'Culture of Poverty'

Oscar Lewis argued that poverty promoted attitudes and behaviour which in turn tended to reproduce the position of the underprivileged. These attitudes characteristically involved a sense of fatalism, an emphasis on short-term aims and an inability or unwillingness to sustain enduring and stable personal relationships. These cultural traits prevented the poor from improving their lot, and those who grew up in such a culture were unlikely to overcome its limitations. Lewis, like other theoreticians and policy-makers, believed that where strong class or ethnic identities were absent, the problems of the urban poor could only be solved from above (Lewis 1968).

The high percentage of unemployed and underemployed in Naples led Allum (Allum 1975) to suggest that Naples was characterized by duality, having a traditional, peasant-like *Gemeinschaft* on the one hand and a modern *Gesellschaft* society on the other. Using a different perspective but arriving at parallel conclusions, Barbagallo and D'Antonio (1976) argued that economic and social backwardness have entailed political backwardness, since there has been very little development of class consciousness here. This they attribute to the isolation of the industrial working class. Mottura (1973) also considered that the relatively small proletariat was swamped within a larger population of the unemployed, the underemployed, precarious workers and the myriad 'mixed' figures that predominate in Neapolitan social structure. This was echoed by a Neapolitan worker who contrasted Naples and Turin: Turin was a working-class city with a working-class culture, but in Naples the proletarian left the factory, with its combative language and trade union organization, and returned to the 'casbah' (the old city), to the world of the 'lumpen-proletariat' which swallowed him up and defused the revolutionary attitudes which can emerge in a factory context.[3]

That there are differences between the language of the factory, of the trade union, and of the political party and the language of the alleys of the old city is undeniable. The cognitive dissonance which emerges when these are confronted struck Maria Teresa Macciocchi during her campaign in the heart of the city. She describes the confusion created when footage of the Vietnam war, which was a central issue in left-wing politics at the time, was shown in the old city. The women in the crowd thought the footage referred to the Germans and were perplexed to be told that the perpetrators of this violence were in fact the Americans, whom many remembered in a quite favourable light. The realization that there was a war going on created panic, since 'Vietnam', and the geographical space and distance it entailed, was totally absent from their conceptual repertoire.

But it is also important to recognize that in the old city and in Naples as a whole there are many languages, many different points of reference and different conceptual maps. Gender is an important consideration here. For many men mobility out of the neighbourhood was an aspect of work or of the search for work, and this brought them into contact with people from different backgrounds and with different opinions. A majority of women, other than those who worked in factories, rarely left their own neighbourhood. Many remembered that in their youth they had gone to fairs and parks, to the beach or to dances. But after marriage, and particularly after having children, many claimed they never ventured beyond their neighbourhoods. Since the majority had married at a very early age, their map of the world was limited and fairly strictly dictated by their own personal experience.[4] This became clear when I met people for the first time. Women in particular were eager to know where I came from and why I was there. As an Argentine I slotted into many women's conceptual map, since many Neapolitans have friends and relatives who emigrated there. They generally recognized that Argentina was in some way connected (though not necessarily geographically) with 'America'. At the same time this was often located somewhere far away, 'in the North'. One woman conceded that Argentina and, what was generally considered to be far more important, my mother, was very far away: 'as far away as Milan'. In the majority of cases I ended up pigeon-holed as a rather peculiar version (i.e. an Argentine) of an Italian from the North.

Differences in conceptual repertoire do mean that, as Macciocchi discovered, many of the referents used in political discourse and much of the rhetoric of political parties is irrelevant and meaningless. A similar problem emerges with the very concept of 'politics' and 'government'. For many women in particular, the introduction of the word 'politics' provoked an automatic end to the conversation. Women generally recoiled from a discussion of politics, claiming total ignorance on the subject. Men usually had something to say on the matter, and it was clearly seen as a male sphere of discourse.

However, if and when a discussion of 'politics' was initiated, both men and women tended to express frustration and dissatisfaction with the way government worked. Amongst other things, there were strong anti-bureaucratic sentiments and a sense of resentment towards the complexities of government. Their argument was that there were so many different organisms constituting local and national government that it was impossible to grasp the process of government or determine who was responsible for specific policies or grievances. This is why many preferred a more personal government, one which was in the hands of a single, strong man. In some cases reference was made to Mussolini. Those who were active party members were armed with more sophisticated concepts and arguments, but they too sometimes betrayed an unease with the ramifications of State power and its fragmented nature.

Those who longed for a strong government in the hands of a single man such as Mussolini were not necessarily sympathetic towards the fascist party, the MSI (*Movimento Sociale Italiano*). There were those who supported Fascism past and present, and many who opposed it and whose *raison d'être* in the political world was inspired by a history of anti-Fascism. But for the many who were not aligned to one or other camp, views of Fascism were patchy and anecdotal. Some of the women of the older generation remembered Mussolini as '*un bel uomo*', a fine figure of a man. Some had witnessed the parade in which Mussolini presented Hitler to the Neapolitans. He too, it was suggested by one woman, was a '*bel uomo*', and the pomp and ceremony made this a memorable day in their lives. Mussolini had special plans for the city of Naples. Naples would be developed into the third largest city of the country and a major port for overseas traffic, which Mussolini saw as an aspect of his colonialist intentions. Naples was to be the link between Italy and her colonies. This was planned at a material level, but also at a cultural level, as witnessed by the founding of the *Istituto Orientale* and the exhibition centre of the *Mostra d'Oltremare*. Naples inherited these structures and the palm-lined boulevards, planted to add grace and style to the city. But Fascism did little to alter the long-term conditions of the city and its people.

At the same time, Mussolini took the Italian people into a terrible conflict, in which Naples suffered enormously. During the Second World War Naples was occupied first by German troops and later by the Allies. Many women remembered being hidden in cellars or attics to escape rape in the hinterland villages to which many retreated, forced by hunger, as the German army advanced. The disruption to local production and distribution and the isolation imposed by occupation meant hunger for the Neapolitans, and the subsequent Anglo-American landings did little to solve the problem. Even after the Allied occupation supplies for civilians were short and rations were low. Nevertheless, the Allies were practically the only source of food and work. At this time 'living by one's wits' was especially important. One of the most popular myths of Neapolitan folklore tells of the arrival of an impressive US battleship in the port of Naples which disappeared overnight. Neapolitans had disassembled the vessel to sell off the various parts. Some versions offer extra satisfaction to the audience by suggesting that the parts were resold to the US forces.

The impact of Fascism was complicated and uneven. Galasso (1978) argues that Naples experienced a typically 'Southern' form of Fascism. Here there was relatively little emphasis on the ideological aspects of Fascism and on *'squadrismo'* (squads) and a greater emphasis on the themes of a strong centralized and personalized government, of social order, and of traditional values and hierarchies. Fascism was a latecomer in the South. This, as well as the mildness of Southern Fascism, might be explained by the relative absence of fears regarding 'the Bolshevik threat' which fired many Fascists in other areas of the country. Whatever the case, Galasso's account of Neapolitan Fascism is consonant with the views encountered during fieldwork, where the 'nostalgia' was for a man and what he implied for 'good government' rather than for a political ideology or party.

Allum's research on Neapolitan clientelistic politics also indicates a preference for power being vested in a single person. He quotes Grasso (1965, in Allum 1975: 121) when he refers to one Neapolitan as saying:

'Ci vuole solo il re, come un capo famiglia che vuole bene ai figli. Va bene, che quando il re è cattivo allora quelli che stanno attorno a lui lo devono uccidere e fare un altro re.'
'You need only have a king, who is like the head of a family who loves his children. It is true that when the king is bad, those who surround him must kill him and replace him.'

Allum points to a preference for personal, paternalistic relations, the origins of which he traces back to the Bourbon kingdom, arguing that the poor of Naples have never shaken off these archaic views of government in favour of the bureaucratic institutions of the modern republican state. The Neapolitan view of the political remained strictly personal and indeed, their experience of politics has been shaped by a paternalistic and clientelistic system. The people did not see themselves as 'belonging' to the world of politics nor did politics 'belong' to them. It is the affair of others, of the wealthy, of the professionals. Furthermore, their view of politicians is a negative one: they are seen to be motivated by self-interest while the poor remain poor.

This disaffection with politics was extended to the ways in which the State was perceived. Grasso's study, quoted in Allum, indicates that a feeling of distance and separateness from the State was widespread among the Neapolitan poor in the early 1960s: out of 120 persons interviewed only 40 per cent expressed some degree of identification with the Italian state, and when an identification was expressed, this was only in rather vague terms. The majority of interviewees expressed a feeling of complete separateness from the State. Ninety persons replied that they had no faith whatsoever in the State:[5]

'Lo stato è il governo e la chiesa. Noi votiamo ma nessuno può cambiare niente col suo voto. Abbiamo i guai nostri e allora dobbiamo stare a credere a quello che dicono loro per farci votare. Io voto sempre scheda bianca o voto per Mussolini.'
'The State is the government and the Church. We vote but nobody can change anything with their vote. We have our troubles and so we are forced to believe what they tell us to get our votes. I always vote blank or I vote for Mussolini'.

Or:

'Lo stato non esiste ed io mi ubriaco tutti i giorni. Quello che mi dà da mangiare è il governo mio. Ho campato tanti anni ma non ho mai visto nessuno che ha detto: "Io sono lo stato: tieni a te ti spetta tanto per tutto il lavoro che ti hanno fatto fare." Invece uno deve stare soggetto al padrone.'
'The state does not exist and I get drunk every day. What feeds me is my own government. I have lived so many years and I have never seen anyone who's said: "I am the state: here, take this, it is yours, for all the work they have made you do." Instead one must live under the boss.'(Grasso 1965, quoted in Allum 1975: 120, my translation)

The perplexity expressed by many Neapolitans with regard to government can be explained in terms of the history of the Italian state. In the first place, the conditions of expansion and annexation of the different regions are important, and as we have seen the uneven distribution of wealth and resources has tended to be reproduced by successive governments after Unification. A second consideration is the way in which the Italian Republic has evolved, generating a 'distorted relationship between citizens and the state' (Ginsborg 1990: 149, 166). Ginsborg attributes this distortion to the inefficiency of bureaucracy and the discretionary powers of bureaucratic procedure, which plays on the ability of citizens to mobilize networks and resources, an ability which is clearly unequally distributed. This inefficiency has been compounded by the fragmentation of government, the proliferation of bodies and agencies, the low standards of the services provided and the internal divisions of the Christian Democrat Party, which has largely fused with State institutions (Ginsborg 1990: 154–5). As Ginsborg points out, in the 1980s the problem of the relationship between the people and the State persevered, and Italians were the least likely Europeans to feel satisfied with State institutions.

Clientelism and Beyond

Clientelistic relations have sustained the distribution of political forces in Italy since the Second World War, but in the South and in Naples particularly they have had an especially high profile. The provision of funds for the South under various schemes such as the *Cassa per il*

Mezzogiorno has fuelled the construction of personal spheres of influence and political networks. Naples is the city of Lauro and the Gavas. Lauro, who built up his fortune during Fascism, survived the fall of Fascism after spending twenty-two months in an Allied prisoner-of-war camp. He joined the monarchist party and went on to found his very personalized political power on the basis of his control of important economic resources. To this end he used his own personal wealth, which gave him control of the shipping and the building industries, and the State funds which flowed into the South. With the *Legge Speciale*, 35 thousand million lire were given to Naples, which the administration, in Lauro's hands, put to its own ends. Lauro believed in State intervention in the form of funds but was opposed to any State intervention or programming in the allocation of these funds, as this would crush private initiative. His opposition to State intervention was reflected in his populist rhetoric. Lauro gained support and in particular reached the poorer sections of Neapolitan society through his antistatist, Southernist rhetoric, which criticized outsiders and especially Northerners and extolled both the virtues and the suffering of the people of Naples.[6]

The political wheeling and dealing that characterized national policies in the South meant that central government turned a blind eye to the gross irregularities and corruption of which the Lauro administration was accused. But eventually Lauro became a threat to the Christian Democrat Party and was removed. This was achieved by closing the communal council of Naples and refusing credit to his followers, who were thus persuaded to abandon their patron.

Lauro was followed in the Neapolitan administration by the 'reign' of the Gavas. The Gavas had the advantage of being members of the Christian Democrat Party and therefore had direct access to State organs. Since the Christian Democrat Party had established control over most areas of economic activity, including the banking sector, their position within the party was crucial. In Naples the Gavas controlled public funding and manoeuvred public investments, the organizations concerned with local public transport and services, and, since these were in the hands of Christian Democrats, private banks as well. The Gavas based their power on the control of economic resources on the one hand and on their influence in Rome within the party on the other (Allum 1975).

This predominance of clientelism in the life of Naples and the South has had serious repercussions on the social, political and economic fabric of the area. The speculative application of funds confounded any possibility of planning the economic development of the area or of any positive transformation in the South. The more profitable areas were those that saw more public and private investment. In the period of Lauro government these were mercantile commerce and building speculation. In the Gava period there were more opportunities, but the main areas of interest remained building speculation, though interest shifted from private housing towards the construction of office blocks, public works and public services, and tourism. But although Gava controlled the local party apparatus and local bodies representing the State, which were staffed by his followers, he did not have access to national bodies and enterprises. For example, the decision to establish an Alfa car factory in the Neapolitan area required Gava's assistance and provided him the opportunity of clientelistically allocating badly needed jobs. On the other hand, Alfa Romeo's decision against purchasing the components necessary for production in the South was a bitter blow. In spite of his influence in Rome, Gava's and other politicians' complaints went unheeded.

It is not only the functioning of government that raises problems: the very operation of democracy is seen as being problematic. The system of clientelism has determined voting patterns in such a way that votes were detached from class and ideology. Thus Gribaudi (1980) points to the electoral fluctuations in the South as opposed to the relative stability of voting patterns in the Centre of Italy, which she explains in terms of the prevalence of clientelism in the South. Ginsborg (1990) also points out that although clientelism is found throughout the Italian political system, its high profile in the South has given it primacy over religious and political ideologies. Although clientelism was only established in Naples in the early and mid-sixties under Silvio Gava (Ginsborg 1990: 178), Lauro had devised ways of exchanging votes for jobs, favours and goods. A popular anecdote in Naples recounts the way Lauro distributed staples to the poor prior to elections and handed out one of a pair of shoes before the elections and the second one only after the elections, provided that these had proceeded favourably.

Furthermore, the use of electoral 'lists' increases the potential for clientelism and personalistic politics, since the vote is not simply given for a political party but for a particular candidate (Ginsborg 1990). Another problem which in fact contradicts this manipulative view of the system and illustrates the potential for arbitrariness in voting behaviour is pointed out by Macciocchi (1973). Candidates from each party were placed on the list in alphabetical order, and those whose names started with one of the early letters of the alphabet were far more likely to be elected, since many voters tended to simply tick off names at the top of the list. These conditions do not inspire faith in democratic procedure and, coupled with the problems of outright corruption and inefficient government, encourage a diffident view of the political system and the State.

The use of public funds for personal and political ends meant that there was no structural transformation or solution attempted for the

South. It distorted political processes at all levels, from that of the administrators and politicians in their alliances and deals, down to the level of voters, for whom membership in the Christian Democrat Party meant the possibility of a job. The clientelistic organization of local government, and its relationship to national government, further encouraged a detached and negative attitude towards politics and the State.

Hope returned to many Neapolitans with the election of the *giunta* led by Valenzi in 1975. However, these hopes were generally speaking unrealistic. Expectations of Valenzi's capacity to change conditions in the city were almost messianic in character. To many, voting in a Communist-led local government meant that dramatic changes would happen almost overnight, bringing a solution to all the problems of Naples: the poverty, the decay, the unemployment, the neglect. For many it would have a very immediate impact: a job for themselves or their children.[7] In fact, there was bitter disappointment. The *giunta* faced a daunting task. Naples represented a far greater challenge than other Italian cities which were led by left-wing governments, such as Rome or Bologna. Housing was a major problem both in terms of an acute shortage of housing stock and because of the inadequacy of the existing stock.[8] Furthermore, local services were inadequate or totally lacking.

Indeed, the Valenzi *giunta* inherited a city which had suffered both decay and destruction as a result of neglect and fierce building speculation. The financial state of the administration was appalling, and the bureaucracy had grown out of all proportion because of years of appointments made entirely in response to clientelistic interests. The *giunta*'s attempts to clean up the administration and impose austerity measures were unpopular, especially since the new administration lacked the resources needed to create alternative job opportunities. The members of the *giunta* were also limited by the national policies of the PCI, based on the 'historic compromise', which urged cooperation with the Christian Democrat Party, in order to deal with the economic crisis which afflicted the country. Unemployment, perhaps the most pressing and intractable problem of Naples, plagued the *giunta*, which was unable to address the issue effectively because of a lack of resources and of an appropriate national policy on the matter. Finally, the *giunta* had to resort to the allocation of jobs in the *comune*, which left it open to accusations of clientelistic practices. (Chubb 1982: 222).

Yet many conceded that the city had improved, especially as regards provisions for cleaning the city and finding employment for at least some of the unemployed registered on the lists. Between 1975 and 1979, 333 kindergarten classrooms were opened, in contrast to the 210 that had been created in the previous thirty years (Ginsborg 1990:

398). But the preference expressed by Neapolitans on so many occasions for a 'strong-man-in-control' combined with a rejection of bureaucratic organization and an expectation of miraculous cures for the ailments that afflicted the city set very high expectations which were not to be fulfilled. The subsequent decline of left-wing votes in Naples is at least partly explained by the gap between the expectations of immediate relief and a direct resolution of their problems and the actual, concrete achievements of the new administration. I found very little understanding of or patience with the national, international and local factors which conditioned and constrained the local government. These were directly related to local and national power structures, as members of the CD party controlled key positions in state institutions and banking and did everything in their power to stall the *giunta's* attempts at bringing about change. But hopes had soared, pinned to the figure of Valenzi himself, and thus failure was attributed to his personal weakness and shortcomings. Criticism was extended to '*i comunisti*', who, it was often agreed, had now proved that they were 'just like the others' (meaning the politicians, generally Christian Democrats or Monarchists). What was seen as being the failure of the Communists only confirmed their general view of the need for non-bureaucratic government.[9]

But the obstruction posed to Valenzi's administration by crucial local and national institutions, which were under Christian Democrat control, must not be underestimated as a cause of the downfall of the Left in Naples. The problems came to a head following the earthquake which shattered Naples and its surrounding area in November 1980. The emergency funds allocated to Campania were not evenly, or rapidly, distributed. Consequently, the *giunta*, starved of resources, was unable to tackle the dramatic effects of the earthquake: the earthquake added nearly 100,000 homeless to the already critical housing situation of the city; the problem of unemployment was aggravated by the disruption of the informal economy that had sustained so many households in the city. Although the PCI, to the surprise of all, managed to maintain its position in the 1980 local elections, dissatisfaction grew and the Left lost its support (Chubb 1982).

In contrast to what occurred during the left-wing government, a massive amount of funds poured into the lap of the administration which replaced the left-wing council in 1983. This fuelled an explosion of clientelism and corruption that made the activities of the Lauro and Gava administrations of the 1950s and 1960s seem insignificant. According to Sales (1993), for all its shortcomings, the left-wing administration had effectively blocked the expansion of the *camorra* in Naples. This situation was reversed after 1983, when we see the rise of the *Nuova camorra*, or the new camorra, which infiltrated local business and administration. This new, entrepreneurial, *camorra* developed close ties with councillors from the Socialist Party and the Christian Democrat Party, in some cases becoming partners in legitimate businesses. The *camorra* thrived on the funds made available for the reconstruction of Naples and its hinterland, as did local politicians and businessmen from Campania and other regions of Italy. A number of triangles, based on mutual convenience and massive profits, were established, linking entrepreneurs, local and national government officials, and *camorristi*. The objective was to secure the contracts tendered for the construction of buildings, roads, and bridges, securing profits large enough to cover the *tangenti* or bribes required to guarantee access to these funds.

During the investigations referred to as *Tangentopoli*, Naples assumed a prominent position. Investigations revealed a large number of cases of corruption and illegal links between the local political élite, businessmen and the *camorra*. Prominent Neapolitan political figures, some of whom had occupied ministerial posts or other high-ranking positions in the Italian government, such as Pomicino, Di Donato, and Di Lorenzo, were found guilty of corruption. In September 1994, orders were issued for the arrest of 98 Neapolitan politicians and entrepreneurs. The most famous amongst those arrested was Antonio Gava, ex-Minister of the Interior, who was accused of *associazione mafiosa*. Ten months later, Gava was horrified to find himself sharing a court-room with petty businessmen and common criminals. However, there were other prominent figures amongst the accused: the ex-senators Francesco Petrarca and Vincenzo Meo, the Deputy Raffaele Russo and the Socialist Raffaele Mastrantuono.

After another decade of clientelism and corruption, in 1993 Neapolitans again revealed a strong desire for change. As the *camorra* effectively infiltrated local government during the 1980s and as the corruption of the governing parties was revealed, blow by blow, not only in Naples but this time in Rome and even in Milan, Neapolitan distrust of politicians could hardly fail to be confirmed. But in the 1994 local elections their dismay was expressed in the search for an alternative. Antonio Bassolino, a member of the PDS and long-term member of the Communist Party,[10] won against the candidate of the right: the glitzy, hard-talking granddaughter of Mussolini.

The national elections held four months later on the 28 and 29 March 1994 are also revealing. As Italians from the North and the South expressed their rejection of the political establishment, an unlikely coalition of what seemed to many to be new political forces was swept into victory. The victory of the coalition was seen as a victory of the right wing. In the North the separatist Lombard League expressed the disgruntlement of Northerners with what they saw as the inefficiencies of a government based in Rome, which used the wealth produced in the North to sustain its power base in the South. In Rome itself and in the South, the Fascists won a lot of support, under a new leadership with some technocratic gloss and a new name (*Alleanza Nazionale*), arguing for a strong central government and the integrity of Italy and appealing to a sense of lost pride amongst many who felt humiliated by the revelations of scandals and corruption throughout the governmental fabric. Throughout the country the glossy image of Silvio Berlusconi, a successful businessman and media tycoon turned politician who led the coalition, promising economic recovery and new jobs, convinced the electorate that he was the man to bring about the miracle of the 'new Italy'.

But this national trend towards the right following the collapse of the Christian Democrat Party was reversed in Naples.[11] Here the victory of the 'Progressive' alliance repeated the victory of the local elections. The PDS candidates won in the working-class suburbs of Naples and in the Eastern wards. Alessandra Mussolini, for the fascist National Alliance, was elected in the historic centre of Naples. In the interior a number of candidates who had been associated with *camorra* activities were defeated in favour of candidates from the Progressive camp.

It is dangerous to read attitudes and aims from voting patterns, but the results of the 1994 elections do indicate a strong claim by Neapolitans for change in the political system and in the conditions of the city. Whether these changes can be accomplished is problematic, given the composition of national government. The Christian Democrat Party has ceased to exist and a wave of arrests and trials for corruption on the part of local officials has swept the country, with Naples playing a rather notable part in these proceedings. But until the end of 1994 power was held by a majority formed by an alliance led by the media tycoon, Berlusconi, and including a significant presence of the ex-MSI under Fini. Their electoral success derived largely from a generalized dissatisfaction with the politicians and with the corruption that characterized the political system. One of the government's first actions was to restrict funding to local governments. Bassolino, the elected left-wing mayor of Naples, has recognized that governing such a city will be a very difficult task. On a national level, the promise of the *Forza Italia* contingent of creating new jobs was firmly refuted by statistics testifying to rising unemployment. In January of 1995 Berlusconi was replaced by an interim government of 'technicians' led by Dini, whose principal task was defined as restoring equilibrium in the economy and setting the stage for new elections.

The Politics of Protest

The impatience with red tape and bureaucracy and the distrust of political rhetoric and partisanship can lead to support of right-wing or left-wing politics, as suggested by many writers concerned with marginality. But it is hard to see in Neapolitan culture the elements of passivity associated with the 'culture of poverty'. On the contrary, although Neapolitans make much of the folklore of 'getting by', they also have a folklore of rebellion. The Neapolitan populace has taken to the streets in riots and demonstrations on several occasions throughout the history of the city.

The most famous uprising was led by Masaniello. Masaniello was a humble fishmonger who lived in the Mercato area of Naples and who, through his personal charisma, became the leader of a revolt in 1647 against the Spanish Viceroyalty's excessive taxation. In a brief period of time Masaniello rose from rags to at least the appearance of riches, and to enjoy the privilege of dining at the table of the Viceroy. And as rapidly he fell from grace in the eyes of the people and the authorities, losing his mind and his life. Masaniello has been mythologized as a precursor of Neapolitan nationalism and as a leader of the poor. The story of his rise and fall is memorized through a popular song, and it was also the subject of a popular play. The moral of the story seems to be multilayered. Masaniello is at once a hero and an anti-hero. Like so many Neapolitans, he was poor but he was astute, he was able to capitalize on his wits and his charm. His story seems to say on the one hand that you can't keep the people of Naples down for too long: they have the capacity, courage and imagination to rebel and shake the bastions of power. On the other hand, there is also here a warning of the impossibility of real change and of the dangers of dealing with the powerful too closely: power corrupts and the man of humble origins can be used and discarded and die in a state of humiliation.

Protest is not only expressed in stories and songs. It is also an integral part of life in the city. Neapolitans have devised effective group as well as individual strategies to confront the problems of poverty and deprivation. Many of these are considered to be 'unorthodox' methods, verging on illegality and criminality in that they are disruptive of public life and often result in damage to property. Setting fire to car tyres in the middle of a busy road is a favoured form of neighbourhood protest. Protests regarding water supplies or other local problems take this form of direct action, as men, women and children draw attention to their plight. These forms of spontaneous protest are sometimes resorted to by factory workers as well. By taking the issue from the factory to the street, their problem becomes public, they can rally the local population to their cause and, of course, bring about major disruption.

The 'movement of the organized unemployed' during the 1970s is the most publicized response to the acute problems of the Neapolitan poor and addresses the basic question: the unavailability of work.[12] The movement attracted the unemployed, especially young people, and mostly men, but also those whose work was precarious or unsatisfactory, so that even those who had a trade might be tempted to join if business was bad. What is interesting is that the movement attracted people who had never before been involved in any political movement or activity.

During the cholera epidemic in 1973 many unemployed were recruited to help out with cleaning the city. After the crisis the problem of the lack of employment for these people presented itself again and as a solution the lists were created. That is to say, groups of unemployed gathered and created lists which were then presented to the authorities. From then on recruitment of the unemployed for jobs was carried out from these lists. Because recruitment was carried out on the basis of professional categories or specializations, many of the original members of the list were never recruited, since no market opened up for their particular skills (barbers, bakers, etc.). Such people constituted the core of the Sacca Eca group. There were yet other categories of unemployed: the intellectual unemployed, young graduates unable to find an outlet for their university degrees, or the *monumentalisti* who had been employed during the restoration of the city.[13]

The relationship between the unions and the unemployed is a difficult one. The CGIL and the PCI had an established link with the 'league of unemployed', which they recognized as the legitimate representatives of the unemployed in Naples. On the other hand, the situation of the unemployed movement was far more complex. The 'street' movement was beyond the control of the leagues, of the unions and of the parties.

There were many incidents of violence on the streets of Naples involving the organized unemployed. One of these incidents, referred to in the press as '*la guerra tra i poveri*' (the war of the poor against the poor) in February 1978 involved two groups of unemployed: the '*Nuove Liste del '76*' or the 'New Lists of '76' and the *Sacca Eca*. The incident resulted in the destruction of eight public transport buses, an injured ticket collector, an injured passer-by and two arrests. Some journalists interpreted the matter as a confrontation between the two groups that had erupted into violence, whereas others interpreted it as a discussion between two groups which was then severely repressed by the police. The problem was that the *Sacca Eca*, the last remnants of the original lists, felt that they were owed a priority position when it came to the allocation of jobs, while the *Nuove Liste* group refused to accept that they be placed at the bottom of the pile. In all cases observers agreed that the intervention of the police had been unnecessary and excessive.

A perhaps more significant incident which illustrates the difficulties faced by the unions when it comes to the unemployed is the invasion by the organized unemployed of various union buildings and of the *Camera del Lavoro*.[14] The first union to be pressurized directly was the CISL, the union most closely associated with the Christian Democrat party, but the CGIL (Communist–Socialist Union) was also to be a target. One evening the central offices of the CGIL were invaded by a large and fairly noisy group of unemployed men declaiming the shortcomings of the unions when it came to representing them and to fight for more jobs. Many in the union felt that these were 'dangerous elements', led and inspired by Fascists. Many were in favour of calling in the police to clear the demonstrators away. However, the union opted for a pacifying attitude and talked at length to the unemployed, explaining their limitations, problems, and what kind of action the union could and could not take on their behalf. The occupation ended peacefully. But the incident reveals the despair of the unemployed, and the inability of the unions to contain the movement, to channel it and of course to solve the basic problem of unemployment.

The attitude of the CGIL, as revealed by this incident, was ambivalent. There was a recognition of their incapacity to deal with the problem, but there was also among many union members and activists the idea that, with the exception of the leagues which were more or less under their control, the unemployed were manipulated by provocateurs of the extreme left or the right. There was often a misunderstanding of the specific problems of the movement both in terms of resolving their problems and in terms of the instruments that the movement had available to put forward their claims and exercise pressure. The procedures for action and negotiation developed by the trade union movement (for example negotiation between management and workers, strike action, etc.) were not only unsuitable for the unemployed movement but predisposed the trade union movement to a misconstruction and non-acceptance of the 'unorthodox' methods used by the unemployed.[15]

The tensions between the trade unions and the movement reflected the serious rifts and divisions which existed within the working class. These divisions were not restricted to the different interests of the employed and the unemployed. Trades were differentiated and ranked according to status and trade union strength. The metallurgical trades were dominant politically and were perceived as constituting the cream of the working class. The members of these trades were frequently very well informed and highly politicized. The wage levels here tended to be higher than in other trades. Prestige also attached to them because they were considered to be more typically 'masculine' and 'strong'. Workers, male or female, employed in other trades, such as textiles, garments or food, were usually employed in smaller units; their unions were weaker and bedevilled by the fragmentation that characterized these industries; and workers' wages in these trades were lower. Furthermore, jobs in these trades were considered to require less skill and less strength, and to be less 'virile' than work in the automobile industry and, especially, work in the steel plants.

Relations between members of different trades were often distant and even hostile. An example of the feelings current among many workers (and usually the more politicized of them) in the textiles, food and other trades, is provided by a conversation held between Enzo, a young man who worked in a food plant, and an Italsider worker who was a sympathizer of 'Il Manifesto' (at the time an extreme left group) who had only been at Italsider for six months, prior to which he had been a member of the 'organized unemployed'. Enzo agreed that the 'metalmeccanici' were the most politicized group of workers in the city, and the most organized. But he argued that they did not try to use their strength to involve other groups of workers. They were solely concerned with the problems of their own trade and 'don't give a damn about the others'. This allegation of a lack of working-class solidarity on the part of the metalmeccanici was countered by the Italsider worker, who evidently had come to identify with the metalmeccanici in a very short period. Enzo was extremely angry at what he considered to be the élitism of these workers. Many men employed in the 'lesser' trades revealed similar emotions and were critical of the metal trade workers, though many expressed their criticism in less political terms, concentrating on what they saw as the arrogance of these workers rather than their political shortcomings.

The differences in status and degree of politicization were also reflected in attitudes to education. Though of course this did not apply to all members of the trade, involvement in factory politics, in the trade union and in political parties encouraged an effort to self-improvement and towards education and 'culture'. Homes frequently displayed a library, usually small but in some cases very extensive. This might include Marxist works, but also works of literature and philosophy, both by Italian and other authors. There were schemes which facilitated the purchase of books by paying for them in instalments, so even those not ambitious enough to read Gramsci, Marx, or Tolstoy (or Percy Allum's study of Neapolitan politics, which was quite widely discussed at the time) would invest in an expensive multi-volume encyclopedia for the improvement of their children. This, in an environment where even magazines and newspapers were an infrequent presence in people's homes, was quite striking. The heavy industries favoured by the pole of development interventions and the industries which have a longer history in the area, such as textiles and leather goods, have been particularly vulnerable in the changing economic climate of the 1980s. Competition squeezed out many businesses which produced for the international market, and the steel plant at Bagnoli was phased out. The workers employed here have been living on *cassa integrazione*, supplemented where possible by other 'jobs' or alternative strategies. In 1994 the unemployment rate for Campania was 20.44 per cent, one of the highest in Italy, surpassed only by Sicily (23.23 per cent) and Sardinia (21.12 per cent). Further redundancies are expected in Southern establishments: 4,000 jobs are expected to go in Taranto at the steel plant and 1,300 jobs are likely to be lost in the Fiat plant in Pomigliano. Whereas hope is in sight for some companies in the North of the country, the South, which felt the impact of the recession earlier, is less likely to see an end to the crisis in the foreseeable future. Mass unemployment is likely to remain a central feature of Neapolitan and Southern life.

Although, as many workers and academics have pointed out, the high percentages of unemployed and underemployed and the large number of those who survive by carrying out a number of different jobs, those whose jobs are precarious, and those whose jobs are illegal does have implications for political action and ideologies, the problems of the South cannot be approached solely from the perspective of the working class. Donolo (1972) argued, in a similar vein to A. Gunder Frank, that conditions in the South favoured the emergence of a *borghesia dello sottosviluppo*, a bourgeoisie of under-development, whose entrepreneurial interests were based on speculation and over-exploitation rather than the development of an efficient, dynamic and competitive economic structure. These entrepreneurs have a vested interest in reproducing the economic and political status quo (Gribaudi 1980).

Others, such as Galasso (1978), see the nature of the problem as being broader and more complex. He argues that there is a long-standing absence of civic culture in Naples: neither under Spanish rule, nor as part of a unified Italy, was there a drive to develop a sense of government and a sense of civil society. Nor was there ever a group capable of promoting such developments.

An absence of commitment to a community was noted by Banfield (1958) in connection with rural Southern Italian society. Banfield attempted to explain the unwillingness of the villagers of Montegrano to organize (which he thought in turn explained their persisting poverty) in terms of the existence of an ethic of 'amoral familism', that is to say, an exaggerated individualism and focus on the nuclear family. This, he felt, detracted from an identification with wider forms of community, including the national state. In a somewhat more sensitive and sympathetic vein, Carlo Levi (1982) notes that the peasants he met during his period of political exile in Lucania during the Fascist period experienced the State solely in terms of exploitation, repression and the conscription of the young men into the army. The heroes of these peasants were not national political figures. On the contrary, this privilege was conceded to the bandits who once populated the area. He quotes a peasant as saying:

> 'Everyone knows . . . that the fellows in Rome don't want us to live like human beings. There are hailstorms, landslides, droughts, malaria and . . . the State. These are inescapable evils; such there always have been and there always will be. They make us kill off our goats, they carry away our furniture, and now they're going to send us to the wars. Such is life!'

He continues:

> 'To the peasants the State is more distant than heaven and far more of a scourge, because it is always against them. Its political tags and platforms and, indeed, the whole structure of it do not matter. The peasants do not understand them because they are couched in a different language from their own, and there is no reason why they should ever care to understand them.' (Levi 1982: 78)

Conclusion

The history of government in the South, both prior to and following 1861, has generated a difficult or even antagonistic relationship between the State and the citizen. The very concepts of State, government and citizenship are disputed. Although these problems apply to Italy as a whole (Ginsborg 1990) the South has experienced these problems far more acutely as a result of economic differences and political imbalances derived from the very history of the Italian state. In a city such as Naples, which has a history of mass pauperism and which in some respects rivals many a Third world city, the problems appear insurmountable to the political militant, to the bureaucrat and to the citizen. This has resulted in populist alternatives winning the day on several occasions, supported as they were by the cientelistic relationships forged between national and local governments. In spite of this, and of the impatience of many Neapolitans with the bureaucratic procedures which sometimes pass for democracy, it would be a mistake to write off political attitudes and behaviour here as backward or amoral or as simply driven by marginality. On the contrary, just as many Neapolitans attempt to circumvent bureaucratic–democratic procedures because they have been ineffective, so too do they creatively address the question of

change and of improving their lot.   Whether this is through political
parties, autonomous social movements or individual or family
strategies depends both on the time and the place occupied by these
individuals or groups in Neapolitan and Italian society.

Notes

1. This is discussed by Marx in *Capital* Volume I, quoting many others
concerned with these issues.
2. See the fascinating, detailed account of the life and customs of the
Neapolitan poor, written in the late nineteenth century by Matilde Serao
(1988).
3. Interview with Michele Gargiullo, September 1976.
4. Although in many households television brought into the home images
of distant realities, these were often talked about as being either assimilated
into the immediate environment, or remaining as a vague and distant place.
5. The attitudes described by Grasso were reflected in a country-wide survey
reported in *la Repubblica* in June 1994, in which a majority of those interviewed
expressed grave disillusionment with their government and the functioning
of the State. The Italian state compared unfavourably with other European
countries, whose citizens tended to have a more positive view of their State
and government institutions.
6. Allum (p.385) indicates that 40% of the monarchist vote was from
housewives.
7. Chubb (1982) emphasizes the significance of the electoral shift in favour
of the PCI, in a city with a history of such strong Monarchist and, later,
Christian Democrat sympathies. She stresses the importance of the cholera
epidemic in 1973, which exposed the degradation the city had suffered during
twenty years of clientelism. Furthermore, the Christian Democrat authorities
were unable to deal with the crisis, whereas the PCI effectively mobilized Party
members to assist in the crisis, and came to be seen as the party of 'good
government'.
8. Ginsborg (p. 398) shows how in 1978 47.3% of homes had no shower or
bath and 17.7% only had outside toilets.
9. See Pardo (1993) for an account of local perceptions of the left-wing
administration and an interesting discussion of some of the causes of the
decline in the PCI vote.
10. The PCI was replaced by the *Partito Democratico Socialista* at the Rimini
Congress in 1991. Not all PCI members agreed with the changes brought about
by Occhetto, the then party leader, and they reformed as *Rifondazione
Comunista*.
11. And the left maintained its hold in the areas with a long history of left-
wing voting traditions, such as the Centre regions of the country.
12. See Pugliese and Pinnarò (1985), who see the organized unemployed
movement as a form of resistance against informalization.
13. Many of those interviewed during the period of the Valenzi government
had obtained work through these lists. A handful had been taken on for

training as hospital nurses. The majority were employed as municipal street-cleaners. Problems arose when subsequent administrations privatized this service and the jobs became open to clientelistic and *camorristic* controls.

14. The *Camera del Lavoro* is a local institution which operates as a meeting-place and representative of all unions within a given region.

15. In connection with the unemployed movement's unorthodox methods, Ginsborg gives an account of a week-long protest called a *sciopero a rovescio* or strike in reverse, which took place in the Policlinico, one of the largest hospitals of the city. Two hundred members of the movement worked side by side with the regular staff for the week to draw attention to the needs for additional personnel in the hospitals. Ginsborg points out that this tactic was used by rural workers in the late 1940s (Ginsborg 1990: 365).

four

A Brief History of Urban Space in Naples

Naples was founded by the Greeks, at a date which remains uncertain, given that the city shifted its location a number of times. However, the grid of one of these settlements still provides the outline to the shape of the old city. This original and restricted space was expanded at different times in the history of the city, which grew from a small port exporting grain to the Hellenic world to a quiet retreat for high-ranking Romans and to the bustling capital of a Kingdom. The geographical history of the city could be characterized as a sequence of processes of expansion followed by processes of involution. When expansion did take place, this was usually carried out in a haphazard, unplanned way.

By the fifteenth century Naples was a large city, and in fact remained second only to Paris until the end of the seventeenth century, when it was superseded by London. Naples was a pole of attraction for the populations of vast areas of the South. In the sixteenth century, immigration from the impoverished and oppressed countryside swelled the city. Expansion of the city into the present historic centre was insufficient to accommodate the growing population. This led to vertical development: Naples was unique in Europe as a skyscraper city, with buildings consisting of four, five and even six floors. This in turn resulted in a peculiar pattern of residence, where nobles, middle classes (artisans, etc.) and the poor working class lived side by side, or rather one on top of the other: aristocrats on the upper floors, middle classes on the middle floors and the populace on the ground floor (Galasso 1978).

Naples was at this time an important European centre both because of its size and because it was an important political centre with a splendid court life. It was the spin-offs of this courtly existence, alongside the enterprises founded and promoted by the State, that supported the population. But, with the massive influx of immigrants into Naples which the economic structure of the city was unable to absorb, a large lumpen-proletariat came to dominate much of the city.

71

These were the *lazzaroni*, who managed to survive against all the odds. The city did have industries, notably a silk industry, and later a ceramics industry which was established by the Crown, and a significant number of artisans' workshops. One of the long-standing characteristics of artisan production was the use of outworkers, who have been a presence in the old city at least since the sixteenth century.

The defeat of the Bourbon kingdom and the incorporation of the South into a unified Italian state had immense repercussions for the city. Not least was the withdrawal of royal patronage and of protectionist measures which exposed local producers to competition from the North, with dramatic consequences. Again the city turned in on itself for survival. The situation was eventually addressed by a number of laws and interventions by the Italian state, such as the establishment of the steelworks to the North of the city to form part of a pole of attraction in a regional development strategy. This created the conditions for the emergence of a strong, militant male working class. Another important intervention was the construction of rail communications between the centre and outlying towns and villages, thus effectively incorporating them into the dynamic of the city. It also facilitated the expansion of the city when, after the Second World War, people were relocated from the overcrowded centre to outlying regions. Expansion took two major forms: the massive building speculation in some areas of the centre, but principally on the hillsides and in the bay-side regions, transforming the famous view of the Bay of Naples. Here again, the growth of the city was haphazard, inspired as it was by the profit motive, and unrestrained by any standards of urbanization and planning. The second was the investment of State and local government funds in popular housing projects which were built in outlying regions and which rehoused many of those affected by the destruction caused by the war.

The lack of investment in infrastructure and the long-term neglect of the city's housing and services have resulted in growing deterioration. The outbreak of cholera in 1973 brought the problems of Naples home to the government and to the people, who conducted a vigorous campaign to fight off the spread of the disease. Yet nearly twenty years on Neapolitans were forced to take to the streets to protest over the lack of safe drinking water.

The plight of the city came to the attention of the world once again in 1980 when an earthquake left thousands of people homeless. Political patronage saw to it that they remained homeless for a very long time. Maurizio Valenzi was the Communist mayor of Naples at the time of the earthquake. In an interview with the *Guardian* in 1990 he explained that State funds aimed at the reconstruction of the damaged areas were held back until after the local elections of 1983, contributing to the downfall of the Communist-led authority, which was seen as having failed to deal with the crisis. The funds that were made available were principally distributed through clientelistic links and invested in large-scale, ultra-modern buildings which did little to resolve the housing problems of the city. At the same time, they offered a window of opportunity to the *camorra*, who had until then operated in fairly well-defined arenas, such as the fruit and vegetable markets of the hinterlands, and who were now able to expand their interests into the construction business. Their enhanced economic position was matched by a much closer association with the political structures. According to Ed Vulliamy, in the same *Guardian* article, out of eighty local councillors of the Comune di Napoli in 1990, thirty-eight (all but one of them, who was a Communist, were members of the parties in power at the time) were being investigated for association with the *camorra*.

The legacy of these different historical moments and events have implications for the contemporary residents of Naples. The 'historic centre' is characteristically composed of a labyrinth of narrow alleys cut across by the wider avenues constructed during attempts at 'risanamento' (improvement) of the city. The population density of these areas is high. Historically, high population densities were accommodated by the outmigration of the nobility from the city centre, which resulted in further subdivisions of the decaying *palazzi*, different sections of which were rented out to individual families. The status differences between those living on lower floors, particularly in the *bassi*, and those living higher up have been preserved, although they are sometimes contested by *bassi* dwellers who feel that the manners of those in the upper floors leave much to be desired. This central area is still characterized today by the simultaneous presence of middle-class residents and a large number of persons who must 'manage' to make a living on a very limited resource base. At the same time, there is a long tradition of artisanship and there are mechanisms for the transmission of skills. The apprenticeship, whether to an artisan or an outworker was still, in the late seventies, a fairly reliable way of becoming trained and employable (or, often, self-employable). The layout of the central areas and the construction styles of much of the old quarters facilitate neighbourhood interaction and street-to-home contact. In fact, in the ground-floor habitations or *bassi*, there was some degree of continuity between the street and the home.

The *bassi* of Naples are as infamous as the *lazzaroni*. These street-level habitations are characteristic of the narrow alleyways of the old city. Consequently they are often damp and dark. They typically consist of a single living space with a small cooking area and bathroom attached. Some have created divisions within their *basso* so as to create differentiated space. But the majority are too small to allow for much improvization. Although they are kept extremely clean, as is the outlying pavement (one of the early morning sights and sounds of the old city is that of the women washing their steps and the surrounding pavement or street), proximity to the street does imply a threat from the high population of rats which plagues the city.[1] Whereas many are today occupied by old couples whose children have married and settled elsewhere, these families have in the past, and other families still do, bring up their children in this restricted space. Children may carry on living with their parents well into adulthood. Because of the housing shortage, adult children may be unable to find a new home at marriage, so they may live with their parents for some time. This is seen as a problem in terms of organizing space and, for the young couple especially, there is the added disadvantage of lack of privacy.[2]

Some *bassi* have multiple functions: as homes and as work spaces. This is the case with outworkers' homes. They will locate their machines close to the door, often overlooking the street. Other *bassi* dwellers may improvise and set up a small store from their door or window. Others may use their homes as selling points for contraband cigarettes. Although this continuity between the street and the home could be advantageous, it could also render the inhabitants of the *bassi* very vulnerable to crime, which has been a growing problem throughout the seventies and eighties.

Bassi or other flats may also house a workshop, particularly a family workshop. Larger units, or workshops dealing with mechanical, woodwork or other noisy, dirty and space-consuming activities may be carried out in *bassi* which have been turned over to this purpose, or in abandoned churches or other ex-public places. There were also a number of factories in the centre, which recruited labour from the local neighbourhoods, either as factory workers or as outworkers. Recruitment of outworkers could take place on a door-to-door basis here, as there was a strong concentration of homeworkers in the shoe and leather trades operating in these areas.

Finding work as an outworker was not difficult here during the 1970s and early 1980s. Workers in the *bassi* in particular were highly visible, and an interested entrepreneur could recruit without difficulty. Furthermore, many workers had contacts through friends or kin with factories in the centre or further afield. In addition, the presence of workshops in the centre offered further opportunities for employment, in particular for women, although certain trades, such as glove- or trouser-making, recruited men as well, and some, such as the furniture business, recruited only men.

A fairly typical household arrangement here would revolve around a husband's employment in a workshop or in the service sector, and a wife's work as an outworker. In cases where the husband was unemployed or only earning irregularly the burden of securing a steady income would fall almost entirely on the wife. In order to maximize her working time she would try to share tasks with neighbours or kin living nearby, for tasks such as child-care or cooking. If a woman had a daughter of a suitable age (which was often considered to be as young as eight or nine years of age) she might delegate much of the housework to the girl in order to free herself for income-generating work.

Thus, the proximity of kin and/or close ties with neighbours was in many cases a central element in the organization of time and resources. In one household, the wife's mother, who lived on the same street, took responsibility for most of the child-care. Neighbours also helped, though on a less regular basis. It was not uncommon to find a division of labour involving several households. Mother–daughter and sister relations were the most likely to be used in this way, although the mother-in-law and daughter-in-law relationship might also fill this function. It is not surprising that the majority of women interviewed expressed a preference for living near their kin. But this strategy has been undermined over time by pressures from the housing market, which has forced new couples to find homes for themselves far from the centre.

The working-class suburbs were built on the basis of family flats in blocks, usually no more than four or five storeys high. Transfer from the old city to the new suburbs meant considerable disruptions to people's networks. Some housewives attempted to re-create the conditions of the *bassi* by leaving their front doors open for most of the day, thus encouraging contact with passers-by and allowing easy access to neighbours. However, in some complexes this was considered inappropriate and even dangerous, and doors were kept firmly closed and callers looked upon with suspicion. The intensity of interaction between neighbours also appeared to diminish. But although households were more dispersed here, it was not uncommon to find relatives living nearby.

Where kin lived nearby, cooperation was an important feature of people's living strategies. Outworkers here had to rely almost entirely on their own networks and those of friends and neighbours to obtain work, as direct recruitment was more difficult in these areas. Although friends and kin helped with child-care here as well, the assistance appeared to be considerably less intense than in some of the cases encountered in the old city.

Although in one of these areas there was a busy shopping centre, this was some distance away from many of the housing estates. Here trips to the shops were supplemented by the visit of vendors, in particular the fish-vendor, who would typically call out to the balconies offering fresh anchovies, a cheap and popular food.

Housewives often emulated their counterparts in the old city, lowering a basket on a rope from their windows or balconies so that the transaction could take place without having to come down the stairs, perhaps leaving a sauce on the fire or a baby in a cot. The distance to the shops offered entrepreneurial possibilities. In one household, where the male head of household worked in a small shoe factory for a low wage, his wife contributed to the household income by purchasing staples in bulk and re-selling them to the neighbourhood. One of this woman's daughters was married and living nearby, working as an outworker for a friend of her father's. Another was living temporarily with her parents in their house, though married and with a small child, since her husband was settling down to a new job with the railways far from Naples. Convenience and deep nostalgia for Naples and her family encouraged her to prolong her stay. A younger daughter had specialized from an early age in doing the cooking and the cleaning, while the very youngest was still at school.

Pressure on housing was not only a problem in the centre[3] – even in the working-class suburbs people were forced to move further afield. Such a move was often contemplated only by those able to afford a car. However, with a rail link which provided a reliable service linking the centre, the working-class suburbs and some of the outlying areas, there was a growing population clustered around these lines. These outlying areas, which were once relatively autonomous villages and therefore have their own centres, offer a very differentiated use of space, where modern blocks of flats built with a view to maximum profits are interspersed with the fields and farmhouses of those who still hang on to some of their land. Small-scale cultivators and commuters thus lived side by side.

Some of these centres became important as sites for the location and relocation of industries, which might be formal enterprises, or alternatively might be organized on an entirely informal basis. It was primarily in these areas that 'mushroom factories' abounded: i.e. factories that initiated manufacture and then closed overnight at the first signs of trade union infiltration or industrial action by the workforce. The ease with which factories could be established and closed down is related to the small scale of the enterprises, the mobility of the machinery and materials and the total disregard for the legal requirements with regard to health and safety in factory environments.

Relations between the new settlers in these areas and the original population were often slow in developing. In some cases the new buildings were concentrated in one area, almost ghetto-like, although young couples who had been born and bred in the area might also live there. There were also perceived differences between the two groups, with consequent suspiciousness on both sides. Some of the new inhabitants felt that as urbanites they were superior to the locals, whom they considered to be 'caffoni' (rustic, uncouth). For some of the new settlers, especially the women, there was an initial problem of being far from kin, which deprived them of important sources of support and of an intensity of interaction which was difficult to replace in the new setting. On the positive side, housing here was generally spacious and modern. Many prized the clean air, the relative quiet, and the presence of cheap local produce, which was in most cases considered to be superior in quality to the goods purchased in shops and markets in the city centre.

My own household fell into the category of new arrivals in one of the outlying areas. The flat was extremely spacious and comfortable, and it was surrounded by fields and, less fortunately, by a pig-sty. Our household was very unusual in Naples since it was based on rather different principles than those that generally obtained. I lived with a young married couple who originally came from a working-class suburb not too far away. They aimed at establishing egalitarian domestic arrangements. All three of us had an income for most of the time. The husband worked in the Italsider plant, the wife was an employee in the trade union. Pooling of incomes was not complete, since I paid my share of rent, bills and food, but other costs were covered singly. Although as mentioned, there were generally three incomes available, there was little money to spare, since investment in a number of modern appliances involved heavy monthly repayments. On the other hand, these appliances were important parts of a strategy aimed at keeping costs and – more unusually – labour-time down to as low a level as possible. A car allowed bulk purchases of seasonal goods in distant markets and bulk-buying in supermarkets for other items which could be stored in a freezer compartment.

A very narrow strip of land under the balconies provided the opportunity for the husband to grow lettuce, aubergines, carrots and spinach. This gave him enormous satisfaction, and, although it may not have made a great impact on the household budget, it did provide us with very fresh produce. We also took advantage of local producers. Whenever possible we purchased the local log-fire oven-baked bread from a woman who lived nearby but produced only a limited batch of bread, which sold out rapidly. Next door to us was a slightly larger than usual holding, shared by a group of brothers who ran a fairly intensive mini-agribusiness. From them we purchased the occasional rabbit or chicken, eggs, apples and pears. Our own block of flats had been built on a piece of land that had belonged to the same family. This particular plot had been inherited by a woman whose husband (not a Neapolitan, as we were frequently reminded) was a policeman. They decided to convert the land into residential property. Our landlord supplemented the income he gained from the rent and from his pension by buying grapes in bulk and fermenting wine in our basement for his own consumption and for sale.

For those who were long-term residents in these areas the options were different again. Distance from kin was unlikely to be a problem, and married children found it easier to find accommodation they could afford near their families of origin. Many householders had inherited their homes and therefore had few worries in relation to housing costs. Some also had small plots of land, which, depending on size, they could exploit commercially or for their own use.

Monetary incomes may be less significant for such households, and they could manage to get by on very little cash indeed. In one case, the male head of household was a rag-and-bone man whose income from this activity was irregular. He also worked on a small plot near the house. His son contributed towards his keep but earned very little, and was expected to save up for his marriage. A married daughter was a daily presence in the household, although she lived in a modern flat in the same area. However, she found it convenient to spend most of the day with her mother and sisters, who took it in turns to feed, clean and play with her toddler. The unmarried daughters organized their day around domestic duties and unskilled outwork which brought in very little money. This money was intended primarily to build up their trousseau and therefore it made little or no impact on the household budget. The wife–mother spent her day doing housework, which in her case was particularly onerous as it coincided with what is sometimes described as 'self-provisioning'. On a very small patch of land, which was usually tended by the mother, the household grew vegetables. The women also cared for the chickens, some rabbits and a pig, which was slaughtered before Christmas. Through a variety of activities and different sources of food and income this household managed to get by with very little dependence on commercial outlets and little contact with the cash economy.

Yet further away, and in areas not served by commuter train services, the encroachment of commuters was less significant. Although factory work was available in some areas, especially for young women, agriculture was the most important activity here. Some agricultural work was primarily geared towards self-provisioning. But there was also the commercial production of fruit and vegetables for local, national or international markets, which provided opportunities for work. Women were the main workers used for picking, turning and packing fruit, and most of the women encountered in this type of work were in the higher age group. As Allum (1975) points out, there is a striking contradiction in Neapolitan agriculture, between the net income generated by agriculture and the poverty of the rural population. Landholdings are very small, and few cultivate their own land. There was a heavy reliance on casual labour for picking and turning the fruit, but this work was seasonal and badly paid. The difficulties faced by these people were exacerbated by the grip of the *camorra* over many local markets and distribution points. So here too incomes were low and irregular, and household members were forced to resort to a number of different strategies and activities, not least that of attempting to provide some security by signing on to the official list of agricultural workers. A trade unionist with ample experience in these areas argued that many of the women present at the trade union meetings attended to ensure that their name was on 'the list', even though they had never picked an apple or a pear in their life.

In all the different areas examined, households and individuals frequently bridged formal and informal activities, and it was often difficult to draw the line between these types of activity. Such interconnections have been pointed to by a number of people working in the South. Mingione (1983) rightly suggests that the analysis should focus on households. He defines these as units of reproduction, and analyses the relationship that exists between different kinds of activities of households, whether they are income-generating or subsistence-oriented. A number of factors impinge on households: the demand for specific types of labour and the ability of households to supply this demand; the capacity of the State to provide support in terms of income and/or services; the conditions which may allow for subsistence activities; and having access to the support and assistance of neighbours, friends or kin. Given the specific conditions that obtain in each case, households have to choose how to allocate time and energy: whether to allocate preferentially to activities which generate a monetary income or to spend more time and energy on intensified domestic work which may help cut expenditure. Mingione argues that what is specific to the Southern Italian case in comparison with more industrialized areas is that in Southern Italy the informal sector has a longer tradition, the population is poorer, and the informal sector is less complementary *vis-à-vis* formal economic structures and positions. In the case of Naples it is true that there is a history and a tradition of informal activities, but their context has changed and is constantly changing, and strategies developed over time may become obsolete or impractical. This is the case with networks which are broken down as a result of housing policy (or the lack of it) or as local enterprises succumb to the competition of cheaper goods produced in South-east Asia, depriving entrepreneurs and workers of an income.

Mingione also identifies differences in respect of the informal sectors of underdeveloped countries. He argues that in such countries the informal sector has an impact on the reproduction of labour and has a structural effect on the cost of living and, therefore, on the cost of labour. In Southern Italy, on the other hand, informalization is principally to do with the reproduction of what he considers to be 'by now a chronic strata of surplus population' (Mingione 1983: 36). In other words, here the informal sector supports (and barely) a fraction of the population which is almost definitely and permanently excluded from the accumulation process of industrial capital. His assessment is in fact reminiscent of the arguments put forward by Nun (1969) and Quijano (1974) regarding the 'marginal mass' or, a preferable concept, the 'marginal pole' of the economy, which suggested precisely that sectors of the population in Peru were permanently or semi-permanently excluded from the economy.

There is a growing contradiction between population and employment, albeit to different extents and in different ways, evident in cities within the new world economy. The State plays a determinant role in providing (or not) services and support for those marginalized as a consequence of current economic trends. The majority of peripheral and semi-peripheral countries lack the resources to deal with this problem in a satisfactory way. Core countries, on the other hand, have behind them a history which has provided them with the means to implement policies to support these sectors, but they too are facing a crisis. Fiscal difficulties mean that core states find it increasingly difficult to fund these policies, and there is a consequent decline in welfare provisions and community services. This forces ever-larger sectors of the population to devise alternative methods of survival. In the case of Naples, poverty and unemployment are both massive and long-standing. But equally long is the history of survival strategies in the city.

The Household and the Allocation of Labour

Because of high levels of unemployment and underemployment and the precariousness of work, it is uncommon to find a household which can rely on the wages of the household head on a permanent and long-term basis. In most cases the household is an important pooling unit to which the various members contribute income and/or labour, often from a very early age (cf. Belmonte 1979). Women too may be expected to make a monetary contribution in addition to their domestic labour. Women may also be involved in the activities of the 'informal sector', selling contraband cigarettes in the street or from their homes. Some specialize in dealing with the bureaucracy as intermediaries in transactions for arranging pensions and other documents. This is generally a lengthy, time-consuming affair, which many women, especially those who work in factories or as outworkers, would rather delegate. Women who have sewing skills may mend or adjust clothes for a neighbourhood clientele, or if they have sufficient skills and time they may work in a factory or workshop, or as outworkers.

From my own and others' material it seems clear that women constitute the majority of outworkers, and that they are the last link in the subcontracting chain generated by decentralized production. They are also likely to be employed in small workshops run on the basis of family or friendship relations, and may be involved in other activities which fall under the rubric of the 'informal sector'. Whereas men and male children are more likely to perform street activities such as petty trading, car attending and so on, women are likely to carry out activities closer to home or at any rate organized on the basis of personal networks. They may turn a street-level window into a small sweetshop or they may buy sugar, flour, and other staples in bulk and re-sell to neighbours, sell contraband cigarettes or work at market stalls. In most of these activities profit margins are low but nevertheless considered to be worthwhile.

That apparently unrewarding activities may be worthwhile can be understood if we locate the individual within the context of the household, seen as a cooperating unit where pooling of various resources takes place. It is therefore important to consider the Neapolitan household and its strategies for survival before considering the outworkers themselves.

Ideally, marriage in Naples is neolocal. In practice various arrangements are made to adapt to a situation of scarce and expensive housing. These arrangements may be permanent or very temporary and may involve members of a single household or several households. The definition of 'household' presents several difficulties (cf. Harris 1981), not least in Naples. If we take as our starting-point a definition of household as all those who live under a single roof we would face difficulties in those cases where, for example, a number of children will leave their parents' home nightly to sleep (and sometimes also eat) with their grandparents. If we define the household in terms of sharing food we again face difficulties in that there are cases of kin who might live some distance away from each other and yet regularly share a meal: in some cases people may share the midday meal or all meals, yet sleep in separate houses; in other cases people (usually women and their children) may take turns to have a meal at each other's houses; in yet another case a woman who worked with her sister ate and fed her children at her sister's home and in the evening prepared her husband's meal in her own home. Thus when we talk of households in Naples we are referring to very fluid arrangements both in terms of residence and in terms of sharing food or pooling resources: they are resource-sharing units which frequently overlap. Which particular arrangements prevail will depend on circumstances, that is on what income is available, on proximity to kin and resources, and on personal orientation, which will depend in particular on the quality and intensity of the relationships maintained with kin and neighbours. While bearing in mind these qualifications, it is nonetheless useful to retain the term 'household', because it constitutes the site for sets of key relationships, and entails activities which constitute the creation of survival strategies.

Survival must be understood in relation to the relatively immediate confrontation with the difficult economic situation of Naples as well as to long-term strategies designed to improve the conditions of the household members. With regard to short-term survival strategies, one of the central features of the working-class household is pooling. Pooling within the household takes various forms. What was seen as the 'classical' form was where a man was employed and a woman was not, or was only employed in occasional work, where a husband took what he needed for his personal consumption (cigarettes, enough money for his own coffees and drinks at the bar and to treat friends and acquaintances) and handed the rest of his earnings over to his wife, who was expected to manage the expenses of the household with this sum. Where both worked regularly it was common to have a division of responsibility for paying bills and rent. Where the husband was unemployed, the income provided by his wife or children was likely to be the only basis for survival. However, even where a husband was unemployed or irregularly employed, children were often not expected to contribute more than an approximation of the costs of their own upkeep. Most women said that they felt their children had needs of their own, they had to think of their future and had to accumulate in preparation for it. The income of the various children, or part thereof, was generally handed over to the mother, who, together with her own earnings and any possible income deriving from State pensions or subsidies, would use this total very carefully to feed her family and meet all necessary costs. Many of the women who were interviewed had a very precise idea of exactly how much they spent on each item, how prices fluctuated and varied from shop to shop. Their immense generosity belied a constant accounting process whereby each and every item was costed.

The Organization of Consumption

Households frequently carried out activities intended to reduce the costs of daily reproduction. Many of these activities were labour-intensive and required the labour of all the household or indeed might bring together members from different households. This was the case of *u pummarola*, or preparing the tomatoes. For this task tomatoes are bought in bulk. The tomatoes are then washed and trimmed and prepared for storage. There are various ways of preparing them: cut into fine strips with their skins on for one kind of dish, peeled and whole for another kind, puréed with basil for yet another. The job is labour-intensive, and several people were likely to be involved, male and female. Given that tomatoes are a cornerstone of Neapolitan cooking, they were the most important vegetable conserved in preparation for the winter months. But other vegetables such as aubergines and mushrooms were also popular, and some families liked to preserve fruits and make liqueurs. This work ensured that a family could cut down on the considerable expense of buying canned items; furthermore the home-treated product was considered to be superior in flavour and quality.

Other households who lived on the outskirts or who had rural links could also invest in fattening a pig, which was then slaughtered in the autumn and prepared to provide the household with fat and meat for the winter. Pieces of pork are salted and dried, sausages are made, lard is prepared. It is said that every inch of the animal is used. For those who have the space to keep one or two pigs it is a worthwhile investment: the young animal is bought fairly cheaply and it is fed on scraps and leftovers, causing no extra expense to the household in return for some meat and animal fat which, given the skilful use of animal protein in Neapolitan cooking, will almost see a family of five through the winter. The animal is slaughtered by a professional and the members of the household, often helped by friends or kin, prepare and cure the meat.

As we have seen in the previous section, those who have access to even a very small plot of land are likely to grow some vegetables: tomatoes, carrots, lettuce, aubergines or spinach. In these areas it may also be possible to purchase vegetables, chickens or rabbits, fruit and wine in local markets or directly from neighbouring producers.

Whatever the environmental conditions which offered opportunities for different kinds of strategy, households established an informal division of labour, which had significant repercussions for the future of its members. The effects of these strategies were enduring, and it was therefore necessary to consider current household strategies in the light of earlier strategies pursued by the household, or even by the households of origin of the adult couple. This is because different decisions regarding the allocation of tasks had an impact on the distribution of skills and resources between household members.

The case of the Arenella household illustrates the process of differentiation which took place in the household. The Arenellas lived in a two-bedroomed council flat in a working-class suburb. Mr Arenella had worked for most of his life in the steel plant, but had been forced to retire as a result of severe illness. His wife came originally from the agricultural hinterlands, and although she was an accomplished cook and knitter she never worked for a monetary income. Other skills she had acquired in her own household were redundant in the urban environment where they lived. Their eldest son, Antonio, 'inherited' his father's place in the plant when his father became ill. He was eighteen at the time and became the only breadwinner, together with his father's disability pension. He remained the most important source of income for ten years until he married.

His work at the steel mill allowed his younger siblings to carry on their studies. The second-eldest graduated in electronics and went on to train with a large Italian electronics conglomerate in the North of the country. The other two children, one male and one female, also continued their studies at university. None had contributed money or labour to the household during their years as university students, although it was hoped that the second son would be able to help a little after his training was completed. However, when he completed his training he married his childhood sweetheart and the family recognized that the new couple would be on a very tight budget and could not help his parents. But Mr and Mrs Arenella hoped that all the younger children would enjoy a secure future in some kind of white-collar or professional work.

Antonio, on the other hand, was made redundant and placed on *cassa integrazione* when the steelworks closed down in the late 1980s. Antonio's marriage had caused a lot of trouble and his family, in particular his mother, had opposed it. She felt the bride-to-be was unsuitable, although another interpretation for her reluctance to accept the marriage was that it deprived the household of their main income. They remained estranged for approximately two years after the wedding, after which the imminent arrival of a child brought the two families together again.

As we can see, in the Arenella household the long-term and short-term survival strategies involved unequal treatment of the children. The eldest son had carried the household for more than ten years and his dedication to wage-labour freed the other children from an early introduction to work, allowing them to study and to lead lives more typical of the children of a middle-class family than of a working-class family. This was perceived by Antonio as being a situation of inequality, and despite his loyalty to his parents it generated considerable resentment.

Work in the steel plant was the best-paid blue-collar work available in Naples. So the Arenellas were in a relatively privileged position. Other households have had to rely on smaller incomes, and therefore their ability to sustain children through the education system has been more limited.

This was the case of the D'Angelo household. Here too there had been a division of labour between family members, so that the actions of one member had significant consequences for other members. In this case the role of the mother–wife as the pillar of the household, typical of so many Neapolitan households, is particularly clear.

The D'Angelos lived in a one-bedroomed council flat on a working-class estate. The family had been moved here by the council from the area of the Port. Although the flat had three rooms plus kitchen and bathroom, one room was a well-furnished dining-room with glass cabinets containing displays of glass and china items, a sofa with various soft toys and other purely decorative items. It was kept shut except when an important visitor was entertained. A second room contained a large double bed where Mr and Mrs D'Angelo slept. The third room was the *de facto* dining-room where the television was kept. This room also doubled up at night as a bedroom for the children.

At the time of research there were six family members in the household: Mr and Mrs D'Angelo, two sons in their late teens who lived in the household until they left temporarily to do their military service, a son of thirteen and a daughter of eleven or twelve years of age. However, here, as in the previous example, we must consider earlier strategies adopted by the household and the contribution made by members who had since left the household.

The eldest son, who was then in his mid-thirties, was married and lived with his wife and three small children in a separate household. He had started out on his own business while still very young. With very little capital he had started petty-trade activities and built up a business in which he regularly employed family members, including his youngest brothers. He had married quite young and lived some distance away from his parents' home.

The eldest daughter, who was about thirty years old at the time, had been taken out of school while still young (around twelve years of age) in order to work for wages and learn a trade. She had lived at home and contributed to the household. But unlike Antonio, she claimed that she had had a lot of money to spend on clothes, for example, and was much better off while living at her parents' home than she had been since she had married in her late twenties. She had searched desperately for a flat near her parents' home, but was unable to find anything nearby. She now lived approximately 20 minutes away from her parents' home and was a very frequent visitor there.

The second daughter, who was then in her mid-twenties, had left school and home in order to marry when she was only sixteen. She had married against her mother's will by getting pregnant. She lived with her husband and three small sons in a very small council flat which was in the same neighbourhood as her parents' home.

Mr D'Angelo suffered from ill health and only worked irregularly. Mrs D'Angelo was responsible for all the housework and in addition did some paid domestic cleaning work. During their military service the sons spent a considerable amount of time away from home, but when they visited they were unable to make any contribution. In any case, their mother explained that in spite of their good intentions their contributions were erratic even when they were at work. The youngest son, who was in his early teens, was still at school. During the afternoon and weekends and during the holidays he often worked in his elder brother's workshop. The youngest daughter, Valeria, was at school, and her mother hoped that she would continue her studies to become a secretary or clerical worker. She was expected to do very little at home. Valeria was also encouraged to study by her elder sister, and she did in fact complete her schooling. She subsequently became a nursery school teacher and continued living at home with her mother after her father died. All but the younger sons eventually left the household to set up their own homes.

This household had to manage on very little income: the father's pension and occasional wages, the small amounts the mother could earn as a cleaner, the small and erratic earnings of the sons who still lived at home. It would appear that some of the children who had left home made occasional gifts of money, food or special items which were given to their mother. There was some indication that this had to be done very carefully so as not to offend and especially so as not to anger the daughters' husbands. Christmas time provided the opportunity for openly making gifts of food and drink.

Mrs D'Angelo was the key to the organization of the household. She explained that she took a proportion of her sons' incomes to cover the cost of their food. They were responsible for clothing themselves. However, if she saw cheap socks or hankies or underwear at the market she would buy these for them and did not like to ask them for the money, since she had bought the items on her own initiative. She would take shoes to be repaired, and this was expensive; but again she paid for it out of her own pocket. When her sons visited from their military service she could not ask them to contribute because the army only gave them a pittance. In any case, the older boy in particular had always worked hard while still at home and had helped out since he was a young boy. But what this meant was that this woman had to juggle with what little her husband gave her, what her sons might contribute and what she herself might earn. Managing on this income meant investing a great deal of time and energy organizing, shopping around and cooking to a very tight budget. All the work and worries involved in this fell to the woman.

Again in this household we see an unequal distribution of tasks and responsibilities. It could be argued that the eldest daughter had been sacrificed, for although she had shown a good deal of promise at school she was not allowed to continue her studies. Instead she had had to become a wage-earner from a very early age. At the same time, she had not been expected to contribute significantly in terms of household labour. In her case, work gave her independence, money and a sense of self-worth. She did not feel that she had been exploited and maintained very close ties with her family and especially with her mother.

In any case the younger children might benefit from the labour of the older ones, unless these were to 'escape' by marrying and leaving home. It was thought that the second daughter had done precisely this, for had she stayed at home she would probably have carried the burden of housework and child-care to help her mother. With greater effort and to a lesser extent than in the case of the Arenellas, the mutual support of the household, managed by the mother, had allowed each child to find its feet and, in the case of the youngest daughter in particular, to obtain the kind of work she and her mother had wished for her. The activities of the parental generation are crucial here. Where a father has a well-paid secure job, children are able to complete schooling or opt for an apprenticeship. Since this was rare in the households encountered, it was common for more diversified activities to be carried out by all household members. Here the eldest child, especially the eldest son, could be forced to take the lead in providing for the group. As we have seen, his labour could enable younger siblings to extend their childhood and adolescence, complete schooling and even graduate from university. The mother's activities had direct implications for her daughters. Where the mother was not involved in income-generating activities, daughters could study or work. However, where mothers were forced to spend a considerable amount of their time in income-oriented work, it was usual for one of the daughters, often one of the younger ones, to take responsibility for the household. This meant that, when it came to setting up their own households, different daughters could count on different skills. So, a frequent pattern was that elder daughters were trained for factory work and could therefore find income-generating work either in a factory or as an outworker, while having very few household skills. Younger daughters, on the other hand, often had developed household skills and were efficient householders and managers, but were not equipped for income-generating work. This meant that when in need they were likely to be forced into low-pay unskilled outwork to fill the income gap of their households. On the other hand, where the division of labour in the household was successful, younger children, male or female, might leave housework and manual work and move up a notch or two in the labour-market towards clerical or other kinds of white-collar employment.

Relations of Cooperation: The Role of Women

Cooperation was the basis of the household's survival in Naples. But built into this cooperation, there were significant inequalities both in terms of inputs of labour and money and in terms of the distribution of these resources. Women had to bear the brunt of household labour, and frequently they made a monetary contribution as well. The division of labour between children was often unequal, the young ones benefiting from the sacrifices of older siblings. These inequalities could generate conflicts and resentments which sometimes simmered beneath the surface or sometimes exploded, causing serious rifts in the household and the family. The vagueness and the ambiguities detected in the statements of many Neapolitans regarding family and kin reflect these conflicts.

Most Neapolitans with whom the topic was broached agreed that mothers were the most important person in anybody's life. This opinion seemed to be unconditional, since it was put forward even in cases where there had been open conflict within a family (usually to do with some kind of rivalry between siblings) and where the mother had either not taken an active part in the informant's defence or had sided with the other party against him or her. There were always mitigating circumstances which redeemed the mother from blame and left her image or memory unblemished. For a number of women, relations with their mothers had been difficult, and there had often been confrontations at the time of courting. Mothers often attempted to prevent daughters from marrying men they considered to be a bad match, usually because of their profession. In such cases the conflict was often resolved by forcing the situation, through running away or becoming pregnant.

Apart from these exceptions, on the whole relations between mother and children appeared to be strong and enduring. Children visited their parents regularly. It was frequent for children, especially daughters, to live nearby, often on the same street. In these cases contact was continuous. Children might be taken to a grandmother to be looked after while their parents were at work. Slightly older children (twelve or so) might sleep at their grandparents' home. Cooking and eating could take place in one household (usually the mother/grandmother's), pooling resources of different households and thus saving money and labour.

Mother–daughter–sister solidarity was perhaps the most common. An interesting example of this was a group of women who were working together in a *basso* making flowers. The group consisted of a mother and some of her daughters (and at one point one of her sons came in, while he waited between his second day-job and his night-job). One woman who was 38 years old and whose husband was unemployed, had five children to support. She survived by intermittently doing outwork making artificial flowers, and ate with her mother and sisters. From them she borrowed bread, pasta and other staples. Another sister, 28 years of age, whose husband was a

salesman in a small shop, had the advantage of a steady income; but
their rent (they lived on the same street as her mother) was so high
that she too was forced to save by eating at her mother's home with
her two young children. Another sister, in her forties, was widowed
and had two children, and she too often ate at her mother's. So on a
regular basis it was the mother and father, both of whom received
pensions, and one daughter with her five children sharing food, and
on a less regular basis the other two daughters and their children. Since
the parents' pensions were inadequate they had resorted to outwork.
Here again, whoever was around joined in the flower-making.
They put the question to me: 'Who can a woman turn to when she's
in trouble?' 'Her mother' was their emphatic reply. The daughters
wished to avoid being ridiculed by their sisters-in-law, to whom they
presented a trouble-free façade in order to 'save face', and turned to
their mother and sisters for help. This link between mother and
daughters seemed to be widespread and very important. Relations
between mother and daughters were often easy and friendly,
contrasting with the relation of father to children, which was often
distant and might even verge on the hostile. The feelings of distance
towards affines expressed by the women in the above example was
encountered frequently during fieldwork. Most women would turn
to their mothers and sisters and would rarely be totally open with
their affinal kin. Yet there were many exceptions to this, for even if
relations may be more difficult between a woman and her mother-
in-law, the latter played a very important part in the life of the young
couple, especially with regard to the care of children. Many women
declared that they had a good relationship with their mother-in-law,
and a few said that they regarded their mother-in-law as their 'real'
mother, or as good as their own mother.
     Although family and kinship relations generally provided the raw
materials for cooperation, neighbours were often a source of support.
In several households in the old city women might exchange child-
care and shopping tasks, borrow staples and offer each other support
through friendship. For some, neighbours were more important as a
source of help than kin. This was more obviously so where there were
intrafamilial tensions or where women had not enjoyed a good
relationship with their mothers. Sometimes distance from kin also
encouraged a heavier reliance on neighbours. In the working-class
suburbs many households encouraged the movement of people
between households. Front doors were often left open to allow people
easy entry into each other's homes. One way of encouraging friendly
relations with neighbours was to make gifts of food when special food,
such as cakes or biscuits, was prepared. In the neighbourhood, as in
family-based cooperation, women were the principal agents, creating
and maintaining relations of support.

Conclusion

In the difficult conditions that prevail in the city of Naples households show considerable flexibility in arranging residence and commensality. Pooling of resources within the household was an important means of supporting family members. This meant that even very small monetary incomes were important. In some areas self-provisioning activities were significant in that they could reduce the extent of dependence on a monetary income. In addition, these activities increased a sense of self-sufficiency, which was a source of satisfaction to many.

The characteristics of the urban environment were central here in that they broadly determined the range of options open to different households. This involves both the physical environment, as for example the availability or otherwise of some land to grow vegetables or to breed a pig, and the social environment, including the proximity of kin, the density of the networks that each household in a particular area could mobilize, and the expectations and 'codes of practice' of neighbours in different areas. This might vary not only from area to area, but from *vicolo* to *vicolo*.

Upwardly mobile couples and/or those who could count on a regular and relatively good income might benefit from moving out of the old city or the working-class suburbs, because they gained in terms of having more spacious and better-equipped homes. But it is hard to imagine that such a move would be possible for the many households in the old city which survived through pooling multiple and often small and irregular incomes. For these households, being in the midst of dense networks of cooperation and solidarity was central to their survival. Moving to an area where no such networks were available to them, and where they would be removed from these multiple if erratic sources of work, would block their current strategies. Of course, for those who had been born and had grown up in the outlying areas of the city these networks were in place and were frequently mobilized. They often had the added advantage of being in a position where they could supplement their incomes through some degree of self-provisioning. On the other hand, they might well be at a disadvantage because of distance from sources of work.

So the history of the city, and the policies and interests that have shaped its growth, have generated a number of different 'urban' environments. People adapt to these environments but also try to shape them themselves and use them to their advantage, although clearly there are different limitations and possibilities attaching to each case.

The household was the primary unit in all these strategies, however much they might vary in size and composition. The deployment of household strategies, such as pooling, cooperation, and the division of labour between household members, relied heavily on people's recognition of the family as a positive entity based on reciprocity and love. Here the mother played a central role, both in reproducing these ideologies and in acting as a centre through which a number of relationships were articulated.

Although reciprocity was the ideal that guided and legitimized many of these strategies, there were often underlying tensions and conflicts. These derived primarily from the differential impact of strategies on household members. These strategies often relied on a division of labour which created work or educational opportunities for some whilst they limited these opportunities for others.

In the majority of households men were only expected to contribute a monetary income, or in some cases an equivalent such as garden produce. Given the economic situation of Naples many men were unable to guarantee this. Partly as a result of this, women were often expected to contribute an income as well as working at the domestic chores necessary to the upkeep of the household. This was central to the husband–wife relationship; but it also had implications for sons and daughters, in that from an early age girls might be expected to spend time on household chores. This was often simultaneous with schooling and/or training within a profession. The future careers of girls were therefore quite directly determined by their responsibilities in the home. Other divisions were implemented on a more flexible basis, although it was often the case that the eldest children were the most likely to start paid work at an early age, and it was common for the youngest daughter to take over responsibility for domestic chores for longer than was the case for her older sisters, who might marry out or be encouraged to work.

These strategies also had implications for the functioning of the economy. In particular, the divisions of labour in the household produced different categories of workers. Some members might be highly educated and achieve advanced professional training, thus being recruited into technical or management levels. Others would obtain solid training in skilled and semi-skilled tasks within specific trades, whilst yet others would have few recognized skills. The household therefore reproduced workers who could be slotted into different categories and different niches of the labour-market. This had implications for the organization of small enterprises and of outwork, as did the prevalence of ideologies grounded in ideals pertaining to the family and to kinship relations.

Notes

1. On the other hand, it is said that the vast rat population of Naples lives mainly on the rooftops.

2. In this chapter I consider some of the implications of the material conditions of housing and residence patterns, such as the potential for building and maintaining networks. There is also the important aspect of the symbolic construction of space, which is discussed by Pardo (1992).

3. In spite of the shortage of homes in the centre and in Naples generally, there are instances of houses being withheld from potential occupiers. According to Pardo, some houses acquired ambiguous status, which could be related to the fact that houses are not mere commodities but also are imbued with symbolic value (Pardo 1992).

five

Outworkers – Lives and Careers

The definition of an outworker in the trade union contract of the Italian textile and clothing industry is any person who, within a subordinate relationship, carries out at home or at similar premises, work which is paid for by one or more entrepreneurs, with or without the help of family members or resident apprentices, using their own materials, accessories and instruments, or those of their employers. Outworkers are usually resorted to by entrepreneurs to cover the more labour-intensive phases of production, without having to increase investment. In fact, the use of outworkers offers the entrepreneur many advantages in relation to flexibility and cost-cutting. As such, outwork is attractive to large and small businesses, traditional and modern industries.

Although the subcontracting system is often associated with underdeveloped economies, this is not necessarily the case. In Italy outwork is a feature of all regions, but is especially important in the industrially developed areas of the North and in the Centre of the country. In the South it is most frequent in the more industrialized areas, such as Naples.[1]

In Naples the vast majority of outworkers encountered during fieldwork were women.[2] In some trades, such as the glove trade or in trouser-making, there were men working at home; but even here they represented a very small minority. Men were more likely to be represented in the ranks of small enterprises, some of which would be based entirely on family labour. It is likely that at one time they represented a higher proportion of home-workers, but the decline of the industries concerned would have restricted their opportunities here. For women, on the other hand, outwork continued to be a viable or, sometimes, a unique option for generating an income. Women have worked at home for artisans and industries for many generations in Naples. Particular trades have been passed down from mother to daughter, and then again to the next generation of outworkers.

The case of trouser-making is interesting because it was an industry

93

in obvious and dramatic decline. In Naples, trouser-making had never been a factory-based form of production, operating instead through small independent tailors, and offering work opportunities to many men and women as apprentices or outworkers. Many men and women had in fact trained with a tailor; but by the 1970s trouser-makers in particular were involved in an uphill struggle. The flooding of the market by ready-made trousers and, in particular, the fashion of wearing jeans had seriously damaged the trade. Young people especially were unlikely to use their services, except perhaps in the summer months when they required a light-weight article.

Traditionally, the system's point of departure was the *sartoria* or tailor. The tailor produced a full set of clothes to measure. However, the trousers were sent out to a specialist trouser-maker. The trouser-maker or *pantalonaio* cuts the trousers according to the measures provided by the tailor. The *pantalonaio* has a group of people working for him who will do both the hand-sewing and the machine-work as well as the ironing. The trousers then return to the tailor for a fitting with the customer. They are then sent back to the *pantalonaio* to make the necessary alterations. The *pantalonaio* checks the alterations and distributes the labour amongst his workers. The finished pair of trousers are sent to the tailor.

A young man who had trained as a trouser-maker gave me the example of a *pantalonaio* with whom he had worked in the early 1970s. At that time he might be paid L6,000 for every pair of trousers he completed for the tailor. His wife worked for about half an hour on each pair, marking out the measurements on the cloth. She received no part of the earnings. Machine sewing was done by a woman who received L300 per pair; the ironing was done by a man for L300 per pair; hand-sewing was done by three women – two of whom were outworkers – who were paid L600 for each pair. The *pantalonaio*'s job was to cut the cloth – a very skilful job – and coordinate the entire procedure, as well as to work out the defects and alterations. As overheads he had to take into account the costs of electricity, the lining which was not supplied by the tailor, the tools and the workshop itself, which in this case however was the *pantalonaio*'s own home. So the total costs of labour were equivalent to L2,400 per pair and gross earnings were of L3,600 per pair, from which he had to deduct the overheads.[3]

Mimmo was also a *pantalonaio*. He was 37 years old and had five children. He had started his apprenticeship at the age of eight with a *mastro*,[4] while attending school up to the *5a elementare*. Having learnt the trade, he then worked for a number of different tailors. After he married, he rented a workshop on the ground floor of the building in the *Quartieri Spagnoli*[5] where he lived. At the time he was helped by an aunt, who did the machine-work, and his wife, who learned to do the hand-sewing tasks. Other people, kin and friends, often worked with him on a casual basis. In the old days he used to make 7 to 8 pairs of trousers a day – now he made only 6 or 7 pairs a week. He explained that, although he enjoyed the work, he found it difficult to make ends meet. Work was too irregular to enable him to sustain a family. He felt that the days of the artisan were over. Factories could undercut the artisan and push him out of the market. In the old days, not so long ago, there was a saying in the trade that the skills of the *pantalonaio* had to be stolen rather than learnt. That was because the artisan was reluctant to impart the skills and knowledge of his trade, so as to limit competition and to maintain his apprentices under his control. The majority had learnt through careful observation rather than through any directed learning. But nowadays it was difficult to find any apprentices. Nobody was interested in learning the trade because it was '*molto sacrificato*', it involved a great deal of self-sacrifice because it was a lot of for little money. In spite of this, a good *pantalonaio* is much sought after.

But because of the irregularity of work and the low income it brought him, Mimmo had joined the *disoccupati organizzati,* and through them he had got a job with the *comune* as a street-cleaner. At the time of interview he was actually doing both jobs, working on the trousers in the evening. He employed two outworkers to do the sewing. He was paid at the end of every week at a rate of L7,000 per pair. He was considerably more generous than the *pantalonaio* who operated in the early 1970s. Only five years on, he paid the machinist at a rate of L1,000 and the hand-sewing at a rate of L2,000 per pair. He calculated that the thread, buttons and other material he had to purchase amounted to about L1,000, and on top of that he had to pay the electricity and the rent. His net income from each pair of trousers was probably between L2,000 and L2,500.

He himself spent only 2 1/2 or 3 hours on each pair, although again here he thought he was 'uneconomical' as most in the trade only spent 1/2 hour on each pair of trousers. He calculated that the total number of hours required to make a pair of trousers was somewhere between 5 and 7 hours. At the time of interview he worked mainly on his own, with the help of the outworkers. Sometimes his daughter, who was then only 7 years old, would help him when she was in the mood. Her help however was minimal, since all she could do was prepare the loops for the belt or other such small jobs. The other children did not wish to help and he did not wish to force them. His strategy remained to keep the two jobs until a better opportunity presented itself, perhaps a stable and less tiring job in the *comune.*

Nella was 37, married and had four children. Her husband was unemployed and she worked as an outworker in the trouser trade. She had learnt to sew as an outworker, apprenticed to a married couple when she was around 14 years old. She later worked in factories until her marriage, when she left factory work in the hope that she would no longer need to work. However, two years later she had been obliged to start working at home. Nella did the hand-sewing tasks, finishing the inside of the trousers. Although she worked irregularly, she calculated that she made about 15 or 20 pairs per week. She worked for four different artisans, but even so work was seasonal. Pay varied, between L1,000 and L2,000, though this higher figure was rarely paid. She managed to complete 4 or 5 pairs a day.

Seasonality meant that sometimes she had little to do, and at other times, in the summer for example, she had to work day and night. Her timetable was very flexible, adjusting to the amount of work to be done. Housework was also her responsibility, though she was helped by her daughter, who in fact seemed to bear most of the burden of the household chores. Another daughter who was 12 had to work in order to clothe herself: she was an apprentice in a small handbag workshop.

The question of the gendered nature of outwork is a complex one, which responds to a number of different factors. One of these is of course choice and the motives behind women's decisions to take up outwork. The individual's life-cycle is relevant here, for although the full range of age-groups is represented in the research, the age-group of women over 25 predominates, followed by the very young (10–15). The greater importance of the older group can be explained in terms of the sexual division of labour and the organization of household tasks. The importance of the younger age-group is attributable to the practice of apprenticeship.

The women involved in outwork in Naples were poor working-class women. The majority were married or engaged to be married. The activity of the husband/fiancé varied. Menfolk might be factory workers (frequently in the same trade as their wives/fiancées), irregularly employed, independent workers or unemployed, or a combination of several of these categories. Even where the husband was unemployed he was likely to be involved in some kind of income-generating activity, however sporadic or unsatisfactory. The important difference lay in the regularity and dependability of income. Frequently, the outworker's earnings were the only stable income of a household. However, in some cases at least, the choice in favour of women's work responded to a desire to improve the standard of living of the household, so an important consideration is the consumption aspirations of particular families. In some cases, the woman's contribution could supplement a husband's wage and allow the family to improve its material conditions or maintain the children in education for longer.

Apart from offering low-cost labour and flexibility, outwork provided a mechanism for training new workers in a number of trades. Once trained, these new recruits might continue in outwork or, as was the case of many, they might enter factory work. Since many young girls trained by outworkers would at some point be producing in a factory, outwork can be seen as operating as a bridge between factories and their requirements for skilled labour and an undifferentiated pool of labour.

Many outworkers in the leather trade, especially in the shoe trade, considered that the training afforded in the context of outwork was superior to that offered by factories or workshops. Those who knew the trade often preferred to send their daughters for training by an outworker, as this guaranteed a thorough, careful training to a high standard. From the point of view of the factories, the system is advantageous, since they can draw on a supply of ready-skilled workers, and the risks of error were absorbed by the outworker/teacher, as were the costs of labour, although these were generally very low.

Skills were an important focus of discussions regarding work. Many of the outworkers interviewed were – and saw themselves as being – highly skilled, and some had in fact acquired particular and rare skills which made them much sought after by employers. The awareness of skills acquired over time, of the long periods of apprenticeship undergone by many of the women, was central to their self-esteem. This was especially important where formal education was lacking. Few of the women interviewed had gone beyond the primary level of school, and some had been unable to complete even this. These women were particularly keen to emphasize their natural abilities, which they felt were borne out by their skill at work and the ease with which they had learnt their trade. Frequently women asserted that they had 'la testa buona', a good head, because of the speed with which they had picked up a skill or because they had learned a particular skill on their own. Although this might also apply to some housewives, in relation to certain skills such as knitting, it was generally the outworkers who emphasized this aspect of their experience.

Their own recognition of their skills gave these women some degree of confidence. However, all outworkers lacked the skills and knowledge required to complete the entire process of production. Their partial knowledge, both of the production process and of the characteristics of the enterprises they worked for and their subcontracting networks, restricted their options and in many cases made them dependent on individual entrepreneurs. Many were unwilling to reveal details of their employers, since they had been threatened that work would be withdrawn from them if they talked. But many were genuinely ill-informed as to the name, the owners, the turnover or the outlets of their employer enterprise. Some of the more experienced would hazard a guess as to the profile of the putting-out enterprise, judging this from the quality of the shoe, the materials and the design. Others were quite uninterested in this, and had never given any thought to the matter.

Although acquiring the skills is the first and foremost step to becoming an outworker, it is also essential for a woman to have access to the instruments she needs to carry out her professional tasks. Access to or ownership of the instruments of production is of course an important pre-condition, although some tasks require very few specific skills, or skills which can be acquired fairly rapidly, and few if any instruments. This was the case with jobs like making artificial flowers, assembling plastic toys, or packing various products. The more highly skilled activities, such as sewing in the shoe, glove or garments trades, did require expensive machinery. There are some exceptions, of skilled work such as hand-sewing or cuttings, and there are some intermediate tasks, such as the finishing of shoes or gloves, which require a limited amount of capital outlay.

Older women in particular had been given a sewing-machine by their parents as a dowry or *dote*. In the past, it was common practice for workers to bring their own instruments into the factory. But even in the late 1970s, when this practice was maintained in only a very few, very small units, girls were often given a sewing-machine as a gift. It represented an important contribution, giving her a start in life. She might later on trade in this machine for a newer one, and in this way her parents' gift accompanied her and assisted her throughout her adult life.

Another way of acquiring a machine was by purchasing one in instalments. Alternatively, when a woman had been working for a factory and decided to leave, her boss might well suggest that she take the machine she had been using and that she repay him every month through a deduction from her wages as an outworker. In very few instances, the employer provided a machine for the duration of the time the women worked for him.

The less skilled tasks, which tend to pay lower rates, are more easily and widely accessible, and therefore we can assume that recruitment of workers for them was considerably easier. But for other tasks, the worker had to attain a certain level of training and have at her disposal a machine and other tools. This tended to place certain restrictions on the supply of outworkers in these trades. In the production of artificial flowers, for example, entrepreneurs or intermediaries might go from door to door offering work. For other businesses this form of recruitment could only be useful if there was a population with a very high density of trained workers. This was the case of areas such as Sanità or Stella, which were traditionally associated with outwork in the leather trade. But the more usual mechanism for recruitment is through the mobilization of kinship, friendship and neighbourhood networks. This was also applicable to the recruitment of factory or workshop workers. Many young girls entered a factory or workshop as a result of parental friendships or kin relations. In the case of outworkers, many not only obtained work from a particular boss through kin, but it was often a kinsman/woman or friend who delivered the work from the factory to the outworkers.

It is generally believed that outworkers are paid much less than their counterparts in the factory. In fact in a high percentage of cases rates of pay were lower for outworkers than for factory workers, but there were also cases of outworkers who considered their rates to be the same as for factory workers. A comparison of earnings confirmed this, especially since in many trades factory workers are also paid on a piece-rate basis. The main difference in any case was to be found in the general conditions of employment applicable in each case. Outworkers had no legal protection and no possibility of making any claims in respect of an employer. They had no sick pay, no holiday pay, no insurance. Of course, many small factories and workshops also employed their workers without complying with legal statutes affecting these matters.

But the outworker was very vulnerable. She could have work withdrawn from her without notice. She could have payment for work carried out withheld in a situation of conflict with an employer. She usually had to take full responsibility in case of accidental damage or theft. Although some outworkers would find an alternative employer quite easily, others would risk the possibility of several weeks, or longer, without work. Given this vulnerability, conflict was avoided at all costs.[6]

Rates of pay varied with the trade and the task. But the total income earned was very much determined by the number of hours a woman was able and willing to work and by the productivity of a worker. Thus, tasks which called for lower piece-rates might, because they allowed for a higher turnover, produce similar incomes to those for which the piece-rates were higher. There was also variability within a trade and task, according to the employer and to the worker's ability to demand better rates or conditions.

There was a correspondence between the degree of skill required for a job and the number of hours dedicated to it. Tasks such as that of the *orlatrice* were usually carried out for several hours per day, there being quite often a division of labour in the household which totally or partially freed the outworkers from housework. Unskilled tasks, on the other hand, tended to be carried out more sporadically, although the cases of flower-making that were examined indicated that this was often a full-time activity. Where a woman was unable to lighten the burden of household or child-care duties, she might switch to an 'easier' task.

Weekly or monthly incomes therefore varied enormously. As Giovanna, an outworker in the leather trade pointed out, even a very small income was important. Giovanna, who had stopped working as an *orlatrice* in the shoe industry and switched to working in the glove industry, which she found less demanding, explained that if a 'rational' calculation were to be made of the worker's costs in terms of time and expenses, very few jobs in Naples would get done. However, such 'rational' calculations were not always rational in relation to the conditions of existence and survival of the people concerned. Thus, according to the calculations of the outworker and her household, her contribution was important, however small. Of course there were also those whose financial condition, though not exactly comfortable, did allow them to make such a calculation and to decide against involvement in outwork.

Many of the women interviewed refused to give details about their earnings. Others were vague; they would know the range of rates they received per unit, but their daily and weekly earnings were not carefully worked out. This was not only because of an understandable reticence in giving too much information but because in many cases wage-work was interspersed with household chores. This meant that working hours were irregular and production levels – and thus earnings – varied considerably from day to day. The lowest daily earnings were of 1,200 lire per day and 1,500 lire per day. These low incomes applied to the most unskilled activities such as flower-making, assembling toys, etc., and to the case of a trouser-maker who, however, only worked 2 hours a day. The highest daily incomes were of 20,000 lire followed by 12,000 lire per day, and were earned by the organizers of teams of workers. This sort of level of income was rare, however, and most of the higher incomes clustered around the 5,000 to 7,000 lire mark.

But clearly, daily intakes depended on the number of hours worked. On this question, the women interviewed were even vaguer than in respect of their earnings. Some claimed they worked a 12-hour day, and this might have been an exaggerated statement aimed at emphasizing that they had no free time. Others, who quoted similar hours, were able to give fairly detailed breakdowns of their time-use and task distribution throughout the day. Many refused to give a figure, and preferred to describe their day, which consisted of various household chores interspersed with outwork activities. Where women worked in couples or teams figures were more precise, and here it was clear that individual flexibility was restricted, there was much greater organization, and rigid timetables were adhered to. In some cases it had been possible to calculate the hourly rate of earnings. This again covered a wide range: from a minimum of 250 lire per hour (for apprentices) followed by 320 lire per hour (for flower-making) to a maximum of 2,000 lire per hour (for a team organizer in the shoe trade). In the majority of cases payment worked out at approximately 600 lire per hour.[7]

Just as the wage-work was interspersed with household chores, so was this work an integral aspect of the spatial arrangements of households. The vast majority of workers carried out their work in a space used also for eating, living and – often – sleeping. In the least skilled jobs, such as flower-making, the table used for work purposes had to be cleared and cleaned in order for the evening meal to be served (the midday meal could be consumed without too much fuss so long as no adult men were present). Other types of work involving the use of machinery, as for example in the case of the shoe trade, demanded some degree of separation, although this might be minimal, especially if the worker lived in a *basso*.

The *bassi* usually consisted of a single room into which had been built a small kitchen and toilet. In some cases there was a second space available, often a room which had been built over the main room. But given that the average composition of each *basso* was approximately four people, the 'front room' almost invariably doubled as a dining-living-bedroom and, where there was an outworker in the household, as a work-room as well.

It seemed clear that outworkers living in the *bassi* and their families were the most affected by the inconvenience of work carried out in the home, and by the health hazards of several trades. Where leather was worked dust and dirt were a problem, though more serious yet was the health hazard posed by the glue generally used in the leather trade (De Marco and Talamo 1976; Berlinguer *et al.* 1977). Those outworkers who did not live in a *basso* generally enjoyed better working conditions. Many of those living in apartments had a separate space or room for their work. This meant that food did not come into contact with the dust and the fumes produced by work. However, where there were children, they were generally allowed or even encouraged to play in the same room where their mother was working.

The Case of the Leather Trades

The most interesting case of outwork production in Naples was undoubtedly that of the shoe industry. This was the most significant numerically, and was also noteworthy for the levels of skills required to operate in the trade, and the degree of organization of the trade. In Naples, the important shoe industry included a number of very different types of units. Some were large and modern, investing considerable capital in the update of machinery, and producing a high-quality shoe for Rome or other Italian cities, or for export, at the time mainly to the United States. Some of the specialist producers had their own outlets in Naples and elsewhere. At the other end of the scale was the small unit using labour which was generally recruited through networks formed by kinship, friendship, or neighbourhood ties. Machinery was often antiquated, bought second-hand from a factory where the owner/boss had been employed. A retirement payment or a redundancy settlement might provide the capital to start off a small business. But these small units were unlikely to be able to accumulate enough capital to purchase more than the sewing machines. Unequipped to perform a complete cycle of production, they were likely to produce part-products for other, larger factories, or in some cases, they might produce a cheap shoe for local markets. Outworkers were used throughout this range of enterprises.

Within the factory, the steps towards the production of a shoe were:

(a) *the design of the model*. This was carried out by the entrepreneur or by a hired designer. This was a male job and was highly paid.

(b) *cutting the leather*. This was also a highly skilled task and was generally well paid and male.

(c) *sewing*. The leather pieces making up the upper part of the shoe were sewn by skilled and well-paid female workers (whose rates of pay were nevertheless lower than those of the highly skilled men).

(d) *attaching the upper part and the sole*. This is now done by machine and it is a male task. In better-quality shoes, additional stitching may complement the machine. This hand-stitching was considered to be a highly skilled task and to be male. The bottom part of the shoe can be prepared by a male worker or, more frequently, may be bought ready-made from a factory specializing in the production of sole and heel pieces.

(e) *cleaning and finishing*. This is an important though not highly skilled task carried out by women workers.

Sewing and finishing are the two operations most likely to be handed out to outworkers. Sewing of the leather uppers was a very skilled task carried out by the *orlatrice*, who was undoubtedly the most prestigious and highly paid outworker in Naples. To become a fully-fledged *orlatrice* required a long period of training of three to five years. This was usually initiated under the guidance of an outworker, who was often a kinswoman or neighbour, and continued either in a factory or as an outworker. The shoe trade, and the skills of the *orlatrice*, were considered to be traditional in Naples, particularly in the old city in neighbourhoods such as the Sanità. But, probably as a result of outward migration from the densely populated centre of the city, leather trade outworkers are now dispersed throughout the city and the working-class suburbs.

The trade was often passed on from mother to daughter, as young girls assisted their mothers in their tasks. It is now considered a female trade *par excellence*, but although most informers saw the genealogy of *orlatrici* stretching back in time over several generations, others pointed out that originally this had been a male trade. While the task was exclusively carried out by hand, it had been carried out by men, who were displaced by the introduction of the sewing-machine. No explanation could be offered for this, other than that the sewing-machine was defined as being an inherently 'female' instrument.

The *orlatrice* was generally very proud of her skills and spoke of her work with enthusiasm and confidence. If the employer produced a lower-quality shoe, which was not aesthetically pleasing to her, she would speak of her work in quite a different tone and express dissatisfaction and even depression at having to use her skills to such an unsatisfactory end.

Although all *orlatrici* were highly trained, some had specialized in rare skills. This meant that they were sought after and were in a far better bargaining position than other workers. Maria had learnt a double-edged moccasin stitch which very few *orlatrici* in Naples knew how to do. In fact, at one time a Roman company was sending her stitching work to do. Maria started work at the age of 8, in what was then considered to be a relatively large factory (with a daily turnover of 50 pairs of shoes) owned by a neighbour; and by the age of 15 she was a fully qualified *orlatrice*. In later life, her special skills placed her in a very advantageous position. She worked for several firms, but one of them took precedence over the others, in exchange for paying her national insurance contributions. The demand for her work also allowed her to set up a successful team with her sister (see p. 129).

The *orlatrice* needs a special sewing-machine, adapted for leather work. In most cases the machine belonged to the worker. In the case of older workers their first machines had often been part of their *dote*. When a worker arranged to purchase a used machine from her employer, she was tied to that entrepreneur at least until she had paid off the machine with her work. The thread used for the stitching had to match the leather, and was therefore usually supplied by the entrepreneur, though many older outworkers remembered their efforts at trying to find matching thread themselves. The costs of electricity and machine repairs were usually shouldered by the workers. A driver, a relative or a friend working inside the factory, or in the case of small units, the entrepreneur himself, might deliver the ready-cut pieces of leather. The finished uppers were collected about one week later. Payment, which was also made one week later, was on a piece-rate basis (*a cottimo*). The rate of pay varied considerably, and depended on the particular shoe and the difficulty entailed in its preparation, as well as on the skill and reputation of the outworker and the financial means of the entrepreneur.

Most *orlatrici* worked with the assistance of apprentices, which increased their productivity and ensured the continuity of the trade. Apprentices were paid very low wages – the general perception of their work was that they benefited from the training they received in a useful saleable skill. This justified the low pay they received. Most of the women interviewed started training at about the age of 10 or 11. During the 1970s and early 1980s many girls started learning from their mothers or from a neighbour in a rather casual way, sitting near the worker, watching her and helping out. At about the age of 11 or 12 they might be apprenticed out to a neighbour or relative, when they would be involved in the work on a more rigorous basis. Most completed schooling at least up to the level of primary school. However, this was achieved by the fact that many young girls divided their day between school and training as well as helping out at home, which was expected of most girls. Their training was more or less arduous depending on their teacher – most girls quietly sat at the table concentrating on their work with very little to say, but in one case the apprentice seemed to spend more time playing with the *orlatrice*'s toddler than working on the shoes (this was probably as useful to the *orlatrice* as the girl's leather work, but did little to advance the apprentice's technical skills). As a girl reached the age of 14 or 15 she was likely to dedicate her time exclusively to the trade and might enter a workshop or factory, where her apprenticeship would be continued (the legal working age in Italy was 15).

The *orlatrice*'s job was divided into two tasks: the first was folding and glueing the edges of the pieces forming a hem and the second involved actually sewing the pieces together. The apprentice started by learning to fold the edges tidily and then glueing the edges and ensuring that they were flattened by using a small hammer. Young children (usually girls) frequently joined in the first part of the operation. After many years of perfecting this skill a girl might start to learn to use the sewing-machine. Although small boys might sit around a table where these activities were taking place, I never came across a boy working on this task, and no boy was ever apprenticed to this trade. Older men, trained under the less mechanized artisan structure, claimed they were skilled in every task of the production process, including the work of the *orlatrice*.

Within the context of being a working woman in Naples, the trade of *orlatrice* was considered to be prestigious, relatively well-paid and convenient, in that it allowed a woman to leave the factory and work at home after marriage. It was therefore considered to be 'a good trade' for a woman, although many *orlatrici* said they wished their daughters would leave the ranks of manual labour altogether and become secretaries or teachers, professions which bring with them a higher status and in addition may be better paid.

Another source of concern for mothers thinking about their daughters' future was the alarm concerning the effect of glue fumes, the inhalation of which causes a disease in the central nervous system. This causes headaches, dizziness and, in the worst cases, paralysis. Pregnant women were at risk of aborting their babies and, given that the majority of women worked until the end of their pregnancies, this was a cause for concern. There was also the fear that the glue could cause malformations in the unborn child. Most outworkers were aware of the dangers because of the considerable publicity given to the problem. *Orlatrici* might take some precautions, such as keeping the glue pot covered and using a brush rather than a finger to apply the glue, or keeping a door or a window open in spite of the cold to increase ventilation. But on the whole women felt impotent and resigned. It was unlikely that their employers would change to the safer but more expensive adhesives, or that they would provide safety equipment. In any case, most found that the use of safety gloves hampered their movements, making them slower and clumsier.

The problem was not restricted to outworkers, although in their case concern was raised because of the close proximity of small children or indeed their actual involvement in the most dangerous phase of the work: the folding and glueing stage. Cramped workshops with inadequate ventilation that were obliged to cut costs as much as possible also placed the workers at risk. Although some cases of polyneuritis had been reported amongst workers in the most modern and careful factories, they usually had the advantage of enjoying trade union representation, which would almost certainly guarantee them compensation.[8] Furthermore, the symptoms would generally be detected earlier in this kind of workplace. Rita, who worked in one of the most modernized and prestigious factories in Naples, which had an excellent record with the trade union, had decided to carry on working as an *orlatrice* even though she was pregnant. She had had the relevant tests and no traces of the substance were found in her blood, although some of her colleagues had had positive results. She explained that the factory had recently installed new ventilators; gloves were available for use, though few if any chose to use them; and finally, pregnant women could ask to be transferred to another *reparto* of the factory, where they would be far away from the glue fumes.

There can be little doubt that the *orlatrici* constituted the cream of the outworkers. In fact their skills conferred on them considerable potential: there were cases where *orlatrici* organized a team of skilled and less skilled women, thus greatly increasing their production capacity, income and status *vis-à-vis* employers. Although single *orlatrici* often worked for more than one employer, teams were in a better position to do so. Clearly, this required considerable organizational skills in order to meet the different requirements and deadlines of several entrepreneurs.

Examples of Orlatrici

Anna

Anna was 32 years of age at the time of interview. She was married, had two daughters and was 7 months pregnant. Anna had attended school until the *5a elementare* (when she was about 11 years old). At 10 years of age she started her training, under her father's supervision, and on her own machine, in a small factory. She remained in factory work until her marriage at the age of 21. When she married, her husband put pressure on her to give up factory work and to start working at home. Then, after her children were born, it actually became practical to give up work in the factory, since she had nobody to leave the children with.

When she first started working at home her father took work to her from the factory where he worked. Her father worked for low rates of pay, and persuaded all his daughters to do likewise, because he considered the boss to be his friend. He was later dismissed without proper compensation by his friend, when the factory closed down. He later worked for his ex-boss's brother, still underpaid and still without any legal status and protection. Anna's boss at the time of interview had also been found through her father. She was aware that her rights were not being respected and that she had a case for legal action, but she decided that this was not worth the effort, since she would surely lose her work and her next employer would impose exactly the same conditions.

Anna was working for a very small factory set up by a worker with very little capital. The worker in question did not know the whole process of production, unlike Anna's father. Putting out solved a problem faced by entrepreneurs with gaps in their knowledge of the production process. This way he also avoided the responsibilities entailed by employing workers in a factory.

The factory owner collected the consignment himself every two or three days. He often stipulated the dates of delivery, which determined Anna's pace of work. She produced 18 to 20 pairs of shoes per day, working from 10 a.m. to 7 p.m. with a lunch-break. She always worked on Saturdays. Some days she worked shorter hours, if for instance she had to go shopping, or sometimes she had to work longer hours, if for example there was an urgent consignment to complete. The sewing-machine was her own – the same machine her father had bought for her when she had started work. She paid the electricity bills (about 5,000 lire per month) but the factory provided all other necessary items.

Anna worked with an 18-year-old assistant and a 12-year-old apprentice. Anna did most of the machine work and the assistant concentrated on the glueing, folding and hammering. When Anna had finished all the sewing work for the day she sat at the assistant's table and did some glueing. The assistant had been working at this job for two years. She would eventually learn how to sew. She was engaged to Anna's brother, who was away doing his military service at the time. He felt happier knowing that his fiancée was working 'in a family atmosphere'. The apprentice was the daughter of a neighbour who found it convenient to have his daughter trained by someone he knew and who lived very close.

The shoes they were preparing at the time of the interview were very difficult. The assistant glued and folded strips and pieces of leather and passed them on to the *orlatrice*, who sewed them together. Then the back pieces were passed to the *orlatrice*, who sewed the two halves together. The inside of the backs were then taped and smoothed down (both women did this) and the linings were joined. They thus assembled the entire upper part of the shoe. Once they had completed the consignment, the assistant started to glue and prepare a new model so that there would be work ready for Anna to start sewing immediately the following day.

Anna did all the housework herself between 7 and 10 in the morning, when she also cooked the evening meal and prepared the lunch. She intended to continue work until the last day of her pregnancy, since she was not entitled to any maternity assistance.

Anna was obliged to work because her husband's salary was inadequate to cover all their expenses. He was an assistant in a butcher's shop and earned 50,000 lire a week, out of which he gave 40,000 to his wife for household expenses, and kept 10,000 for his own personal expenses, such as cigarettes and coffees. Rent and other charges for the flat came to 60,000 lire per month, added to which there were also the costs of the telephone, gas, electricity and grocery bills. Anna and her husband lived in a council flat which had been built in one of the workers' suburbs in the 1950s. However, the flat was sublet to them illegally by the legal tenants, so that their position was precarious and their rent was higher than it should have been. But the flat had the advantage of being quite spacious. Anna had a separate room for her work, which was large enough for the three workers, plus visitors and the children, who played there. A balcony door was kept open in spite of the chilly temperature, because she was conscious of the dangers of the fumes from the glue to herself and the children.

Anna would have preferred working in a factory. But she found it hard to imagine a situation which would free her from her household duties. Working in a factory on a piece-rate basis would earn her much better wages, even if she were paid at the same rate. This was because in a factory she could concentrate on her work from 8 until 5 o'clock with no interruptions other than a half an hour for lunch. Since she was a good worker, with twenty years' experience, she would produce much more than she did at present, since she would not have to stop work to see to household affairs or to the child. As it was, Anna generally earned about 30,000 to 40,000 lire per week, but she could earn as much as 50,000. She had to pay the assistant 5,000 a week and the apprentice 2,000 lire a week.

The assistant, on the other hand, did not want to work in a factory. An older neighbour who was visiting explained that the girl was used to being 'in famiglia', in a family context. Even though she might earn less money this way, here she was in good company and had time to do the housework in her family's home, which she had to do before coming over to work with Anna. Another factor was her fiancé, who had found this job for her. He did not like the idea of her working in a factory. Another four years were likely to go by before they could marry, and he felt more secure with her working 'at home'. The neighbour explained again that men in Naples wanted to have their cake and eat it: 'Women must work because this is necessary, but they must do so in the home. In a factory women may meet the wrong kind of person. In fact, there is jealousy and gossip there, whereas if they work in the home or with kin all these dangers are avoided. So, thanks to *lavoro a domicilio* the men protect their sense of personal dignity, keep their jealousy at bay, and at the same time are assured of a second and necessary income.' Anna's case had been different because, although she had worked in a factory while young and even once she was engaged, she had always worked with her father. The neighbour felt she summed the whole situation up by saying that 'in Naples we're still very backward about these things'.

Assunta

Assunta had attended school until the Second World War broke out. She then left Naples for the greater safety of the countryside, where no schooling was provided. Furthermore, she explained, schooling was not considered so important in those days. By the time the war had ended, she was too old to start school again. She started work at 15 as an apprentice to an outworker who paid her a little money as well as training her. Her apprenticeship lasted between one and one-and-a-half years.

Assunta liked working at home because she could set her own pace of work. She calculated that she worked 7 to 8 hours a day on the shoes. In the morning she cleaned the house and started working on the sewing-machine at 10 or 11 o'clock. At lunch-time she and her niece, who worked as her assistant, had a break. She prepared a meal for herself, her niece, and her mother and mother-in-law, who lived with her, and who were 78 and 84 respectively at the time of interview. At about 7 in the evening she stopped work. She then had a bit of time to herself to read, watch television or chat. However, this was rare, and this was generally only the case at the weekend when she did not work on the shoes. Assunta had no children.

Her niece was 21 years of age, and was engaged to be married, waiting until she and her fiancé were able to find a house. There was a very simple division of labour between them. The younger woman took the pieces of leather from the bag delivered by the factory owner. She then put the lining and the outside pieces together, and glued and sewed them with great speed. The older woman finished off the more intricate sewing, which took longer. Assunta explained that they both worked at the same pace, and because of this all income was divided equally between them.

They owned their machines. The older woman's machine dated from 1953; the younger woman's was newer, and she had bought it on a hire-purchase basis. The cost of electricity was covered by them, as was the cost of any repairs to the sewing-machines. Their boss provided all other materials, including the glue. No applicator was provided, so they applied the glue with their bare fingers. Assunta took a fatalistic view of the dangers of the glue, but pointed out that so far, after so many years' work, she had suffered no adverse symptoms.

Payment was made for every dozen pairs of shoe uppers they completed. Assunta was unable to calculate the rate of production, which she said varied from day to day, and from model to model. There was no adjustment of payment in respect of more difficult models which required more time.

Assunta would have preferred to give up work, but although her husband would have supported her if she decided to do this, it was impossible, since on his income alone they could not meet all the household costs. Her husband, who also worked in the shoe trade, earned enough in the factory to cover the food bills, and no more. Her niece was not interested in factory work nor for that matter in outwork. She hoped that at marriage she would have children immediately and give up work.

Assunta and her husband used to live in the centre of Naples, but they were rehoused to a block of council flats in the early 1960s. She preferred living in the centre, but prohibitive rents and the severe shortage of housing made this impossible. The area where they lived was at the time nothing more than blocks placed in a desert-like wasteland. The area was scarred by large ditches and heaps of rubbish, which were often smouldering, with children playing among the rubbish heaps. Subsequently, much of the wasteland was converted into small gardens by groups of residents concerned to improve their environment.

The Azzeccatrice: Annunziata

The task of the *azzeccatrice* or *apparecchiatrice* requires a great deal of care and concentration. Training, on the other hand, is less demanding than in the case of the *orlatrice*. Generally speaking, apprenticeship for this skill takes between one and two years, although some women claimed that they had taken up to three years really to perfect the skills necessary for the job. Assistance is not so important here, there is little scope for a division of labour, and so most *azzecatrici* worked without apprentices or assistants.

The job of the *azzeccatrice* is to clean the shoe, removing all traces of glue or paint and any other marks, ironing the leather into shape and packing the shoes in boxes. The equipment needed for this task is simple and inexpensive: some cotton wool, a solvent, and a special iron. The task was less prestigious and rates of pay were lower than for the *orlatrice*. Because the task is accomplished more rapidly, however, a good *azzeccatrice* could earn as much in a day as an average *orlatrice*. The *azzeccatrice* outworker was not as common as the *orlatrice* outworker, and most seemed to work inside the factories.

Annunziata was 35, married with two children, who at the time were 7 and 4 years of age. She had got as far as second grade at primary school and at 10 she had started to work in a factory where her mother worked. Her mother taught her the job of finishing the shoe. She had always done this work. After her marriage, when she was pregnant, she had left the factory and had started to work at home, for a different employer. She then received the boxes of shoes and her job was to clean, paint over the edges and iron the insides. She complained that the shoes were ugly and of inferior quality. She found this discouraging, and got little satisfaction from working with this kind of shoe.

Annunziata knew the name of the company she worked for, but had never met the factory boss. An employee (a driver) brought the work to her every day and collected the boxes containing the finished shoes. He brought 30 to 40 pairs and she usually managed to work through the lot in time for collection the next day. She was paid 180 lire per pair and made about 6,000 to 7,000 lire per day.

Annunziata had to get up at 4.30 or 5 o'clock in the morning to start work. At 8 o'clock she got the children ready for school. The 3 or 4 hours' work in the early morning meant there was less pressure on her during the day. She was able to do some cleaning and prepare lunch, and then recommenced work on the shoes at about 12 o'clock. At 5.30 or 6 o'clock she prepared the dinner for the children. She went to bed early, at 9.30 or 10, and estimated that she worked about 10 hours a day. The work was totally manual, and each pair of shoes normally required about 15 minutes' work. The instruments she used were a pair of scissors, a little knife, a brush, alcohol, petroleum and an iron or *palletta*.

Annunziata lived in a relatively new block of flats, in an apartment which consisted of a kitchen, a bathroom, the main bedroom and two living/dining-rooms. One dining-room was for everyday use, and it was here that she kept her work. The second dining-room, which was very well furnished, was for display only. The bedroom was also lavishly furnished in 'modern-gothic' style, made by the factory where her husband worked. The couple slept in the main bedroom and the two children shared the everyday dining-room with Annunziata's two younger sisters. Annunziata worked in the kitchen.

The rent was paid by the youngest sister, who worked in a shoe factory as an *orlatrice*, and by the husband. The second sister worked as a cashier in a *rosticceria* (cooked food shop) and earned 3,500 lire for a 7-hour day. Her earnings were thus barely sufficient to cover her own personal expenses, and she therefore made no financial contribution to the household. She did some housework in the morning before leaving for work at 10 o'clock and in the evening she prepared the dinner for the adults. The outworker did some chores in between her work and looked after the children. On Saturday, a thorough cleaning of the house was carried out by all the three women.

The Glove Trade

Like the shoe industry, the glove trade has a long history in Naples. It was introduced by the Bourbons in the early nineteenth century and was safeguarded from outside competition by the protectionist policies of the Kingdom (Esposito and Persico 1978). The industry grew in importance, and by the early 1970s 85 per cent of all Italian glove production was concentrated in Naples (De Marco and Talamo 1976). Production was largely geared to export markets and included a range of products, from very fine-quality leather, through to sports gloves, especially ski gloves. However, the trade was clearly suffering a decline, at least partly related to competition from cheaper producers abroad. The factories which were visited appeared to be no more than assembly and packing points, employing very few workers, most of them men. And yet few outworkers in this trade were encountered.[9] A number of men working in their homes refused to grant an interview. Their task was to stretch and cut the leather into the appropriate shape and size. The majority said they could not afford the distraction.

The industry had experienced very little technological change since the introduction of the sewing-machine, and although the question of skills was important, access to the appropriate tools was much less of a problem than it was in the shoe trade. This would facilitate the recruitment and use of outworkers, so that it was quite surprising that they should have constituted such a small percentage of my sample. However, a study carried out amongst 10 artisan units in the areas of Stella and Materdei, in the centre of the old city, found that only three of the ten carried out a complete cycle of production. Seven of those interviewed handed work out to home-workers, although the researchers were unable to find out how many outworkers were involved. Of those employed in these small units, 85 per cent were female and 61 per cent were under the legal working age. The average size of the units was approximately 13 workers and, rather atypically, only one out of the total number of workers in each unit was a member of the family of the artisan. The conditions were bad, since the workshops were located in small, cramped rooms which in a number of cases were also the living quarters of the artisan. In four of the enterprises they worked an 8-hour day, in five they worked a 10-hour day and in one of them the working day lasted more than 10 hours. Conditions were such that the authors preferred to define these units as 'group outwork' rather than as artisan production (De Marco and Talamo 1976).

Francesca

Francesca was around 55 years of age and lived in a *basso* with her husband and four of her eight children. Her husband had retired some years ago and had a small pension. She explained that he had also been ill for the last four months, implying that he was therefore quite unable to make any further contribution to the household. However, all her children were employed, with the exception of one of her daughters, who took care of the housework. Her daughter had also picked up the skills of the trade from her and helped her sometimes.

Francesca had to cut the glove fingers. She would take what seemed like mere scraps of leather and would push and pull them against the edge of the table to stretch the pieces and she would then cut out the shape of a finger. She did this with an astonishing speed and confidence.

Her employers were a small factory which collected the pieces from her every day, and paid her on a weekly basis. In a single day she was able to produce fifty pairs, for which she was paid L30 per pair. This meant that her usual earnings were around L1,500 a day. This was what she could earn working nearly full-time on the gloves. Francesca had been doing this work for 45 years. She had started at the age of 10 when she learnt the trade from a woman 'teacher' *a domicilio*, in her home. She had never worked in a factory. The tools she needed were simple: a pair of scissors and the table. The sewing of the pieces was carried out by other workers whom she did not know.

Giovanna

Giovanna was 40 years old. She was married and had two children. Her husband had been unemployed for the last sixteen years and was a member of the *disoccupati organizzati*. She had originally trained as an *orlatrice* and had worked as such until her marriage. When her children were born she decided to abandon the shoe industry and start to work with gloves because she found this less demanding. As an *orlatrice* she had found it hard to concentrate while attending to the children and the housework.

Giovanna made ski gloves, which have a plastic foam lining. The procedure was fairly lengthy, as she first had to sew a red leather strip to the centre of a square of foam. Once she had done this on all the squares, she had to stitch on a piece of red leather as an ornament. She then sewed a bottom piece of leather to the foam, and subsequently added a top piece with the fingers. A similar process was repeated to make the underside of the glove. She was only able to prepare the top and the bottom pieces, but did not have the skill required to sew these together or to add the thumb-piece, which, she said, required a lot of skill.

In spite of the amount of work required, she was paid L100 per pair. The amount she was able to produce in one day varied enormously, depending on the housework and other factors. But she usually made somewhere between 20 and 40 pairs in a day and earned around L3,000 a day.

Giovanna had had her machine since her days as an *orlatrice*. It was her responsibility to buy the thread, the cost of which had increased enormously over the years. A large reel of black thread now cost as much as L6,000. Because of increasing costs she had asked for a rise, and her boss had agreed to up the rate to L100. She preferred not to calculate the exact costs per pair of gloves. She suspected the result would be depressing. Yet her income was essential to the household. She also sold contraband cigarettes from her doorway, which is where she sat at her sewing-machine. She mentioned that her husband did 'odd jobs', and unwittingly gave the impression that he too was involved in contraband.

She would prefer to work in a factory, but household duties made that impossible. During the week she did very little cleaning, so

Saturday was a busy day, mainly dedicated to cleaning the house thoroughly and doing the shopping, although a neighbour provided many items which she sold in the neighbourhood at low prices.

Giuseppina

Giuseppina was a 66-year-old widow. Two of her three sons lived at home with her. She had to work to keep herself and pay the rent. She felt it would be unfair to expect her sons to contribute, since they were of an age when they had their own expenses and their own future to think about. One son worked in a glove factory and another worked in a shoe factory. She did all the housework, although her daughter-in-law who lived opposite did the shopping for her. A nephew's wife who called her *zia* (aunt) and lived nearby also helped out and kept an eye on her.

Giuseppina had had no schooling whatsoever. She had started being trained at the age of 11 by a friend who was an outworker. She had later worked in a factory until her mother became ill, when she was forced to give up work in the factory and took up outwork. Her particular skill was ironing the ready-made glove. She had a special glove iron which ran on electricity. The finished glove was placed on the iron and a fork with four points was placed between the fingers so that the middle piece of each finger, which joins the top to the bottom, was folded inwards. The glove was then removed and placed under a marble stone until it was cold. The iron should have had different moulds to cater for different glove sizes; but she managed to do all sizes on a 37 size mould, because she was very experienced and understood what could and what could not be done, how far to push the glove down on the iron, and how much to stretch it. The gloves she was working on were a good-quality sporty model lined with sheepskin lining.

She was working for two different factories. The factory managers delivered the pieces, collected the ironed gloves, which were paired and carefully placed in boxes, and delivered payment. She was paid L10 per pair and ironed around 100 pairs in a day. On a good day she might bring up the total to 200 pairs; but on average she would earn about L1,000 a day.

Artificial Flowers

There were a number of activities carried out at the level of outwork, such as the assembly of toys or making soft toys, which required no specific training. Recruitment of workers for these tasks was therefore easier. But from the supply side this kind of outwork provided much lower incomes; the work was frequently dull, and was therefore not an attractive option. However, for those in need and without more strategic skills, these jobs provided an opportunity of bringing some money into the household. One of the most widespread was flower-making. It appeared that in this trade there had emerged women who specialized as brokers, recruiting workers for the workshops by going from house to house.

The flowers were of the small cloth kind which in Naples were used mainly to accompany *bomboniere*.[10] Generally speaking those involved in flower-making were young girls trying to earn some money to build up their *corredo* (trousseau) and older women. Because the skills required can be learnt very rapidly, anybody, including very young children, can join in. It was common to find groups of people working on the flowers, although usually each person worked on their own pile. There was little scope for a division of labour here.

The part of the flower that would be the petals was stamped and cut out mechanically in a workshop. These were distributed in bags together with bags of stems to be assembled.

Caterina

Caterina was 20 years old, single and living at home with her parents, a brother and a younger sister who, like her, 'worked with the flowers'. They lived in one of the semi-rural suburbs of Naples. She had completed primary school and then trained as an embroiderer in a small workshop. But her parents did not wish her to leave the house 'after she had reached a certain age', so she started working at home. First she made metal hair-clips, which she found heavy going and badly paid. She then learnt how to 'make the flowers' from an outworker, who then handed work out to her so that she could work in her own home. She later became independent and worked directly for a factory that came recruiting to her door.

She and her sister received packs containing the pieces of the different types of flower. They would pile up the different types of petal and work through them, pile after pile. Payment was per flower and varied according to its complexity, but on average they were paid L3,000 per thousand flowers. If they worked all day without interruption they could make up to 2,500 to 3,000 lire. This money was handed over to their mother, who used it to buy items for their *corredo*.

They started work at some time between 9.30 and 10 o'clock in the morning. Before that they would help their mother with the housework. Neither did they work with the flowers on Saturdays, because this was the day for general housework. They broke at midday and carried on after lunch until 5 o'clock. They worked in a room which was also a living-room and a dining-room. At the centre of the room was a very large table. Here they would sit, often accompanied by their mother, who would sit and 'rest' and help them assemble the flowers. They were often joined by two young neighbours who brought their bags of petals and stalks with them, working through their pile whilst chatting and listening to the radio.

Caterina didn't enjoy this work. However, she was obliged to do it in order to buy what she called her *dote* or dowry. This was bought month by month as the wages arrived.

The advantage of this kind of work is that it requires little concentration, no equipment beyond one's finger and the glue, and that anybody can join in. This was one of the few activities where I ever saw men (though never Caterina's father or her status-conscious brother-in-law) joining in, albeit cautiously.

Conclusion

People are drawn into outwork for a number of reasons. Those who are too old to compete on the labour-market, those who are constrained by their roles as wives and mothers, those who are constrained by their family from working outside 'a family atmosphere'. In some cases adequate incomes are made; in others only a very small amount of money was made in this way. However, for many households this small amount was nevertheless significant.

Outwork had two important consequences: on the one hand it reproduced segmented labour-markets by passing on different skills to different categories of people. This was especially so through the apprenticeship system and because of the division of labour organized by individual households. This meant that some children learnt saleable skills and others did not. Both were likely to fit into the outwork system, either as skilled outworkers or as unskilled outworkers assembling flowers, toys, etc. Outwork also provided good training for the factory, thus removing from factories the important costs of training.

Gender is an inevitable factor to be considered here. Women were far more likely to become involved as outworkers than men. This trend in Naples reflects the Italian national trend, and indeed also reflects what happens globally. Women are far more likely to find outwork attractive, given the centrality of their domestic role. Indeed, their aspirations to become wives and mothers are central here, in that the *corredo* provides a strong incentive to work for money. Once engaged or married they are likely to be influenced by their fiancés or husbands to leave factory employment, and once they are mothers there will usually be very concrete limitations to their working outside the home.

Notes

1. Because of its invisibility, and its characteristic absence from official statistics, we are forced to rely on localized or rather general inquiries and estimates. In the mid-1970s the estimate for Italy as a whole ranged between 1,100,000 workers, a figure suggested by De Marco and Talamo (1976), and 1,800,000, as suggested by the trade unions.

2. This was supported in the case of Naples by De Marco and Talamo (1976), and coincides with estimates for other areas of Italy or for Italy as a whole, as seen in De Cecco (1972), Frey (1973), Frey *et al.* (1976) and Bettio (1988).

3. The figures quoted in this section relate to the period from 1975 to 1980. In 1976 the average rate of exchange was 1,498.248 *lire* to the pound sterling, which is fully representative of the exchange rates during the entire period.

4. *Mastro* or master is the term used to refer to the artisan. It implies that he is a specialist, a fully trained and expert member of his profession. Because of the widespread use of the apprenticeship system, it also implies the role of teacher.

5. The *quartieri Spagnoli* or Spanish quarters are a very poor area of the old city.

6. The *Legge No. 877, 18 12, 1973* was intended to protect the rights of outworkers. According to this law, enterprises handing out work must be registered. Three years later, only 53 enterprises in Naples had registered: 21 of them were glove producers and only 8 were in the shoe trade. There were also 2 garments factories, one handbag factory, one tailor and one trouser-maker. The recipients of work were also supposed to register, and at that time in Naples not more than 20 outworkers had registered. Many employers attempted to persuade their outworkers to register as 'artisans', which meant that they themselves were responsible for the payment of various state contributions. The law demands that outworkers should be paid at the same rate as that established by the trade's contractual agreements, and that they should be fully insured. Thus an outworker did have a legal case to make against an employer who, like the majority, did not comply with these conditions. But as the outworkers themselves pointed out, an attempt at putting legal pressure on an employer was hardly worthwhile, since the outworker would certainly lose her work and she would then face exactly the same problems with her next employer. Furthermore, rumour had it that the name of a 'trouble-maker' got around and she or he would find it difficult to get work. This was confirmed by the experience of a factory worker who had been a ringleader in a factory dispute. She was unfairly dismissed and took her ex-employer to court. She won the case and received compensation. But in spite of her skill and experience, she was subsequently unable to find employment. Eventually the trade union interceded on her behalf and a firm which was on good terms with the union offered her a job.

7. In the study carried out by De Marco and Talamo (1976), 49.7% of outworkers earned up to L2,000 a day; 26.3% earned up to L3,000 per day; 20% earned up to L1,000 and 4% earned up to L4,000 per day. My findings indicate that outworkers can earn considerably more. The discrepancy may be due to the time difference between the two pieces of research, or it may be that their sample includes a higher proportion of the less skilled tasks. Furthermore, their questionnaire was distributed in some of the very poorest areas of the city, where I did hold some interviews; but a high proportion of the material in my research came from areas such as Stella and Sanità, which were then the 'heart' of the leather trade. Another factor may be that many of my interviews were arranged through personal networks, which may have

led me to contact outworkers who were in a more favourable position rather than concentrate solely on those living and working in the *bassi*.

8. The trade unions had been involved in a number of fierce battles to gain recognition for the disease and to obtain compensation for those affected. However, the families of some of those affected in Naples claimed that the unions had been slow to take up the issue and that they had done most of the pushing. The union had jumped on the bandwagon subsequently when it became obvious that this was indeed a big and serious issue.

9. Interestingly, no contact was made with glove workers, neither through the trade union nor through personal networks. Given that a high percentage of my personal contacts were in the shoe trade, they tended to generate contacts with other workers or entrepreneurs in that trade. There is the implication here that the shoe trade and the glove trade are very distinct economic and cultural entities. The segregation appeared to be greater than with other trades such as clothing or even agriculture or food, given that the trade union provided many opportunities of contact with workers from these other trades – but none with a worker from the glove trade.

10. *Bomboniere* are small china or glass objects which are distributed at weddings and baptisms. They are an important item of prestige and considerable sums of money are spent on them. Those who receive them often collect them, displaying them in the glass cabinets found in many Neapolitan working-class dining-rooms.

The Petty Producer and the Mirage of Independence

Neapolitans talked a lot about work: about the need for work, the lack of work, the absence of job security and stability, the problem of low pay. Many people described their life in terms of their work experience. Many felt their entire life was geared to work and that work dominated their existence, leaving little time or energy for other activities. For many work was an important source of appraisal for themselves and others, and in some cases it was a source of pride and self-confidence. But clearly not all kinds of work provide the kinds of satisfaction aspired to. Frequently people expressed a concern for autonomy, and some were quite hostile to the discipline and authority involved in most forms of employment. This preoccupation with autonomy affected people's opinions about work and their decisions concerning this. Clearly, for many if not most, survival outside the 'formal' factory and services sectors was a consequence of necessity. But beyond the question of economic need and objective opportunity many individuals – even or especially those with proper employment – wished for independence.

Wanting to 'be your own boss' was a sentiment that was shared by petty traders and workers, even when these were employed on full contractual conditions and with high wages, as were the workers at the Italsider plant, who were considered to be the 'élite' of the Neapolitan working class. Several members of this élite manifested deep discontent with their routine, with the unpleasant environment of the factory or plant and with the authoritarian relations which prevailed in the factory. As a matter of fact, the dream of many went further than having their own enterprise or workshop or wanting a plot of land which would allow them to feed themselves.

Many workers did attempt to set up their own enterprises. This they might do on the basis of compensation payments received if they had been discharged from work. When discharged illegally, some workers successfully took their employers to court, and thus had a substantial sum of money at their disposal. Similarly, if the company they worked for had gone bankrupt – a not infrequent event – they would receive compensation. In any case the initial capital sum was, typically, small. On the other hand the ex-worker/neo-entrepreneur would probably have some machinery. Sometimes machinery was bought from factories which were renewing their stock, and sometimes items of machinery were part of the household paraphernalia. This was because many women had been given or had bought for themselves a sewing-machine and, if they had worked in the leather trade, it would be adapted for working with leather. A very important factor is having access to labour. A male worker who contemplated the possibility of setting up a small enterprise usually had direct access to the unpaid labour of his family and the cheap labour of kin, neighbours and friends.

A not untypical profile of a neo-entrepreneur in the Neapolitan shoe trade, for example, was that of a factory worker who retired or was dismissed with compensation and whose wife and/or daughters were skilled in the female tasks of the trade and who might own their own machines. Such a man was in a good position to start up a little workshop. If he had learned the full process of production he might with time be able to set up most, if not all, the different phases of production. In this case, if he had contacts which allowed him access to the market, he could operate autonomously rather than remain a dependent link in the subcontracting chain.

It is likely that the majority of such attempts at autonomy did not succeed. From anecdotal evidence it was clear that many units collapsed and at that point the different people involved were forced to find other solutions for their survival. Some units could carry on operating at low levels of production but still ensured some form of income, however meagre. Yet others succeeded in becoming independent, and might even be able to expand. An important factor in the relative success of small enterprises was State intervention, principally via the *Cassa per il Mezzogiorno* funds, which were made available to assist small units of production. To qualify for such funds enterprises had to meet a number of pre-conditions. One of these was the official approval of the trade union – based on their assessment of how workers' rights, levels of pay, safety and health regulations were respected.

The family played a central role in providing the structure for the small enterprise. In many cases prospective artisans or entrepreneurs could not get started without the backing of their families. Sometimes the family was the enterprise, in other cases it had constituted its origin and core. An example of the first case is provided by the Carnevale family. They worked in a *basso* in one of the old neighbourhoods in the centre of Naples producing handbags. Their living quarters were behind and above the room that served as a workshop.

The workshop itself was quite spacious. Mr Carnevale worked at a high bench and at a sewing-machine, while Mrs Carnevale worked at a sewing-machine which like her husband's had been adapted for leather work. There was a third, ordinary sewing-machine left free. They had three children who worked alongside them. The eldest, who was nearly 15 years old, had a bench to himself. The other two, who were 12 and 10 years old, worked together. The eldest boy applied a rectangle of leather to a rectangle of cardboard, and then glued them and hammered them together. He carried out his task quickly and efficiently. The two younger children glued long strips of leather, which were then sewn by their mother, after which the children applied metal pieces to the strips. These were the removable shoulder straps of the handbags. Mrs Carnevale attached the zips and sewed the pieces together to make the front and back of the bag. Her husband turned these inside out and sewed the back and front together as well as the lining, to which the zip had already been attached. The model they worked on was a simple black bag with two inside sections and two small pockets in the front. The materials were not of the best quality, but the bag was of a tasteful design and was well made. Mr Carnevale designed the models himself, producing a new one every week.

The entire process of production was carried out in the workshop: from the design, to the cutting, the sewing, and every operation until the finished handbags were filled with paper and placed carefully in plastic bags. How many they consigned was up to them, but the wholesaler wanted as many as they could produce, and they in fact worked to their maximum potential, making between 10 and 11 bags a day.

Mr Carnevale claimed he worked 24 hours a day. He started work at around 9 o'clock and paused only for a brief lunch. At 1.30 the children went off to school for the afternoon and their parents carried on working until they stopped for dinner at about 9 o'clock in the evening. Sometimes they worked for a further couple of hours before going to bed. Mrs Carnevale claimed that if she got up to do some cleaning or cook some lunch, her husband complained and told her to come back to work. She stressed that they worked 'every day, Christmas day included; Saturday and Sunday'. Mr Carnevale said that only in case of serious illness or death in the family did he ever stop working – and with him his family. He was concerned that lately they had lost working time because first his brother and then his mother had died. Their entire day, and their whole life, was totally determined and dominated by their work. They both insisted that work was the most important thing in their life and had to be a priority.

Life and work was not without pleasure however. Mr Carnevale said it was immensely rewarding and satisfying to see the bag ready-made and finished. 'To think that out of ordinary material I was able to make this useful article. Artisan work is fulfilling. In a factory they don't know how to make a complete bag. They can either cut, or they can sew, but they are unable to make a bag from beginning to end. The ability to do this, to make something out of nothing by oneself is very satisfying.'

He had no doubts about preferring work on his own to work in a factory. He argued that if he worked in a factory he would earn much more. And, his wife intervened, he would have all the benefits, for example the *mutua* (health insurance), and holiday pay. Their independent status did leave them vulnerable. At the time they were worried because their eldest son had inflamed tonsils and needed an operation, and they had no money to pay for the operation.

Mr Carnevale claimed that they were neither better off nor worse off than when they started. They had managed to pay for the machines, but it was impossible to expand the business. This meant that he was at the same point and producing the same quantity of bags as when they started out. In order to survive they had to work full-steam, and there was no 'break' in sight. He pointed out that not all artisans were in his position. Many had had a 'break' and had been able to expand and make a good living for themselves. It seemed to him to be a matter of luck or perhaps dishonesty. All he needed was a bit more money to employ one or two other workers. That way they could produce more and the children need not work as much. But workers have to be paid: 30,000 40,000 or 50,000 lire a week or more.[1]

He had not started out in the leather trade. He was first trained by his stepfather, who was a tailor. But he claimed that his stepfather had withheld from him knowledge about the most important stages of production, such as cutting. This meant that he was permanently dependent on his stepfather and unable to set up a unit on his own. When he returned from military service he decided to train in another trade. That was when he learned to make bags with his uncle. In the daytime he would do his training, doing the most menial jobs and earning very little. In the evenings he made trousers to pay for his food at home. As he gained more speed and skill in the leather trade he asked to have his wages increased, but his uncle refused. He therefore found a job with a *mastro* (qualified artisan) who had a small factory. Here he was soon promoted to the position of supervisor; but after he married he quarrelled with his boss and left work. It was then that he started making bags at home. He and his wife had an ordinary sewing-machine, and they did most of the work by hand. Later on they bought the other machines, paying for them in monthly instalments. The wholesaler they worked for was an old personal friend and had always helped them: they could ask him for whatever they might need and he provided it, deducting the cost from the payments he made for their bags.

This man's biography was constructed around his working life. The history of the little enterprise was his own history. Although his wife intervened, commented and joked, it was his story that dominated their account of their life and work. But although this story was seen and felt to be about his life, his initiative and his ability, his marriage had played a crucial part in this story. His search for an independent solution to subsistence seems to have dominated his life, yet this particular solution would not have been an option had he not married. Only with a wife, one with specific skills, could he have walked out of the factory to set himself up as an artisan. It seemed obvious that his wife and children would have been better off had he taken a factory job (assuming this was a real option). But it had been his decision to remain independent, motivated by his commitment to be free from the authority of a boss, to have control over his work and to enjoy the satisfaction of turning raw materials into a product he found aesthetically pleasing.

Aesthetics was not high on the agenda for Carmelo, who also ran his own small business. Carmelo was in his mid-thirties when he was first interviewed, and he owned and ran a small workshop which produced religious mementoes. These were designed by the boss and manufactured in the workshop. At the front of the premises there was a small area with a counter for selling their own produce as well as other merchandise. Many of the sales were made outside the shop by the boss or his partner/accountant at the various fairs, exhibitions and religious festivities which took place all over the country.

The workshop predominantly employed Carmelo's relatives. At the time there were two young girls, one who was 14 years of age and the other 16, who were his cousins. They earned very little (about L5,000 a week). Their tasks were to assemble the religious objects, serve at the counter, stock the produce, and clean the floor and the toilet. Carmelo's younger brother, who was around 12 at the time, also worked here, mainly serving at the counter and, when there were no customers, assembling the mementoes. His other brothers and sisters had also worked there when they were younger, or in between factory jobs. When there was a lot of work Carmelo and his wife Anna also worked at home; but he tried to avoid this.

Timetables in the workshop were rather flexible. Work started sometime between 9.00 and 9.15 in the morning, depending on when Carmelo arrived to open up the shop. At lunch-time they stopped for half an hour or an hour, depending on how much work they had, and finished their day at 6.00 o'clock – again, depending on the pressure. When work was over the girls had to sweep the floor and tidy up the workshop before going home. If there was an urgent consignment they would stay on until the work was finished.

Relations between the boss and his cousins were extremely friendly. In spite of the jovial atmosphere, the girls did not question his authority or his rights, and in fact they worked fairly hard. The banter and joking that went on, seemingly endlessly, came mainly from Carmelo. The main tenor of his jokes was sexual. Carmelo was capable of an extremely crude though ingenuous use of language, and was quite uninhibited when it came to expressing whatever sexual fantasy passed through his mind at any particular moment, or of asking very direct and personal questions. The girls barely flinched at this display. The younger one blushed at the more daring comments or giggled briefly, but both carried on working without interruption.

It was difficult to reconcile Carmelo's overtly sexual view of the world, his irreverent and anarchic wit and his extraordinary sense of ease when delivering crude observations, with the world he became involved in through his professional duties. His customers were all of a religious inclination, and his most important customers were personnel from the Catholic Church, especially nuns and priests. It was a testimony to his intelligence and entrepreneurship that he was able to maintain good relations with his clientele.

Carmelo started off with no capital. He had a very small sum of money he had earned, which he used to purchase cheap religious mementoes. These he then resold from various improvised stalls. He did quite well, and decided to start designing and making his own. The advantage of this kind of product is that it requires few and very cheap materials: a lot of plastic, fake velvet, cheap prints and cheap braid. At first he and his wife (and other family members) had made the objects at home, and he would then sell them wherever he could. Looking back on these early days he felt satisfied with his progress. He had been able to rent the premises where they worked, and his wife hardly ever had to do any work nowadays. The business carried on prospering, and much later he set up a proper shop on a busy central street and was able to ensure an even better and more secure life for his family.

Carmelo employed three or four outworkers to cope with the demand. He distributed the work by car, or in some cases it was collected by the workers. He invited me to accompany him on one of his visits to his outworkers. The first outworkers we visited were in fact a couple. The husband had a full-time job as a semi-skilled worker at the Alfa Sud car factory. In spite of having a fairly good job, one which was considered to be amongst the most prestigious and well-rewarded in Naples, his salary was inadequate to meet living costs. Therefore in the evening after work he and his wife worked for two or three hours to earn a little extra. During the daytime his wife was too busy with housework and shopping to work on the mementoes, so this was their 'leisure time' activity. It was, nonetheless, essential to the family economy, even though they earned very little doing this work: L15 per piece. They managed to assemble between 15 and 200 pieces a day, and could earn between L2,000 and L3,000 a day between them for 2 to 3 hours of work.

When we arrived and the woman opened the door Carmelo broke the ice immediately by making a heavy sexual joke. She laughed and seemed to enjoy the banter, but told him to be quiet because they had guests. We were immediately ushered in to the dining-room, which was in perfect order, and the door was closed behind us – they were careful to avoid any mingling with the guests, who were the man's sister, her husband and their children. But behind closed doors the joking continued. Carmelo was given a drink; he did not like it so he helped himself to another one from the modest collection of liquors on the mantelpiece.

His 'friendly' behaviour contrasted with what he had said about the couple on the way to their home. He had said he disliked the man because he was a Communist and he was dishonest – he had stolen from him. He later said the man was all right, but his wife put him off: she was dirty. This man had borrowed a sum of money from him (about L100,000) which he now needed urgently. He decided to deduct this sum from the work they did for him. Carmelo was rather upset because they had accepted work from another entrepreneur who, to make matters worse, was his ex-associate. This worried him in case they mixed up the consignments. He would now have to count the items when they were returned to him.

He left them a roll of velvet, two boxes of plastic pieces and a length of cord. The work they had to do was simple: the velvet rectangles were cut and used to line cardboard rectangles. Cord was then sewn round the edges and a transparent plastic cover was cut to fit a frame and all the pieces were assembled. The picture of a saint was glued on and all this was then glued on to the velvet rectangle.

The woman asked if he could give some work to a poor widow with small children who lived downstairs. He agreed to this and promised to bring some work round for her. The finished work was loaded on to the car and we drove home.

Another success story, though on a different scale from Carmelo's example, is the case of Tino, who had a small shoe factory. The factory employed 15 or 20 workers and was located in one of the outlying towns in the Neapolitan periphery. The workshop area was very small, although not unpleasant. They produced about 40 pairs of shoes per day. It was defined as a mixed factory, where artisan production dominated but modern machinery permitted a higher rate of productivity. Machines were used for *montaggio* (joining the upper part to the sole) and for some of the cutting and filing down of the soles. The rest of the work was done by hand or with the sewing-machine, which was also very labour-intensive work. The shoes produced were of a very high standard, catering for expensive and fashionable retailers in Italy and abroad.

At the time of interview Tino was in his late thirties. He was married and had four children. He had started to work as a young boy, when he was around 10 years of age, learning from an artisan. He had in fact learned the full process of production as well as various trade secrets. After his apprenticeship he worked in a series of factories. In his last factory job he rose to the position of manager. He left with very little compensation after quarrelling with his boss, but his experience there as a manager proved to be invaluable.

After this he was unemployed, so he started making a few pairs of shoes. He had a buyer thanks to the contacts he had made as factory manager. He then got together with a friend and later persuaded another one to join them. One by one, the workers were recruited through personal networks. By recruiting workers in this way they knew exactly what they were getting, how skilled the workers were, what their attitudes and personality were like – all of which helped to set up a successful unit.

The skins were probably the most expensive items of production. Most skins were imported, although they were often treated in Italy. Since they produced for a luxury market they had to use only very good-quality skins. These were selected by Tino himself. He calculated that for a closed, lined shoe, the cost in skins was equivalent to L5,240 per pair. The total cost including labour was around L17,000. The shoe was likely to sell at around 30,000. All the workers lived locally and they were all communists, belonging either to the PCI or to one of the smaller groups to the left of the Communist Party. Relations in the workplace were extremely friendly, and the men teased each other and joked. The women, however, remained quiet, apparently excluded from the men's discussions.

During my first visit to the workshop the workers in turn each explained their jobs. They were extremely proud of their work, each claiming that his specific task was the most important. The young women were quiet and didn't participate in this rivalry. The men explained that few workers knew how to make a shoe in this way any more. This was because mass production had taken over in most factories, and consequently workers were increasingly dependent on machines, and their skills were increasingly narrowly-defined. All the men in this workshop had been trained as artisans while they were still children. Later they had gone into factory work, so that they did in fact end up being specialized in a single stage of production, unlike their artisan teachers.

Tino explained that, as he was a communist himself, and a friend to the workers in his workshop, work relations were complex. On the one hand he sometimes had to take decisions and impose them on others. On the other hand, the nature of the relationships between himself and the others, both inside and outside the factory, made any imposition of authority extremely difficult. They all frequented the same branch of the PCI, they had known each other for many years and they belonged to the same neighbourhood. Also, the fact that he worked alongside the others made him an equal. Although all of these things seemed to be considered positive, he pointed out that sometimes he was forced into confrontations with his workers/mates.

Tino's success was probably largely due to a grant from the *Cassa per il Mezzogiorno*. He had been backed by the trade union, which had seen in his unit an example of good practice. With these funds he had built a new and larger workshop. He proposed to improve the work environment by making it more spacious, providing good toilets, and showers. Above the workshop he was building a flat for his family's use. He planned to employ at least one more worker for each section as soon as they were able to occupy the new premises.

Personal networks were a crucial resource to all three entrepreneurs. In the first example the family had to rally around the family enterprise as a matter of survival. The choice of this particular strategy of survival was the result of Mr Carnevale's personal trajectory and skills and his need to feel autonomous, to be his own man. In the case of Carmelo, family labour again played a very important part in the take-off and later success of his enterprise. Here the combination of low-pay, kin-based labour and the work of outworkers were the key to success, as was targeting a line of production where materials were cheap and where few specialist skills were required. However, Carmelo's opportunistic choices and his idiosyncratic self-taught marketing skills undoubtedly were crucial too. Although all workers in the cases examined were recruited through personal networks, family and kinship relations are specially significant in providing especially cheap and flexible workers. This is because familial ideologies generate sets of differentiated rights, so that some have rights over the labour of others, while at the same time they foster ideals of communality and reciprocity, where demands for better wages or improved working conditions appear to be inappropriate. Not only is kin-based labour cheaper, but it also predisposes workers to accept requests to work late or to work harder. The authority relations that characterize family and kinship ties, and in particular cross-gender and cross-generational ties, underwrite the authority of work relations. Mr Carnevale had rebelled against this and left both his stepfather and his uncle, but his own marriage and his authority in his own family had later been central to his strategy of avoidance of undesirable positions of subordination.

In Tino's case it seemed as though he and his wife had initiated the core of the enterprise, which later expanded, again through personal networks. However, the relationships which characterized Tino's enterprise were of a very different order and carried with them quite different expectations from those discussed above. Here workers were friends, mates and comrades, and egalitarianism was the accepted norm between them. Workers were paid in accordance with national trade agreements; they were legally employed, and every effort was made to make the work environment safe and pleasant. Tino saw the disadvantages of this, given that there was a direct conflict between doing his job as owner/proprietor and his role as mate/comrade. On the other hand, the owner's and workers' knowledge of each other's skills and competence had allowed for very high standards of achievement.

The desire for 'independence' is a powerful incentive to work outside the factory context, although external constraints are such that the entrepreneur is forced into relations of subordination *vis-à-vis* other factories or merchants in the majority of cases. However, the pursuit of independence was an important factor contributing to the existence of small units in Naples. Availability of capital was an important consideration here. Where capital had been obtained through a process of accumulation or through grants or credit, expansion had been possible and, in the few cases observed, successful. But most Neapolitan artisans and petty entrepreneurs were starved of capital and were constrained to maintain their enterprise at what one might call a subsistence level, and this they only managed to do precariously and on the basis of low wages or even unpaid labour.

The 'entrepreneurial spirit' was not lacking amongst those interviewed in Naples. On the contrary, what was surprising was the resourcefulness and drive that many revealed in their accounts of their work experience. Skills are important, and in no case was any petty entrepreneur trained through the formal system. Those without formal training or indeed without full schooling could find a niche, as Carmelo had. Alternatively, if apprenticeship had taken the place of school, they had the skills that enabled them to set up a production unit, albeit in a restricted number of trades – and the leather trade tended to predominate. But with the decline of artisan production described by Tino, amongst others, there is the risk that younger generations will not acquire the quality and breadth of skills necessary to set themselves up independently. This, coupled with declining numbers of factories in the area, implies a growth in the large sectors of displaced people unable to find work in the factory sector yet ill-equipped to survive outside it.

The ideal of working independently represents one factor in the proliferation of very small units of production. The examples discussed suggest that the prevailing relations of gender and the organization of authority relations in the household and the kinship system have important implications for the potential of men and women to operate in the arena of small-scale production. Women will generally work under the authority of a man, who may be her husband, her father, or a kinsman or family friend. But the extent of the differential effects of expectations regarding gender roles on men and women workers is illustrated most clearly when we compare those cases of men and women who have chosen to work independently.

Outworker Teams

Groups of women, who are generally related through kinship ties, may get together to form outworker teams. These teams offer a number of advantages over single outworkers because their productivity is higher and they are able to work on a fairly regular basis for several employers. This means that they are in a less vulnerable position. In addition, because of their productivity and efficiency and because generally they cluster around a woman with special skills or experience, it is in the interests of an entrepreneur to try to guarantee access to the team's labour. Because he must compete for this with other entrepreneurs, he may decide to create a privileged position for himself by legalizing the working status of the outworker. This means that she will be on the official payroll, which gives her cover for state sickness benefits and pensions, and that her rates of pay will be in line with trade contracts. The entrepreneur may also pay the cost of electricity or in some cases a portion of the telephone bill, in order to ensure his consignments will be given priority.

Some women were interested in expanding their output and building up a more secure position for themselves while becoming more independent from individual entrepreneurs. The only way to accomplish this was by setting up a team. The cases of teamwork encountered were successful. They required a great deal of organizational skill as well as the usual – or above average – trade skills. But in spite of their success they could never achieve the relative autonomy gained by small artisan enterprises. They were and remained expanded outwork units.

Anna Maria

Anna Maria was 35 years old and had been married for 13 years. She had three children, the eldest of whom was 12 while the youngest was only 9 months old. Because her family of origin was very large she had been obliged to start work at an early age to pay her way. By the age of 15 she was a fully qualified *orlatrice*. She met her husband in a factory when she was only 10 years old. When he returned to work after completing his military service she was 12, a *signorina* (young woman). So they began courting and by the age of 14 she was engaged. She carried on working in the factory until after their first year of marriage, when their first child was born. She then started working at home for the same employer, and when he later went bankrupt she rapidly found another.

At the time of interview she worked for a medium-sized factory with a turnover of about 130 pairs of shoes a day. This factory was her principal employer, which insured her and to which she gave priority. However, she also accepted consignments from other factories, according to how much time she had available. The sewing-machine was her own. Her very first machine had been given to her when she had started working in a factory. It was her *dote* as an *orlatrice*. She had subsequently exchanged it for a newer model and kept updating it. The factory provided the special thread needed for the specialist work she did for it.

Anna Maria specializes in sewing moccasin ridges. Because this is a skill which very few workers have, she was very much sought after at the time. A moccasin single ridge earned her L150 per pair; a double ridge L200. For non-specialist work her principal employer paid her L370 per pair, while other factories paid between L400 and L450 per pair. Work was delivered and collected daily, but payment was made once a week. She calculated that she worked 12 or 13 hours a day and she was able to finish 50 pairs of shoes or between 50 and 150 pairs of moccasin ridges. In all, she earned somewhere between L80,000 and L100,000 a week, although she could sometimes earn more.

Work was carried out in her home, which was a fairly new and spacious flat in a central neighbourhood of Naples. She had a separate room for work, which was quite spacious. Working at home was convenient, because her children were still young and she now had the baby to consider.

Anna Maria shared the work with her sister Lorena. Lorena seemed to be the one principally responsible for the housework and especially the cooking. After cleaning her own home in the morning she came over to Maria's house to clean up and cook. She then spent the entire day at Maria's with her children, sharing the daily meals there and only returning in the evenings in time to prepare her husband's meal. In between the housework she sat at the work-table and concentrated on the task of folding the leather edges.

Lorena was 33 years old and had two children aged 5 and 3. Her husband was a bus driver and earned good money. She found it hard to concentrate on work when the children were around, which was why she would have preferred to work in a factory. But her husband would not accept this because he was jealous. She thought that if she were to work in a factory she would be able to make arrangements for child-care at the school or with one of her sisters. She had worked on her own for a while, but had mostly worked in factories, with her sister. When her sister left to work at home she followed suit and also started to work *a domicilio* (at home).

At the time of interview Anna Maria and Lorena were helped by two sisters, aged 15 and 16, who worked for them as apprentices. They explained that in the past they would have had up to five apprentices working with them. The girls were neighbours who were unsure of what they would do once they completed their apprenticeship. One was close to achieving the status of a fully-fledged *orlatrice*, although her teacher thought she was not very good at her work. Their main problem in terms of thinking about the future was that their father was extremely strict and very jealous of them, and would not allow them to work 'outside'. As it was, he had opposed the idea of them training with Maria and Lorena, although he had eventually agreed because Maria lived so close to their home. Because of this situation, they thought their only option would be to complete their training, buy a machine and work at home. As apprentices they earned very little, and so it was not advisable to extend their training period more than they had to.

The work was divided as follows: Maria did the sewing and her sister was in charge of the glueing, although she too could sew. The senior apprentice folded the edges and the youngest completed the glueing. As well as being in charge of sewing, the team organizer dealt with the administration of the unit, receiving consignments, working out work schedules, and negotiating with entrepreneurs. Because they worked for a number of factories and prepared different types and models of shoe, organization had to be meticulous to ensure that they fulfilled their tasks properly and completed the consignments promptly so as to meet all the different delivery dates. The difficulties involved in planning work schedules could be compounded when factory owners failed to collect their consignments when their firm was in difficulties. In this way they postponed payment for the work that had been completed. The delay not only affected income calculations but also had a knock-on effect on future production.

Maria's and Lorena's children played in the work-room. The baby's play-pen was also in the room close to her mother's sewing-machine. Maria was not teaching her daughters how to fold and glue. She and her husband did not want their daughters to follow in their mother's footsteps, because the job was hard and the 'atmosphere' in the factories was undesirable. But at the same time they were reluctant to allow them to carry on their education into intermediate and high school because of the drug problem that afflicted many schools in the area. Lorena's daughter enjoyed sitting at the table with the women, helping with the folding, even though she was no older than six at the time.

Rosa

Rosa's team consisted mainly of herself and her sisters. There were twelve children in her family. Two of the elder sisters had recently married and lived in their own homes, but their father's sister was living with them. Both her parents worked in the shoe trade. The girls worked in a room which had been set aside specifically for the purpose of outwork, although it also doubled as a storage room for a number of items, most of which were *corredo* items for those of the sisters who were already engaged.

Rosa, who was 20 years old and was the eldest of the group, organized the entire affair, did the machine sewing and distributed their earnings amongst the members of the group. She had completed primary school and had started training with an outworker at the age of eleven. At twelve she started to work in a factory, where she completed her training after three years. She had moved around quite a lot, changing employers according to where wages were higher. She was engaged and was soon to be married. She had only left the factory to become an outworkers six months ago, when her sisters lost their factory jobs and so were free to work as a group. This was an attractive option, because her fiancé did not like her working in a factory, as he disapproved of the 'atmosphere'.

They were working for a fairly large factory with a turnover of about 1,000 pairs of shoes per week. The factory supplied one sewing-machine and paid the costs of electricity and telephone, as well as insuring the head of the unit or *titolare*. The group could produce 70 shoes a day if the model was simple, or 45 to 50 a day if the model was more difficult. They were paid at a rate of L500 per pair, and for boots the rate increased to L1,100 per pair. They worked an eight- to ten-hour day and also worked on Saturdays. Rosa distributed the income as follows:

(a) folding : L30,000 per week.
(b) apprentices (2): L25,000 per week
(c) *azzeccatrice*: L38,000 per week
(d) organizer: L70,000 per week.

All the sisters, with the exception of the youngest who was an apprentice and therefore earned very little, gave L1,000 to their mother. Rosa was putting aside some money and using another part of her income to buy her *corredo*. Two of her sisters were also engaged, and they too had started to collect items for their *corredo*. But their mother focused on Rosa, and contributed mostly to her *corredo*, since she was the next one to get married.

The girls helped with the housework in the morning before they started work. Their mother controlled the pace of work and put considerable pressure on her daughters. Their aunt, who was the main person in charge of cooking and housework, also popped into the room at regular intervals, urging the girls to concentrate on their work.

Rosa's sister Chiara was an *azzeccatrice*. She was 19 at the time and engaged. She hoped to marry in two years' time. She had completed primary school but had already started factory work when she was around 9 or 10 years old. She used to go to school in the morning and spent the rest of the day in the factory. Here she trained for three and a half years. She later left the factory and trained as an *orlatrice* with an outworker, returning to factory work through an arrangement made by her father. He had wanted his daughters to work in this factory, even though wages were low, because the owner was an acquaintance and he knew the people who worked there. He was not concerned about the money: it was far more important that they learn the trade properly and that they should avoid any 'funny business', which he knew often occurred between a boss and his young workers. However, one month their wages were so low they decided to leave. Chiara and her sisters had been working at home ever since, and she intended to carry on in outwork until she married. Her fiancé was also in the shoe trade.

Emilia was 18 and she had left the factory with her sister Chiara. She had completed primary school and then trained as an *orlatrice* in a factory for seven or eight years. Emilia was also engaged. Her younger sister Rita was 14 and had worked as an apprentice in a factory for a year and now carried on learning the trade at home, which she preferred. Marina was 19 and was engaged to Rosa's brother. She had trained originally in the belt trade, but there was no more work available in that trade, which had, in any case, paid very low wages. Seeing this, she had opted for training as an *orlatrice* with her future sisters-in-law. Another sister, Maria, who was 15 years old, lived at home but was not part of the team. She worked with a married sister in her home as an *azzeccatrice*.

The Mirage of Independence

The actual autonomy of small units is limited, and has been for some time. A Ministerial survey dating from 1960 found that 17 per cent of all the units interviewed in the provinces of Milan and Sondrio produced for other enterprises. A study carried out in Lombardy in 1972–3 (quoted in Frey 1973) showed that those artisan units which produced *semi-lavorati* (part-products, equivalent to 13 per cent of all artisan production) in the early 1970s supplied 56 per cent of their output to industry, 9 per cent to intermediaries and 20 per cent to other artisans. Artisan units producing finished goods supplied 13.6 per cent of their goods to industry, 10.7 per cent to intermediaries and 6 per cent to other artisans. In Lombardy just under 30 per cent of artisans had links with industrial units or intermediaries. Thus few artisans have direct access to the market. Whereas in Central and North-eastern Italy a degree of autonomy and regional integration have been achieved, small units in the South remain heavily dependent on other units. However, although autonomy is limited in most cases, the head of an artisan unit does avoid the problems entailed by working under the direct control of another man.

This is relevant to a theme which was frequently addressed by men when they talked about work and their futures. For many, accepting the authority of a boss was difficult, and they often expressed the wish to free themselves from this unpleasant relationship. On the other hand, for many the ideal was a secure job in the *comune*, which hardly guaranteed them independence – but nevertheless the issue of authority did not there appear to be a source of concern. Nor were those men who worked in the shoe trade thinking primarily about autonomy when they wished they could get a job with Italsider, although for those working for this establishment this issue was often seen as important.

Outworkers frequently preferred factory work because of the regular wages, holidays and sickness benefits. But many also liked the idea of a contained working day and of working *in compagnia*, in the company of others. Women factory workers were generally happy with their work situation. Although the majority envisaged leaving work one day, when they married or had children, they considered that factory work was preferable to outwork.

Teresa, who was 27 years old at the time of interview, was single and lived at home with her parents, her brothers and sisters and her grandmother. She had been working in the factory as an *orlatrice* for two and a half years. She had started her working life at 13 as an apprentice to an outworker, with whom she remained for two or three years. Not yet a fully-fledged *orlatrice,* she started work in a factory, where she completed her training. She calculated that it took her around seven years to become a fully qualified *orlatrice.* In her present job she worked an eight-hour day, taking home around 240,000 lire a month. Bettina was a 24-year-old shirt-maker (*camiciaia*) who, like Teresa, was unmarried and living at home with her family. Bettina worked a 40-hour week in a factory and was paid between L220,000 and L230,000 a month. She had trained in a factory, where she worked as an apprentice for 4 years. Bettina found outwork boring, and in any case argued that in her trade outwork was rarely an option. She felt that in the event of marriage she would wish to carry on working in a factory, although she foresaw that there would be problems when she had children. She thought that the problem of child-care could be resolved with the help of her parents, and outwork would be her very last option. Maddalena, who was in her forties, also preferred factory work. As an *orlatrice* she worked an eight-hour day and earned around L230,000 a month. She had been at home for 5 or 6 years when she had had to stop work in order to care for her elderly parents, returning to the factory at their death. Although she explained that there was little time in the factory for conversations, they did manage to have a quick laugh during the breaks. She had no contacts with her workmates outside work, but she nevertheless found the factory more enjoyable than outwork, which she considered to be boring. Maddalena was also unmarried and childless, and lived with her cousin and her family.

Not all factory workers were single or childless however. For married women with children, kin provided a crucial support because of the paucity of good public services, particularly for child-care. Nunzia was 25 when she was interviewed, and had two small children aged 5 and 3 and was expecting her third child. Nunzia had started her career at the age of 6 as a dressmaker's assistant. At the age of 12 she started work in a small factory/workshop, where she trained as an *orlatrice*. She had become engaged at 14 and was married at 19, and now worked in a well-known factory which produced high-quality shoes for export. Her preference for factory work was determined mainly by the higher rates of pay, but she hoped that, as they finished paying for all the important household appliances, she would be able to leave work altogether in the near future. At the time of interview her husband's mother took care of the children. Her decision to carry on working in the factory was clearly affected by her ability to rely on her mother-in-law, and it was also helped by the fact that her husband and all their family were supportive. This she attributed in part to their being Communists and members of the trade union.

The choice in favour of factory work or outwork was therefore directly related to age, marital status and family circumstances. A third possibility falls outside both these categories: some women were able to set up an independent unit, supplying customers directly. This was the case with Nunzia. She was 39 years old, she was married and she had a 12-year-old daughter. She had started work at the age of 9 as an apprentice to an outworker and had then worked in a series of factories. She had now been working on her own for seven years. She made shirts to measure and also had some ready-made shirts available for sale. She had bought two very specialized sewing-machines, one for making button-holes and one to attach buttons. She rented a small workshop in the old city, which was was quite spacious and had a small toilet, and she had recently bought a couple of rings to cook with. She was in the workshop from 8.30 in the morning until about 9 o'clock at night, when her husband came by to fetch her to drive home. At lunch-time her daughter came from school to the workshop for her midday meal.

Nunzia preferred working on her own because she had greater freedom than in the factory and she made more money this way, even though it meant she worked longer hours. But she felt that she was directly benefiting herself by working longer hours. There was enough demand to keep her going, even though this was very seasonal. She was very busy during the summer months, whereas in winter things were quieter.

Nunzia's position as an independent skilled worker was rare; the majority of women who worked independently only earned very small incomes. This was the case for Ornella, who at 34 was married and had a 15-year-old son. She defined herself as a housewife, but she worked as a seamstress. Most of her work was limited to the odd sewing job, mending, shortening skirts and trousers, changing zippers and so on. Her clientele were the people of her neighbourhood. She did not earn a lot, but what little she did earn allowed her to have some extra money without having to ask her husband. She had trained as an *azzecatrice* and had worked in a factory until approximately four years ago. Her husband had decided that she should stop factory work because he wanted to find his dinner ready when he came home from work, and his shirts and clothes clean and ironed, ready and waiting for him. Although she preferred factory work she had attempted to find a contact to work at home as an outworker; but this was difficult for *azzecatrici*. So she had compromised and taken up sewing.

Gender and Autonomy

It is difficult to reconcile a need for income with a desire for autonomy. This is as true for men as it is for women. However, men were in a better position to attempt the semi-independent option of the artisan or petty entrepreneur. Family structure and gender roles dictated the possibilities open to both men and women. In the case of men, access to labour and indeed machinery could be guaranteed because of their status as heads of households. They could usually claim access to the labour of wives, daughters and other kinswomen, who in many cases were likely to have strategically important skills. The nucleus of husband, wife and maybe children could at some stage be extended to include male friends or colleagues. This was not the case for women, who only had access to the labour of the women of their household and usually only to the labour of young children and adolescents, and this, increasingly, was on a part-time basis only. So whereas men's position in the family often made the dream of autonomy a feasible option, women's position in the family tended to restrict their choice, so that they usually opted for outwork as a compromise between the need for income and the need to be at home.

The question of skills and training is central here. The artisan context trained men so that they learned how each stage of the production process was carried out. This enabled them to set up their own production unit. Those men who were trained in a factory were at a disadvantage, for they lacked knowledge of the overall organization of the trade. Women also benefited from training in a small artisan unit or with an outworker. In the shoe trade proper training was important, since a woman's reputation would give her access to work in the factory and at home. A good reputation and specialist skills were important resources. If such women had access to kinswomen and neighbours (usually as apprentices) they could successfully set up an outworker team. However, expansion beyond this was impossible, since women never learned the entire process of production, regardless of where they had trained, nor could they command the male labour required to carry out all phases of production.

The choice against factory work stems from different concerns for men and for women. In most cases male factory workers and petty entrepreneurs expressed a strong desire for 'being their own boss'. This desire for independence was coupled with the hope that their efforts would bring them success and economic well-being, and provide the means to break out of the poor living conditions to which they were condemned as factory, or even more so, as workshop employees. In reality, the ideal of independence and economic success was rarely fulfilled: in order to secure a minimum income a burdensome pace of work was imposed on the small unit from the outset. For women, the decision to leave the factory was usually determined by changes in their personal lives: they became engaged, married or had a child.

While independence for men was defined largely within the sphere of work, for women it was the household which tended to provide the focus. A woman's aspirations to independence were enmeshed in her duties as wife, mother or daughter. Men were also conditioned by their role in the household and their obligation to provide for the family; but this obligation presupposed their complete exclusion from household tasks and granted them greater freedom and mobility to pursue their personal objectives.

A young woman's struggle for personal freedom and autonomy would not therefore be principally directed against the factory but rather against the household, which was seen as the principal area of control over their lives. Single women tended to identify parental control as the source of oppression, and factory work might represent a means of escaping from or at least alleviating this control (cf. Stivens 1978). At marriage all this changed: marriage might well be seen as a means of escaping parental control and establishing an area of autonomy by setting up one's own home, a space which was directly under one's control. A woman might see her labour and time as being redirected from the parental home, which was not fully 'hers', to her marital home, with which she fully identified.

The division of labour by gender within the household results in important differences for men and women in terms of access to important resources. These may be capital, skill and knowledge or labour-power. There are, of course, independent productive activities requiring very limited capital and skills which are frequently resorted to by the unemployed, but these usually provide low returns and little stability and are unlikely to constitute a long-term activity. In the Neapolitan leather industries the entry requirements for activities were much harsher. Access through inheritance was essentially discriminatory, since the artisan unit would be passed on to a son or other male kin. Where inheritance was not relevant, an individual attempting to establish an independent unit must fulfil certain minimum requirements: s/he must have access to instruments or machinery; must have access to capital; must have an adequate knowledge of the trade; and must have access to cheap labour.

Whereas the instruments required by some workers (such as the *azzecatrice* in the shoe trade) were quite affordable for most, other workers required costly machinery. Any attempt to establish a full cycle of production, in the shoe trade for example, would involve the acquisition of expensive machinery. Considerable capital sums would be necessary. Capital was usually acquired through an early retirement or redundancy payment. Frequently the ex-employer provided machinery and credit which was to be paid back with work. Alternatively, loans may be negotiated through banks or special state funds. Loans could also be obtained from kin. Men were more likely than women to be successful in such negotiations, because they were perceived as having greater business credibility and were more likely to gain the support of appropriate backers. In either case the new entrepreneur was unlikely to be able to provide the installations necessary to operate a complete process, and was thus likely to concentrate initially on operations which are manual, or which require relatively cheap machinery. Contacts were also crucial, not only to recruit cheap labour-power but also to secure credit and loans and to ensure that the product was commercialized successfully. Because of their greater freedom of movement, men acquired a far wider network and were in a better position to build up contacts which could be economically useful.

Women were far more restricted to kinship and neighbourhood

networks,and even if these expanded as a result of factory work or
trade union activity, their relationships with men were severely limited
by the ways in which appropriate behaviour between men and women
were defined. Male–female patterns of interaction were rarely
conducive to relationships such as friendships and partnerships,
which can become instrumental to the pursuit of successful economic
activity. Since in most cases key positions in the various relevant
institutions, such as banks, local government, or trade unions, were
occupied by men, women were excluded from the personal networks
which were so important for the establishment and survival of small
enterprises. It may be that women face specific difficulties when
attempting to establish contact and organize themselves as a working
group. The teams of outworkers in the shoe industry were related
through ties of kinship or affinity. It was not clear how women could
come together on a less personal, and more instrumental, basis.[2]

Personal relations were crucial for the pursuit of economic activities
in Naples. Both from the point of view of the worker and from the
point of view of the entrepreneur, personal contacts were important
for survival and success. Although women were central to the
maintenance of networks, these operated differentially in the cases
of men and women. Because of the way gender roles were defined
and male and female spheres of action were perceived, men and
women did not have equal access to these relations. The distinction
extended from here to affect women's access to other important
factors of production and commercialization.

Thus there were significant differences in the possibilities open to
men and women workers in relation to their survival outside the
factory. The content and extent of the meaning of independence was
different for men and women. Yet the independence of both men and
women was subject to a series of parallel constraints. These constraints
are related to the physical, economic and political environment of
the city of Naples and, more generally, of the South of Italy.

Conclusion

Autonomy at work was a more plausible alternative for men than it
was for women; but it was a partial autonomy in either case. The
spaces available for independent work were few and quite clearly
delimited. Much depended on the functioning of certain key
industries, such as the shoe industry or the garments industry. These
have showed a decline over the years. In the period from 1971 to 1981
there has been a decline of micro-enterprises[3] in the South both in
terms of the number of units and the workers employed in such units,
in contrast to the trend elsewhere in Italy, especially in the Centre.
Larger units have fared better (Giannola, n.d.: 82–3). Again, contrary

to the trends shown in other regions, light industry has been in decline, especially in the shoe and garments industries, which have been of great strategic significance in the expansion of businesses in the Centre and North-east of the country.[4] In these industries there has been a tendency for enterprises to grow in size, while there is a parallel decline in the total number of units. In the shoe and clothing industries there has also been a drop in the total employed in these sectors (Giannola, n.d.: 85). These statistics would indicate that the spaces available for the strategies described in this chapter have shrunk. Petty entrepreneurs in particular have not fared well in the South, contrary to what has occurred in Italy as a whole. This has implications for outworkers, many of whom are attached to the smaller enterprises.

There are also important implications here for the Southern economy as a whole. There is evidence that a clear majority of the larger firms are not Southern in origin. For the South as a whole 55 per cent of medium-sized units, which employ 70 per cent of the workers, are owned by non-Southern entities. Even in the case of units with 50–90 workers, 30 per cent of these are non-Southern-owned. Giannola observes that within this category of unit the tendency is that in the units which are not owned by Southerners employment is more contained than in those which are Southern (Giannola, n.d.: 87). In any case, Southern capital is concentrated in small enterprises with less than 50 employees, and only maintains a position of strength in the shoe and garments trades, which, however, have suffered a decline. Growth has taken place in the sectors dominated by non-Southern capital. But Giannola suggests that, on the basis of past trends, small and medium-scale local capital are able to take advantage of the opportunities offered by this external investment, and contribute to local processes of growth. Of course, the success and sustainability of this growth will depend to a large extent on what kind of support is available to encourage, channel and develop the entrepreneurial attempts of men and women.

In the examples we have discussed, dependence on a larger firm or wholesaler did not detract from the sense of satisfaction and control experienced by the petty entrepreneur. Expansion from a very minimal level of production has been possible to the extent that particular entrepreneurs have been able to capitalize on funding and/ or on cheap labour. Personal relationships were crucial here, and although women play a central role in creating and reproducing these relationships, their access to them as resources are restricted. The authority of men as household heads and their capacity to mobilize networks outside and beyond the household mean that they are in a better position to establish and sustain a small enterprise.

Whilst material needs shaped the choices of men and women, there were other, non-material considerations at play. In particular, the recognition of the need to be autonomous and to be fulfilled. What this autonomy and fulfilment meant was different for men and women, as were the opportunities of achieving them. This was because kinship relations and ideologies impinged in different ways on men and women, sometimes supporting the pursuit of goals, sometimes constraining individual aspirations. In some cases individuals have little scope for choice. This is very clearly so in the case of outworkers, where personal choice in favour of outwork or factory work was so frequently conditioned by the wishes of parents, and especially fathers, and/or fiancés or husbands. But taking all these into account, it must be said that for many women outwork did represent a form of 'freedom', a freedom which was to do with the possibility of organizing their own control over their time.

While factory work provided some women with a sense of freedom because of their earnings and because it enabled them to have some form of relationships outside the home and the neighbourhood, and outwork provided other women with a sense of freedom by increasing their sense of control over their time and space, women's views of freedom were not as strongly focused on work as were men's. For the majority of women, autonomy was envisaged in respect of home life. It was escaping the parental home and setting up their own home which represented the main expression of women's desire for autonomy.

The ways in which men and women view work are significantly different, then. For women work is a means to an end, and they make their choices on the basis of their opportunities and convenience. For men, on the other hand, work was an important area for self-definition. Women did derive pride from their work and their skills, and many enjoyed work and gained a sense of satisfaction from it, especially where the work was skilled. But their self-esteem, though conditioned by the work experience, was primarily derived from the sphere of home and family relations.

Notes

1. See note 3 from Chapter 5 for exchange rates betwen the Italian Lira and Pound Sterling.
2. There have been cases of cooperatives set up by and for women (none that I came across in Naples), such as those of the embroiderers of Sta. Catalina Villarmosa and in Partinico in Sicily. These were the result of a protracted

struggle against the increasing abuse of the system of subcontracting by the middlemen. Cutrufelli (1975) explains that the Partinico cooperative failed because of the restricted mobility of the women who were therefore unable to operate efficiently on the market. 'This impossibility regarding movement results in an impossibility of forming stable organisations, of expanding the movement (of resistance against the middlemen), this being an essential condition to the very survival of the cooperative' (Cutrufelli 1975: 162).

3. Micro-enterprises are units with eight workers or fewer (Giannola, n.d.: 82).

4. On the other hand, there has been significant growth in heavy industry (car industry, engineering, etc.), of 25% from 1971 to 1981. Expansion has been concentrated in the medium and large enterprises.

Part II

Family, Gender and Identities

seven

The Organization of Sexuality

Most of the literature on Southern Italy tends to concern itself with rural areas. This may explain the divergence between the Neapolitan examples and the main arguments suggested in the literature on the Mediterranean. In Naples, young working-class women in the late 1970s might enjoy considerable freedom of movement. This movement, however, was not unrestricted: generally women tended to confine themselves to areas near the home, for example the distance from home to school or work, or to a kinswoman's house or to a local shop or market. For social outings this field could be extended considerably; but the girls were always accompanied by a group of other women or by a brother or kinsman. Since girls were expected to do a great deal of work in the home from an early age, and often assisted in whatever productive activities might take place in the home after school hours, there was not much time left for socializing. Sunday afternoons were usually the time for walks and visits.

On such occasions boys and girls met and established friendships which could lead to a casual form of courtship known as *fidanzamento fuori casa*, or engagement outside the home. These relationships were not considered to be important, and a girl might become involved in a series of these liaisons without damaging her reputation. It was assumed that such relationships were sexually innocent, and in fact many girls considered themselves to be 'engaged' in this way with very little prompting beyond an exchange of glances or a slight flirtation.

Serious courtship, called *fidanzamento in casa*, engagement within the home, involved considerably more formalities and signified a radical change in the girl's life. Her fiancé would visit her parents and, if all went well, the potential in-laws would also exchange visits. With this accomplished, the young man was accepted by the girl's household, and was thereafter likely to become a more or less permanent presence and a fairly regular commensal. The girl was expected to visit her mother-in-law and to develop a close and affectionate relationship with her, reflected in the expectation that she use the term *mamma*, mother, to address her.

Courtships of this kind tended to be protracted affairs. The usual period of engagement lasted around five or six years, although some couples had to wait up to ten years before they were in a position to marry. Serious engagements of this kind were usually entered into when the young woman was between 18 and 21 years old. Given the seriousness of the relationship and the restrictions it imposed on the girl's life, some 15-year-olds or 16-year-olds felt they were too young to become engaged. The young man was also likely to be over 18 – he must have something to offer in terms of future prospects, so that he would generally only make overtures to a girl's family if this was the case. Otherwise he was likely to postpone the confrontation with the girl's father until he was in a better bargaining position.

Engagements are necessarily long because the couple will experience difficulties in establishing a home. The housing situation in Naples is an important factor here, as is the felt need to have everything ready for the new home. Although most young girls started thinking of their trousseau or *corredo* from the age of twelve or thirteen, they started to work seriously for it after they became engaged. Mothers were key figures in the accumulation of a *corredo*. It would be the girl's mother who would start thinking about the *corredo* and preparing it. She may in fact shoulder the responsibility entirely, especially if the daughter is not in wage employment. On the whole, however, young girls found some income-generating activity which allowed them to build up their *corredo*. Even here, though, the mother may be the administrator of the girl's income, receiving it and using it to purchase the various items. These include sheets, towels, bedspreads, tablecloths, and cutlery, but could also include a television, a stereo or domestic appliances. Becoming engaged and building up a *corredo* were important factors in encouraging a young woman to seek some form of income-generating work if she was not already employed.[1]

From the time she is engaged, a girl will no longer be able to go out with groups of friends or, in fact, go out at all unless accompanied by her fiancé or to visit her mother-in-law or kin. At this point, her relationships with her women friends tend to deteriorate. She is likely to give up work or become an apprentice at home or in the workshop of a trusted friend or kinsman/woman. The girl's father officially takes on the role of controller of his daughter's behaviour and reputation on behalf of the man to whom she has been promised.

The sexual content of relationships seems to follow a development parallel to these circumstances: there is very little, if any, physical contact in the engagement 'outside the home', whereas once a couple becomes engaged 'within the home' they may well become involved in sexual experimentation, which can result in full sexual intercourse.

This does not mean that virginity is not important. On the contrary, it is a crucial element in the relationship of men and women. In a city like Naples people are subjected to many influences (and, amongst these, that of the feminist movement). Therefore, no claims can be made for a homogeneity of values or behaviour such as that suggested by much of the 'honour and shame' literature.[2] Some young women contravene the above pattern, talking as though they have had considerable experience, even though some of them have never been involved in long-term stable engagements. Others talk as though they remained virgins until their wedding. It is difficult to assess the weight of most of this talk; but both men and women generally speak and joke with ease and delight regarding sexual matters.

The attitudes of men also vary. Many felt they would react violently if they were to discover that they were not the 'first man' in the sexual experience of their fiancées and wives. But others argued that what had happened before their relationship was of no concern to them. Most men, however, even those who placed themselves amongst the ranks of the left-wing parties, so keen to represent 'progressive' ideas, wanted, even expected, to marry a virgin.

Yet nobody was likely to be surprised if a bride dressed in white (and a white wedding is the dream of the majority of women), was not a virgin, or was in fact pregnant. This was not considered a great problem, although the news would hardly be broadcast. The realization that an unmarried daughter or sister is pregnant will almost certainly cause a stir, and family members will be mobilized to resolve the problem. Once everything has been settled and it is clear that the marriage will take place, tempers will become calmer. Ideally, women were expected to marry their first lover. In the 1970s and early 1980s only three cases of unmarried mothers were encountered in my fieldwork. In all three cases the conditions which resulted in single motherhood were explained and understood. The women with whom the matter was discussed were in no way condemning of these girls.

Although this was not its explicit function, the fidanzamento in casa could provide a framework which allowed women to engage in full sexual activity, should they wish to do so, without forsaking the ideal of the white wedding. Sex in this case could be seen as an anticipation of the right which the couple was expected to acquire through the marriage ceremony.[3] A woman who went through several such engagements could lose her reputation and seriously weaken her chances of finding a husband. The explanation for this was that people would murmur that 'there must be something wrong with her' if she was unable to succeed in any of her relationships, implying that it is the woman's role to adapt to her partner's personality and needs. But it was sometimes suggested that another cause of loss of reputation, which was not made explicit, was that such a woman could have been 'sullied' by sexual contact with one or more of her partners. Marriages were not arranged by the couple's parents. Young women were likely to meet their future companions in a variety of ways, through friends, at parties, or on the street. This rather haphazard way of meeting potential partners was not a new development. A large number of women in their fifties and sixties had also met their husbands on the street, at fairs, and on the beach. At this stage of courtship parents had relatively little control over their daughters unless it was indirectly through the girls' siblings, cousins or neighbours. In fact, given that a daughter's marriage was a central parental concern, one of the problems that had to be solved, from their point of view as much as from the girl's, was to ensure that the young women met prospective partners. In a large city such as Naples, the institution of the *passeggiata* around the village square on a Saturday afternoon or the alternative social relations that can provide a groom without the latter's initiative were largely ineffectual. Some degree of freedom must be granted a girl if she is to marry at all.[4]

Although they have little control in the first stage, parents do influence the sentimental histories of their daughters and sons through their necessary approval and acceptance of the chosen partner with the *fidanzamento in casa*. Once the young man became 'of the house', much stricter control was exercised over the young woman to prevent contact with other men. On the other hand, should the girl become pregnant, parental pressure and control was also placed on the young man to resolve the problem. Marriage *di riparamento* (of repair) was not uncommon.

Ultimately, and of course excluding those cases where violent means were used, it was the women themselves who controlled their sexuality and decided whether or not to dispose of their virginity: the forms of courtship described were attempts to control women but also to provide some protection from error and deceit. In fact, the wrong move can have serious consequences. A woman may decide to engage in full sexual intercourse knowing that it may result in pregnancy. This should have the often desired effect of shortening what is usually a long period of courtship. Alternatively, she may resist attempts by her fiancé to persuade her to give him a 'proof of true love', knowing that she may lose him because of this refusal. Or a woman could engage in some form of sexual activity as a sort of 'promissory note' to try to establish a relationship with a man of her liking and then judge how far she may or must go according to his reactions and behaviour. So every woman must face these decisions carefully, for a miscalculation can have painful, and perhaps enduring, repercussions.

A woman who engaged in sexual activity outside the protective framework of the *fidanzamento* system was in a far more vulnerable position, and might be rejected by her family and of course by her lover as well. On the other hand, a *fidanzamento* may be broken off; but if it became known to the parents that the fiancé was their daughter's 'first man', they would be very likely to exercise pressure to have the relationship re-established. So the withholding or the disclosure of this information allowed the young woman some degree of manipulation. Going to bed with a man could be an insurance in terms of marriage – unless he outwitted her. It was sometimes dramatically stated that, should this happen, the only options were prostitution or a relatively inexpensive and simple operation to re-establish virginity, since generally in a large city the only proofs of transgression are pregnancy or the loss of the hymen; otherwise, suspicions must remain such, and if a woman is careful she may overcome them.

Although many young women dreamt of improving their social and economic position through marrying 'above' themselves, most ended up marrying within their own class.[5] This may be partly due to the fact that one is more likely to meet members of one's own class; but there is no doubt that there are many obstacles to a cross-class marriage. My impression is that *fidanzamento in casa* was less likely to occur between working-class women and professional men, and that in any case the system of control breaks down here. That is to say, in the case of transgression parental pressure is ineffective where the fiancé is not himself working-class. So involvement with a middle-class man carries very high risks, although at the same time many young women (and possibly parents) would be tempted by the idea of successfully establishing such a liaison.

Young women generally avoided involvement with someone whom they considered to be of lower status, but parents especially (and from personal accounts mothers seemed to play a central and energetic role here) would oppose the match. Mothers preferred their daughters to marry either a white-collar or a higher-status worker, such as a metal trades worker, rather than a lower-status worker from the food or shoe trades, or even worse, a construction worker. There were many personal histories involving young love's being either curtailed or victorious over parental opposition. When faced with parental opposition, a woman may decide to *scappare* or elope, or may become pregnant. In other words, a young woman, or indeed a couple, may use the system of values to their own advantage.

The situation of the unmarried, unengaged young woman appears to be quite fluid and contradictory. On the one hand, there is parental control, which is exercised not only directly but also indirectly through the neighbourhood, through kin and friends and also through the girl's peer group. On the other hand, young girls have considerable freedom to leave the house and go for walks, visits and parties. What is most striking is not this, for all these outings are approved by parents, but the apparent ease with which young men and women will meet on the street and talk to each other in a fairly carefree fashion. This relative freedom is cut short from the time a girl becomes engaged 'in the house', and this moment signifies a crucial change in her life. From now on the fluidity is contained, the contradictions are ironed out and the priority of control and good behaviour is clearly established. The contradiction now is to be found only in the relationship of the engaged couple, and this because their relationship has been approved and has official validity, in that it provides the basis for resolution should a pregnancy occur.[6]

The freedom of the engaged girl was due to the fact that women were not passive occupiers of roles. They were active subjects who had a lot to lose if they blundered. The ultimate objective of most young girls was to marry. Even those who had ambitions with regards to work and careers wanted to have a husband and children – a family of their own. This objective therefore conditioned their sexual behaviour from an early age. Virginity was socially valued. Because she was aware of this, each woman had to struggle with the intricacies of personal and sexual relations, of her desires, of the man's intentions and of public opinion. Virginity was indeed an asset, but not necessarily an asset to be clung to at all costs – on occasions the loss of virginity can be tactically important, though of course there are also occasions when such a loss can be disastrous.

From the parental point of view, the problem was a different one, yet the objective was the same: the marriage of a daughter. Control and protection were a concern; and yet in most cases parents consented to their daughters' going out, for otherwise meeting a potential husband could be difficult. In fact, the role of the parents became more clearly defined with the *fidanzamento in casa*, where they enter into an agreement with a particular young man and his family, and their part of the agreement, that is to 'look after' the girl, must be fulfilled if the wedding is to take place.

Sex and the Married Woman

The problem of the 'allocation' of women's sexuality was not resolved with marriage. At marriage a woman shifted from the realm of responsibility and authority of her father to that of her husband. For the woman this transfer was usually seen as a positive one: her husband's authority was generally (and this was increasingly the case) a more fluid one than that of her parents, especially her father's. Furthermore, marriage granted most women a home of their own, a space which they felt to be under their control and to belong to them.

It was far more unusual for a married woman to discuss sexual matters than it was for single women to do so. If and when this occurred it generally took a diffuse form, so that women would talk about whether they were 'happy' with their husbands or not. Although there was a sexual content to this happiness, it was not simply and straightforwardly a question of sexual satisfaction. Most of the older women who broached this subject were not 'happy' with their husbands, and some women expressed hostility towards their spouses. Among the younger women a greater diversity of feelings was expressed, probably owing to the fact that some of the younger women were more deeply affected by a variety of influences, including versions of feminism, whereas others had attitudes which were reminiscent of those of the women of their mother's generation. But even those who expressed rebelliousness regarding the predominant values did not speak lightly of women's infidelity.

Given the fact that discussion of this topic was restricted to a very few intimate friends, it is difficult to generalize about sexual behaviour and attitudes. As was mentioned earlier, however, Neapolitans are not shy about making jovial, and sometimes joyful, references to sex. From these comments it could be inferred that women are thought to enjoy sex and to have certain 'needs', although these were not considered to be as imperative and pervasive as the 'needs' of men. For example, a group of older married women teased a young bride whose husband worked far from Naples and was thus absent from home for long periods. They said that she missed her husband so much that it affected her head, making her distracted, and that she could hardly wait for him to return – it was made very clear through gestures and innuendoes that she missed his physical presence.

But even if enjoyment of sex within marriage was generally considered 'natural' and desirable, chaste behaviour was valued. The infidelity of women was considered to be a grave insult to a husband, and a serious threat to family stability. Many men felt that they would react violently to their wife's infidelity. But all those questioned were 99 per cent certain that their wives had never been unfaithful to them, a belief they stressed emphatically.

On the other hand, it was expected of a 'normal', 'healthy' man that he would take every opportunity for sex that presented itself. In fact, his self-image would be enhanced by his exploits. Most men were keen to recount their sexual exploits and, judging by some of the reports, Naples offers many opportunities for sexual adventures to the right kind of man. The prompt availability of other men's wives in their accounts of their own experience did not appear to them to contradict their certainty regarding their own wives' behaviour. Virginity in a man was not desirable; and in fact a man who was thought to be a virgin when he was past his teens caused concern and pity.

A woman who was to engage in sexually adventurous behaviour

would be realizing her potential corruptibility and forsaking her status as a respectable woman. Although this double standard was generally accepted by men and women in a fairly fatalistic way, many women (and some men) did question the fairness of these views. When a young woman asked why men should be allowed to engage in extramarital relations when women are not, her husband jokingly replied: *'perche l'uomo e cacciature e a femmina e zuoccola'* – 'because man is a hunter and woman is a whore'. The term *zuoccola* also means 'rat'.

This comment suggests that the position of women is a contradictory one. Man is the predator, but woman is not simply the victim that may be preyed upon. Her vulnerability in fact gives her a negative value. It renders her corruptible and therefore, to a certain extent, corrupt and corrupting. In a sense 'woman' is seen as being predatory herself: the rat is to be hunted down, but it is also a renowned and feared aggressor. Similarly, the prostitute is to be accosted, her services bought; but at the same time she must take some initiative, which may well be seen as an aggressive one, to earn her living through selling sexual services.

There are important differences in the opinions expressed by men regarding the link between sexuality and adultery. Women too differ in their views here: many women express an acceptance of a 'natural' difference in the needs and sexuality of men and women. This view offers a static and non-negotiable perspective which can to some extent dissipate anxiety and jealousy by rationalizing male infidelity in terms of men's animal needs. This may require a corresponding degradation of certain women who are considered to be the likely targets for the satisfaction of such animal urges. This rationalization may therefore contribute to women's internalization of male definitions of women and sex.

On the other hand, there are other women who expect from their partners the same treatment they are prepared to give – if fidelity is required from them, they demand fidelity in return. My personal opinion is that in many cases these expectations were fulfilled. Should they be disappointed, such women are more likely to react with anger and would appeal to ideals of justice and equality. Where husband and wife share common or at least overlapping frameworks and terms of reference (usually promoted by trade unions and political parties), opposition and negotiation (but also breakdown) are possible. But for those women or couples embracing the 'naturalist' explanation for male infidelity such terms and references are absent. A woman may not have at her disposal the language to express her objections, and may show greater tolerance to her husband's extramarital adventures. Surely there is a great deal of individual variation in such intimate confrontations, and reactions would vary from situation to situation and from person to person, but my impression was that these latter women would take a more passive stance and would certainly not be likely to have a confrontation as a matter of principle. The real confrontation might come if and when they were to feel threatened, when they feared that they might lose their husbands. Jealousy here seems to be less a matter of sexual jealousy and more to do with fears of a practical nature.[7]

Carlo was married and in his early thirties. He had had an affair with a girl for over two years. When her parents learned that she was having an affair with a married men they threw her out of home. He therefore felt responsible for her, for a girl who is unmarried and doesn't live with her family can end up on the streets. Because he was the cause of her troubles, he felt he should protect her and look after her. Although his wife believed that the affair was over, he had in fact found her a flat and continued to see her. He claimed he loved neither one of them. He had pointed out to his wife that clearly this other woman had something she did not. As far as he understood it, the problem was that he needed affection and warmth. At night when he came home he was too tired to make love. So if he had the opportunity in the morning, that was fine. Otherwise, one simply doesn't make love. So if and when the opportunity arose during the day he would naturally take advantage and find relief (*mi scarico*). Any man who did not take a chance when it presented itself was a fool or a homosexual. A normal, healthy man would never let a chance slip by. And he implied that chances were frequent. Men, he said, are like children. When they see something they want they won't stay still until they have it. Once they've got it, they tire of it quickly. His wife had been very upset and angry with him, but had pleaded with him not to go. She openly called the other woman a bitch and a whore, in front of myself and her two eldest daughters, who were eight and nine at the time.

But whereas extramarital sex was deemed to be a 'natural' consequence of masculinity, such behaviour in a woman would not be understood. Some men would have an unquestioned condemnation of a wife who committed adultery. Others recognized the injustice of double standards. Yet in spite of rational arguments, many admitted that dark passions were awakened at the thought of their wives' committing adultery. Most men with whom I discussed this matter went to considerable lengths to wonder about what they thought their reactions would be, but none pursued their reactions as far as wondering at the possibility of divorce. Although divorce is now legal, it was more common among the middle classes than among the working classes of Naples. It may be that in fact wherever possible the 'errors' or the problems were settled privately, and where they had nc t become too public the marriage would survive in spite of them.

Or perhaps the men are right: perhaps their wives did not commit adultery and were ultimately tolerant of their husbands' weaknesses.[8]

Middle-class professional women appeared to have more opportunities of embarking on romantic ventures than working-class women, who were subjected to greater pressures in terms of time and were more restricted to the space of home, work and neighbourhood. Since public knowledge of such an act could alienate a woman from her husband and possibly her neighbourhood and family as well, neighbourhood control was quite effective. Most people were concerned about provoking gossip. Women were unwilling to allow men who were not kin into their homes if they were alone. And men were sensitive to the problem, and would avoid causing embarrassment to women they respected by not calling when they were on their own.

And yet a case which was covered by the local press proved to be a focus for a great deal of discussion. Several women in the city had complained that when their husband had left home very early for shift-work or night-duty, a stranger had got into their bed and made love to them. This he did to many women many times: the dark had protected him and they had not realized they had a stranger in their bed instead of their husband. This provoked hilarity and disbelief: when discussing the story, many women arched their eyebrows and pointed out that even in the dark a woman has ways of recognizing her own husband. They suggested that this had been a very convenient accident for these women. Whether fact or fiction, this case indicates that it was thought possible to circumvent the network of controls. Furthermore, the reactions of the women commenting on the incident illustrate the view that women derive pleasure from sex generally and that marriage might not fully satisfy a woman's needs.

Just as there were individual variations regarding attitudes to extramarital sex, so there were also important variations in the ways in which married couples recognized each other's space, rights and needs for personal fulfilment. There were women who preferred to work rather than stay at home. There were those who participated actively in trade union activity or in political parties, and many of them claimed to have the support of their husbands here. An example is the case of a young woman factory worker who was married and had a small child. She had positively wanted to carry on working after the birth of her first child, and in addition there were financial motivations for continuing paid employment. She had been able to continue working because her mother looked after the child. She had been very active in trade union affairs and had participated in an extended factory sit-in. She now had three children. Living on two wages meant that they had been able to improve their standard of living, and she could foresee a time in the future when she would give up work. In the meantime, her husband, who like herself was a Communist and a trade unionist, supported her choice to work and to be involved in trade union affairs.

It was clear that on the whole men who were militant on the left of the political spectrum, in parties and trade unions, felt the obligation or desire to attempt to be understanding and cooperative in respect of their wives' careers and interests. However, being militant on the left was no guarantee of supportive behaviour, as the term *compagno-padrone* (comrade–boss), coined in the early 1970s, indicates. In fact, it was rather more common to see militant men, often mouthing the 'correct' position on 'women', reproducing the same situation in their homes as their fathers. Some of these men explained the contradictions between theory and practice by attributing their failure to their wives' unwillingness to change, to read the newspapers, to participate in political activities even on a local, neighbourhood level. They maintained that in spite of their efforts, their wives persevered in their traditional role. In fact, all cases of a more 'balanced' relationship involved women who seemed to conform to the new ideal of a politicized woman, having a fairly clear direction to their lives and considerable experience in work and political and union activities prior to their marriage. So here, too, expectations were clearly defined, leaving little room for women's own exploration and experimentation.

An important consideration here is the question of spouse selection and the criteria that may be relevant to this process. There were, among the 'traditional' couples, those who had married very young and whose relationship had been shaped outside the more recent currents of thought regarding women's rights. But there were also young political leaders and activists who had chosen as their brides young women who were expected to fall into the traditional roles.

The typical explanation for spouse selection was 'being in love'. Love is a sentiment strongly praised and blamed in Neapolitan poetry, theatre and song. Being in love is closely associated with making love or at least desiring to do so. There is a distinction commonly made between physical attraction (*piacere*) and being in love (*'nnamurata/o*), but the distinction is loose and the terms may be used interchangeably. However, it is likely that, as in other societies where love is the basis for the selection of a marriage partner, being *'nnamurata/o* with intent to become engaged and married covers a series of other conscious and unconscious processes of selection, taking into account economic suitability, acceptability of the partnership to the family, etc.

There were couples in which neither husband nor wife felt the need to measure themselves against the changes proposed by the feminist movement. In such cases, it was more likely that the traditional division of labour between men and women would be respected. Even if the woman were employed and made an important financial contribution to the household (sometimes, given the uncertainty of employment in Naples, she might be the only stable provider) the head of household, however nominally, remained the husband. It would be a mistake to assume that all such women were passive, quiet and obedient. Many Neapolitan women, young and old, are vigorous and assertive in manner, outspoken and easy with words (including sometimes the use of very strong language). And yet the impression remains that underlying the marital relationship is the acknowledgment of the husband's authority.

The strong sense of authority surrounding a husband was revealed in the interaction between husband and wife, for example in the strict keeping of the boundary between male and female tasks. When a husband came home, he usually expected to be served food without even having to request it – it should be ready and waiting for him, and it usually was. His clothes must be cleaned and ironed, the house in good order. The husband's role was to provide the money necessary for the household. He was often unable to do so; but his wife would continue to fulfil her half of the bargain, to the best of her ability.

During the daytime, men were usually out of the house. In the mornings, women started to clean at an early hour and outworkers commenced work immediately afterwards. Neighbours, usually women, or kin may come by. A visitor in a household can often notice a change of atmosphere that follows upon the arrival of the male head of household. The topic of conversation may be abandoned, his wife and perhaps his daughters will busy themselves with the meal, and the dynamic of the group is changed and indirectly focuses on the new arrival.[9]

Not all husbands and fathers elicited awe and fearful respect. There were cases of husbands who had easy relationships with their families, or who in fact had weak positions in their households. This was usually due to the compounding of perceived personal and economic ineffectiveness. However, in such cases, the privileges due a man were not withheld, though respect and love may have been withheld at a more intimate level. There were women who said they did not respect their husbands, or who did not like their husbands, and for whom marriage was said to be a 'martyrdom'. And yet the majority remained with them and continued to perform as dutiful wives and mothers.

Although being 'in love' with a man may have been the original inspiration behind a relationship, marriage is in fact to do with more enduring considerations. But whereas in some cases wives were economically dependent on their husbands, in others, women were the principal contributors. Economic dependence cannot, in such cases, provide the explanation for marital continuity where love and respect were absent. One factor to be considered here is the social context in which these women live, which does not favour their leaving their husbands. The inhibitions imposed by public opinion are compounded by structural conditions: housing is a major problem in Naples and, furthermore, women acquire responsibilities as mothers very early on in their marriage. Parents or kin tend to live in cramped conditions and would have difficulty in incorporating a woman with her children into their households.

In addition, the family formed by a marriage takes on a meaning of its own, beyond the marriage itself. For a woman, marriage provides the opportunity of having her own home, which she will consider largely to be her own space, and the possibility of organizing her time and labour towards the creation and maintenance of something she considers to be her own, and so becomes inextricably linked with her perception of herself. A woman would be reluctant to give this up and submit herself once again to parental control and dependence.

The family is also a pooling unit, especially as children grow up. Each member will (usually) contribute to the household of his/her family of origin, whether in terms of labour, or money, or both. This pooling is potentially a source of conflict, but can also have a cohesive effect. The mother is usually at the centre of this pooling process. A married woman living in her own home is therefore likely to see herself as being autonomous (from parental control), and as an indispensable member of the household. To some extent the activities of the household are independent of her relationship with her husband. In addition, there is the socially reinforced willingness of a woman as wife, but especially as mother, to submerge and subordinate her own personal needs to those of her family, and to realize herself through her dependants.

Parsons (1967) points to the lack of conjugality in the Neapolitan married couple. Whereas in courtship the fiancé is expected to plead, to be attentive, to find ways of demonstrating his affection, after marriage the content of the relationship changes. She indicates the sources of friction within the married couple, the most important being the enduring relationship that each maintains with his or her family of origin. This can result in the actual dissolution of the marriage, as each partner moves closer to his or her parents' home.

Couples also face friction because of the strains of restricted incomes. The distribution of income is a source of misunderstanding for many couples. Men and women may have very different priorities when it comes to the allocation of resources. Again here Parsons suggests that men face a disappointment, in that wives don't behave towards them as their mothers did: rather than giving unquestioningly as mothers do, wives make demands on their husbands and have expectations of them which women don't have of their sons.

Conclusion

Virginity is important in a woman's progress towards marriage – a progress which is seen as being desirable by most young women. But its importance is not to be understood in the sense of rigidly adhering to being a virgin, but rather of using virginity tactically. That is to say, it is important to know when to protect virginity and when to relinquish it. The high value placed on virginity was oppressive to women. But at the same time, within these oppressive relations women had a degree of power, since as the holders of virginity they could dispose of it and thus put pressure on various groups (their own family and that of their fiancés, for example). The rules defining appropriate behaviour could be broken by a woman to her own advantage.

Chastity and postmarital fidelity did not seem to lend themselves to the same degree of manipulation. It would appear that there was greater consensus in respect of the advisedness of a woman's fidelity to her husband (which could be seen to be expressed either/both by overt statements to this effect and/or by the non-admission to unfaithfulness on the part of women). Since divorce did not seem to be common among the socio-economic group in question, it is possible to assume that other sanctions, such as public opinion and the reactions of families, are operative here.

But it would be unwise to assume that only women's sexuality came under family scrutiny. As was mentioned, men had considerable sexual freedom, and sexual exploits were seen to enhance their masculine image. However, there may be circumstances under which men would face family opposition. This seems to have been the case when the activities of married men appeared to endanger the integrity of their families or when an unmarried man was thought to be involved with the 'wrong kind of woman', and to risk making an unsuitable match.[10]

What we see in Naples are men and women faced with a series of options and having to assess the implications of their actions in terms of achieving accepted goals. There is some continuity in the behaviour of men and women here: marriage is an important institution and crucial for individual fulfilment. Both men and woman want to marry. This intention will condition people's behaviour, especially that of women, for whom their personal life and sexual reputation are important elements in defining their suitability as partners. At a certain stage of her life, virginity is an important element in a woman's self-appraisal and may be a significant factor in her attempts at achieving marital status. However, virginity need not be adhered to rigidly. On the contrary, a woman may manipulate her virginity as a resource to achieve her aims, and thus she may lose her virginity

without losing her reputation.
The sexuality of both men and women is socially defined and controlled here. Yet the sexuality of women is subject to a greater degree of control and becomes the concern of social groups rather than being an individual affair. Although I have argued that the importance of virginity, and, to a lesser extent, chastity, must be seen in relation to specific situations and circumstances, the question why women's sexuality is so important from a social point of view remains, as does the question why the values of female virginity and chastity (however flexible in their operation) are of such public concern.[11]

Notes

1. Until recently, the *corredo* consisted of bedlinen, tablecloths, doilies, towels and the woman's nightwear. In Lampedusa (Sicily), this still appeared to be the case in the seventies. Here, young women started making their own *corredo* when they were approximately 12 years of age. This is the way they learned to crochet, sew and sometimes embroider. The items were collected over the years and were an important object of display, testifying to the young woman's ability and diligence. In Naples, most women bought their *corredo*, and until about 30 years ago it was common to have at least some sheets and hand-towels embroidered by professionals. Nowadays such items are not valued amongst the working-class of Naples, and instead purchases have been broadened to include electrical appliances and television sets. The difference in emphasis between labour-intensive display goods, particularly those produced in the home, and expensive electrical prestige goods obviously has important repercussions at an economic level, putting pressure on women and their families to secure a monetary income.
2. But Pitt-Rivers (1974) does raise the question of class differences in relation to 'honour'.
3. With respect to premarital chastity, Tentori (1976) observes for Matera that 'the majority of young people has neither the intention nor even the idea of contravening a norm so deeply rooted in customs as this one.' He points out that in any case the organization of life makes sexual encounters of fiancés impossible. The contrast with the Neapolitan case may be due to a time difference (his fieldwork was carried out in the early 1950s) or to differences between a small town and a large city.
Silverman (1975) says with reference to a town in Central Italy: 'Sexual relations between the engaged couple . . . are quite common, as is evidenced by the fact that approximately one quarter of the brides are pregnant at the time of marriage. In most cases (perhaps 90%), marriage to the fiancé follows a premarital pregnancy, generally with the wedding date hastened' (p.315).
Both Silverman (ibid.) and Parsons (1967) refer to the period of engagement as a difficult time, which involves a great deal of risk and anxiety.
4. In Matera (Tentori 1976), as in other small localities, the *passeggiata* or stroll around the *piazza* or up and down the main street is an important means

of seeing or meeting prospective candidates. Thus a more controlled form of seeking a partner is open to parents and their children.

5. Tentori (1976) argues that in Matera there is class endogamy. There are many obstacles to the marriage of persons with different degrees of prestige, and there is a tendency to avoid marriage between craftsmen and peasants. In fact, marriage possibilities tend to be limited to those living in the same *sassi* (meaning the homes that are carved out of the rock and have made Matera infamous) or neighbourhood. Also see Davis (1973) regarding ambitions and possibilities in the field of cross-class marriage in a rural context.

6. Parsons (1967) refers to the ambivalence of mothers regarding their daughters' sexual behaviour. While on the one hand they warn of the terrible consequences of transgression, they also appear to encourage such transgressions.

7. In a fishing community in Sicily a young woman explained that she was not jealous of her husband's encounters with the many tourists who travelled through, since they were unlikely to take her husband away from her. On the other hand, she would have been very jealous of any local woman. It was as though these 'foreigners' were outside her social reality and therefore did not count – they could not pose a real threat. A parallel here may be the denigration of women considered potential rivals as prostitutes – this placed such women outside the social universe of husband and wife, and thus cancelled the threat.

8. The only cases of women's adultery that I came to know about concerned middle-class women married to middle-class men. But a non-middle-class example was provided by the story of a woman who lived with her husband in an area in the outskirts of the city of Naples. Her husband, who was a *camorrista* (i.e. involved in the Neapolitan version of the *mafia*) shot her young lover. Local women commented that it was a shame that such a young man should die for such a reason, and blamed the woman, who should have known better and remained faithful to her husband. Such violent or rather such effectively violent reactions are not usual – not everybody has the means to kill a rival, nor presumably do they have so much to lose as a *camorrista* who loses face. Another case was purely a matter of conjecture: a young woman suspected her middle-aged mother, who was unhappy with her husband, of having a romantic affair with an unmarried neighbour for whom she cooked and cleaned. She hoped that it was the case, because she felt her mother deserved some support and pleasure, which she felt her father had never given her.

9. I have no data on the incidence of physical punishment or domestic violence, but it is not unknown for a husband to strike his wife and/or daughters or sons. On the whole this kind of violence is not condoned. It is understood that some situations might provoke a man to violence, but the too frequent beating of a wife or children is considered to be incorrect (cf. Loizos 1975). T. Belmonte (1979) described the violence he witnesses in parent–child relations during his fieldwork in the old city of Naples.

10. In one case, Carlo, a married man, had lived independently with his wife and children for many years, and was known for his philandering behaviour, which he publicized himself. His family of origin had been aware that he had had a liaison with a young, unmarried woman for some time.

As far as I know, no pressure was put on him until the young woman's parents, on learning about her affair, forced her to leave home, and she turned to him for help. He claimed to have felt obliged to find her an apartment and to help her financially. When he then started to play with the idea of living with her, his wife reacted very strongly, and the man's family intervened. His mother called a family meeting to discuss the matter and bring the man to his senses. This was accomplished and the family was preserved.

Another example refers to a young unmarried man, where again the family intervened at the behest of the man's mother, who had reason to believe that he was involved with a woman who was much older than he was, and maybe even a prostitute. The implication seemed to be that such a relationship could be deleterious to his health and future.

11. Virginity is an important and powerful symbol in many cultural contexts, not only in a Catholic one. See Silverblatt (1981) for the importance of virgin women in defying Spanish domination and Catholicism and in attempting to preserve pre-Conquest knowledge and religion.

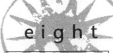

eight

Familism and Gender in Naples

The family provided the core idea behind household arrangements, which were an important element in survival and social advancement for both individuals and groups. As we have seen, individual biographies must be contextualized within the strategies pursued by their families of origin and the particular divisions of labour that these strategies entail. The question is whether such strategies would work in the absence of the appropriate emotional and ideological underpinnings that the idea of the family provides. Without the ideal of family solidarity it is hard to imagine that arrangements such as those made by the D'Angelos or the Arenellas would work, entailing as they do considerable self-sacrifice for some household members.

Similarly, the networks forged through neighbourhood and kin ties were a crucial resource for obtaining work, for making contacts and for finding work or recruiting labour. The pivot of these networks were the women of the household, who were the most likely to invest time and energy in pursuing and negotiating relationships with kin and neighbours. Especially those women who worked in their homes, whether as housewives or outworkers, spent a considerable portion of their time engaged in conversations with neighbours and visiting or being visited by friends and kin, although outworkers were often prevented from leaving their homes owing to the pressures of work. Female networks therefore constituted a central resource for the subsequent elaboration of individual and family strategies.

Anthropologists working in Italy have emphasized the centrality of the family (Davis 1977; Pitkin 1985; Kertzer and Saller 1991) and some have documented the changes that have taken place in the Italian family (Kertzer and Saller 1991). As early as 1958 Banfield drew attention to the family in his attempt to explain the 'backwardness' of Montegrano. He attributed the persistent poverty of the town to 'amoral familism'. By this he meant an excessive focus on the interests of the individual and his or her immediate family, to the exclusion of wider loyalties. This excessive concern with the nuclear family prevented the Montegranesi from building up other, more effective, interest groups. Although not necessarily defined as 'amoral', familism has also been identified as a significant factor in Italian society by other authors (Ginsborg 1990). Ginsborg argues that whereas in the history of Italy as a whole there have been times and places when family interests have been compatible and closely allied with wider concerns and social movements, in the South the tendency has been for familism to prevail over other considerations.[1] Furthermore, here familism has taken a particular form, associated with a struggle for survival, which gives it its specific character.

This character makes for significant differences in the role of the family in the South and in other regions of Italy. During the 1970s and 1980s many families in the Centre and North benefited from improved incomes. In some areas the family became the model and basis for successful entrepreneurial activity, often achieved through close collaboration with local and regional economic and political structures. In the 1980s, on the other hand, a new version of familism based on consumerism has tended to erode collective ideologies and goals (Ginsborg 1990: 414–15). Nevertheless, the major difference is that in the South families still face difficult objective circumstances and the relatively larger family units could reflect the persistence of strategies aimed at maximizing the work and income of as many family members as possible. Furthermore, given the hostile social environment of Southern cities, the family could be seen as a refuge from the outside world (Ginsborg 1990: 417).

The debates concerning familism and the values associated with it tend to assume the existence of an opposition and a distance between the family and society. This view is consonant with a number of anthropological works concerning the political and cultural character of the South. For example, speaking of Sicily, Blok (1975) argues that the Italian state only incompletely incorporated the Sicilian region, creating spaces which were then occupied by mediators who linked the local population with the centres of power. These mediators gave rise to the figure of the *mafioso*, who incidentally, borrowed selectively from familistic ideology. Jane and Peter Schneider's argument (1976) is somewhat different, though nevertheless relevant here. They argue that Sicily has for centuries been peripheral to a number of centres such as Rome at the time of the Empire, North-west Europe or Northern Italy, and as such specialized as an exporter of primary resources. Furthermore, Sicily, and in particular Western Sicily, was for a very long time subjected to raids, attacks and invasions over several centuries. It was this position of peripherality, and the vulnerability of the local populations, which generated cultural responses to these external forces in the shape of the codes of honour, friendship, *omerta*, *furbizia*, which again focused heavily on the family unit as a source of reputation and support. Thus the code of honour, so frequently flagged by Mediterranean anthropologists and associated by them with the Mediterranean family, is seen here as an invented tradition which constituted a response to peripheralization and a defence of the vulnerable sectors of Southern society (Schneider and Schneider 1976).

The Schneiders' analysis of the opposition between community and State, which recognizes the global forces which generate peripheralization, provides a valid model for understanding the South of Italy until the end of the 1950s. Gribaudi (1980) suggests that until this time the South was essentially a recipient of external forces, subject to external powers: first the Spanish and French dynasties, later the Piedmontese. It is therefore appropriate to characterize the relationship between core and Southern periphery, or State and local community at this time, in terms of opposition.

Until the 1950s the Italian state was as distant as it had been during the period of the Spanish Viceroyalty. From the Unification onwards the role of the State was, primarily, that of a mediator and guarantor of the privileges of the landed élite. However the Second World War and its aftermath profoundly changed the face of Italy. One of the most significant factors here was the changes that subsequently took place in the relationship between Italy and Northern Europe. The South had for long been an exporter of raw materials, especially agricultural goods and labour, and entry into the European Common Market consolidated this role, particularly as a source of labour for the industries of Northern Europe. But with the impressive post-war boom in Italian industry located within the 'industrial triangle' in the North-west, the flow of migrant workers to other European countries declined. Later, with recession affecting the powerful economies of Germany and France in particular, but also other areas which relied on immigrant workers, including Northern Italy, there was a shift towards devising policies that might anchor populations in their localities of origin. At this point, the Italian state took a more 'interventionist' approach to the South.

Gribaudi (1980) argues that the persistence of Christian Democrat power has relied heavily on an interventionist policy for the South. The aim of these interventions was not, as we have seen, to foment local development in the area but rather to maintain the status quo and to guarantee Christian Democrat supremacy locally and nationally. Gribaudi describes the intention of State intervention here as one of 'protection–control'. Both the implementation of and the ideologies behind policies emphasized the importance of community and family values and served to underwrite the use of family, kin and neighbourhood networks for survival.

The character of the Christian Democrat Party, which ruled Italy from the early 1950s until the early 1990s, is a significant factor here. This was a very broadly-based movement which tried to reconcile the interests (and attract the votes) of industry, large sectors of the middle classes, small landholders and Catholic workers. Ideologically, the party was composed of two major and somewhat contradictory strands. On the one hand there was Catholic social thought, stressing the values of solidarity, support of the institution of the family, protection for the weak and assistance for the poor. On the other, there was also the individualism associated with the modernization project, which stresses the freedom of the individual and of the market, the development of technology and of consumerism. The party was further divided in terms of groups or *correnti*, representing different strands of these ideologies and sections of the interest groups. These differences and contradictions were reflected in government policies and in particular those policies directed towards the South, which aimed at supporting capital and modernization, while simultaneously 'protecting' the local inhabitants from the most damaging effects of industrialization.

On the basis of these interventions, Christian Democrat governments saw themselves and presented themselves as the party responsible for upholding the Southern way of life, protecting communities from the negative consequences of industrialization. Their aim was to restore the balance that had been lost as a result of the war, to weaken and eventually eradicate the influence of the Communist party and to consolidate the Christian Democrat Party's power base. Funds were made available to achieve this, and they were distributed clientelistically so as to strengthen vertical ties and so discourage the emergence of class-based solidarities, which might threaten party supremacy. An important aspect of policies of protection and preservation was the deployment of the ideal of the family and of family values. Through a number of interventions which took the family as a starting-point, a dichotomy between the private and the public was generated and reproduced, a division which was directly linked to a perceived opposition between the market and subsistence production.

During the course of the 1970s, a growing number of benefits were made available to the population. In the South, invalidity pensions and other forms of subsidies were made available and became a significant factor in the reproduction of a high percentage of Southern households. This, for Gribaudi, not only reflects the changing economic circumstances of Europe and Italy and represents an attempt to anchor persons within their families and localities, linking them clientelistically to the dominant party/ies,[2] but was also meant to uphold the ideal of family and community in the face of what were seen as the destructive aspects of the forces of modernization. But despite its political functionality, the expense involved in sustaining this redistributive policy could not be sustained indefinitely. In the late 1980s pressure on government grew from the IMF and the looming 1992 watershed of European unification, and forced Italian governments to tighten fiscal controls and cut down on government expenditure.[3] Later, and in spite of populist electoral promises, the pressures of the Maastricht treaty were also felt by Berlusconi's government in the last quarter of 1994. Berlusconi was forced to propose a budget which would cut 48 trillion lire (about 20 billion pounds sterling) from government expenses. The cuts were mainly directed at State pensions and benefits, and provoked an unprecedented response, including the largest national demonstration witnessed by the country since the Second World War, held in Rome, with parallel demonstrations in Milan, Turin and other cities on 14 October of that year.[4]

At the same time, Berlusconi's new government of the 'Second Republic' created a Ministry for the Family. This was an attempt to reaffirm the centrality of the family and of family values in Italian society, understood here as an essentially conservative force within society. But many became concerned about possible connections between this official recognition of the family and the dismantling of welfare provisions. Many feminists in particular viewed the new Ministry with suspicion: upholding the family could be a strategy to shift the burden of responsibility for the old, the very young or the infirm from the State to the family. This would have important consequences for women, whose unpaid labour was already a crucial resource in the provision of care, especially in those areas, such as the South, where services were already lacking or grossly inefficient.

More generally, there was the discomfort created by the suspicion that the Ministry might be echoing earlier State interventions into family life, namely the policies generated during the period of Fascist government. The direction of Fascist interventions was pro-natalist and aimed at reinforcing paternal control by strengthening the importance of *patria potestas* while confining women's roles to the family, as mothers and wives. In 1938 a number of laws achieved this by confirming the impossibility of divorce, obliging women to be faithful to their husbands even after separation, and transferring control of women's property to their husbands and, at their deaths, to their children. Women were restricted to enjoying rights of usufruct. The 'crime of honour' was to be viewed more leniently when a man killed his wife, daughter or sister in defence of his or his family's honour. Furthermore, the limitation of women to their role as reproducers was expressed in campaigns in which their maternity was exalted, and in 1938 a system of prizes was set up to honour the more prolific women. A slogan from that period expresses the fascist view on gender and the division of labour: 'Maternity is to women what war is to men.' This track record made many women uncomfortable, and anxieties regarding the dangers of a fascist revival reached a peak for men and women alike when the new president of the *Camera* declared, in the early days of the Berlusconi government, that a positive revision of the Fascist period was in order. Irene Pivetti sent a dagger to the heart of the anti-Fascist tradition that has had a virtually hegemonic status in Italian social and political life, when she suggested that the Mussolini era represented a golden age for the women of Italy.[5] But whether under Fascism, Christian Democrat governments or the new republic, the family has always been a prominent element within Italian political discourse (cf. Caldwell 1978).

The Catholic Church in its special relationship with the Italian state has also been a significant force in placing the family at the centre of social and political discourses. The family has in fact been at the heart of Italian Catholicism's social philosophy. According to this, the family emanates from God and is based on natural rights. Because of this it is prior to and superior to civil society and to the State. The State has the duty of protecting the family from the exterior world, but should not intervene in its functioning except in cases of breakdown. That exterior world could be hostile, and the Church warned in particular against the detrimental impact of industrial society. At the same time, the Catholic Church has been in a position to influence both policy and public opinion, indirectly through the Christian Democrat Party and directly through its myriad activities and organizations. The Lateran Pacts, which regulated the relationship between the Italian state and the Catholic hierarchy, made religious education compulsory in schools. Furthermore, the Church retained control over nursery education, homes for displaced children, hospitals and nursing homes. In fact, the Church's alliance with the Christian Democrat Party had a reviving effect on the Church's social presence, inducing greater activism in the parishes. The Church was also active through numerous confraternities, charitable organizations and other voluntary organizations (Ginsborg 1990: 168–73).

However, in spite of its revival during the 1950s, the influence of the Church has waned since the height of the partnership sealed between the Christian Democrat party and the Catholic hierarchy. For example, church attendance in Italy has declined significantly. In 1956, 57 per cent of men and 80 per cent of women stated that they attended church almost every Sunday or more often. By 1985 only 19 per cent of men and 38 per cent of women stated that they attended church regularly (Nanetti 1988: 66). In addition, in spite of the Church's energetic attack on divorce,[6] the referendum held in 1974 resulted in an overwhelming approval of the 1970 divorce law, with

59.1 per cent in favour. In 1977 a law was passed which legalized abortion, and this was ratified by a referendum in 1981. This too was seen as a victory for the forces of laicism and progress over those of Church hegemony. In 1975 family law was dramatically altered to redefine and equalize the status of family members. The law was not put to a referendum; but it nevertheless resulted from political pressures and reflected a recognition of the demands of the women's movements to change the hierarchical nature of Italian legislation regarding family and sexual rights. It also recognized important changes in public opinion, which was increasingly inclined towards granting greater individual freedom of choice (Nanetti 1988: 37).

The disjunction between recent legislation and a commitment to Catholic values results from the contradictory nature of the Christian Democrat project. But another factor here is the pluralism facilitated by the democratic process, for in spite of the strong political hold of the Christian Democrat party, there have been spaces in the political arena which could be used to advantage by other parties and pressure groups. For example, in 1975 the Radical Party and the *Movimento della Liberazione delle Donne Italiane* were the principal protagonists in the collection of signatures requesting a referendum on the issue of abortion. Their success was thwarted by a premature election, but it did put pressure on the succeeding government to alter the Fascist laws, which were still in force and made abortion a crime punishable by up to 5 years' imprisonment. The referendum on abortion held in 1981 was similarly successful and mobilized women's movements and, somewhat more unevenly, the parties of the left such as the PSI and PCI. The mobilization of these mass parties, as well as of women's groups, had the important effect of bringing to the fore issues which until then had been considered 'women's issues' and 'private affairs' and making of them instead issues to do with civil rights.

We should not underestimate the importance of Italy's foreign relations in shaping legislation. The governments that have led Italy at different times since the Second World War have had to acknowledge and incorporate what were defined as appropriately 'European' criteria for judging the relative development of society, and have at different times had to comply with these values and indexes in order to support claims to the status of an 'advanced industrial society'. The project of European unification has reinforced this influence. So successive Christian Democrat governments have had to juggle with the possible contradictions arising from the combination of aspirations to become an influential member of Europe, a modern state with the continuing influence exercised by Catholic values and the power of the Catholic Church.[7]

What this very brief discussion highlights is that the importance placed on the family and on the values associated with it, such as solidarity and unity, does not stem simply and spontaneously from individuals or communities in opposition to the State. On the contrary, these views, which may well be mobilized as a defence against the outside world, are entangled with the ideals of the Church and the directions of successive governments. Thus the State has itself been an agent promoting familistic values. Any understanding of how individuals in Naples or elsewhere view their families and how their identities are tied up with these views must recognize that Church, State and civil society have been involved in a protracted dialogue within which the family has taken centre stage.

What emerges from what are in fact a variety of dialogues is a process of change in people's attitudes and in the family itself. The divorce and abortion referenda provide good examples of this. But there are a number of other relevant indexes which illustrate changes and continuities in people's behaviour. For example, as many had predicted, following a rush immediately after the law was passed, divorces declined after 1973 from a rate of 31.2 per 100,000 inhabitants to 22.6 in 1983. In Campania, the region to which Naples belongs, there was an even greater drop, from 30.0 in 1993 to 14.1 in 1983.

Relative family size is often used as an index of social change. In Italy the size of the family has declined from an average of 3.3 members in 1971 to 3.0 in 1981.[8] The decline is a general one, but interestingly Campania shows the highest average family size in the country, with 3.5 in 1981, having declined from a rate of 3.9 in 1971. Changes in sexual behaviour are indicated by alterations in the level of fertility. These have also declined, although here too Campania is the leader for high fertility rates in the early 1980s, with 73.5 live births per 1,000 women in the 15–49 age group, whereas the national rate during that period was 53.0. The national figure fell again to 46.7 after 1982. Abortions in Italy decreased by 3,000 units between 1982 and 1983. Yet this decline is proportionately inferior to the more significant decrease in the number of births during the same period (17,000). The campaigns surrounding the referendum provoked much public debate concerning abortion from the mid-1970s. But in spite of this, it remained a very delicate subject. Those who were willing to discuss the matter tended to express a tolerant view, so that while they claimed they would not have an abortion themselves, they could understand that a number of factors, such as health or finances, could make such an option desirable.

In the 1980s, Italy's demographic profile came much closer to that of Northern European countries than it had been in the 1950s. The demographic pyramid is now typical for an advanced industrial society, with declining numbers of young people and a higher proportion of older people, as fertility rates decline and life expectancy increases. The natural increase of the population (births to deaths) for 1979 was 2.5. Many regions of the North have negative population growth, and in 1983 the net increase in population for the country as a whole was close to zero (Nanetti 1988: 33); in 1994 Italy as a whole registered zero growth.

But whereas Italy is now closely aligned with a typical advanced industrial demographic profile, the differences between the North and the South persevere. As has been noted already, Campania is distinguished in the 1980s by having the largest family size and the highest fertility rates in the country. In 1979 the natural rate of increase of the population for Campania was 9.1 (compared to a national rate of 2.5). This rate did, however, show a decline from the rate for 1970–2, which was equivalent to 13.4. At that time Campania had the highest rate in the country, almost double the national average of 7.2.[9] Given these figures it is not surprising that the Campanian demographic pyramid diverges from the national one, for the ratio of young to old population clearly favours the young. In Campania the proportion of older persons is equal to 46.9 of the total, against a national average of 76.6 (with many regions in the North scoring a rate greater than 100).

These figures could reflect a number of factors. The overall decline in the birth rate could be the result of a growing availability of contraception or a greater willingness to use it. This in turn could be related to changing ideas regarding the family and especially children, as the role of children changes, or as the perception of children as economic contributors or economic burdens shifts, along with parental aspirations regarding their children's futures and careers. In Naples all these factors were relevant. Many adults (though women were the adults most likely to discuss these issues with me) expressed a wish to have smaller families. This was often attributed to the costs of bringing up children 'properly' and to lower expectations regarding what children might contribute to the household. For many it was preferable to have fewer children and see these through school and university or proper training. For many working women there was the added consideration of managing their own workloads while caring for small children.

In a number of interviews in the old city, women who argued in favour of limiting family size were critical of neighbours who had large families. Their criticisms contained a moral evaluation of these families, which seemed to be grounded in ideas of respectability. One woman, Marina, felt that some of her neighbours bred like animals; they were unable to control themselves. Another woman, Anna, who had only one son, thought that her neighbours' larger families were a result of 'ignorance'. In other cases it was thought that poorer members of the neighbourhood were operating according to a strategy that was no longer desirable, having many children who could contribute to the household from a young age. Most men and women agreed that the ideal was to have a larger number of children, but they recognized that under the present circumstances couples were well advised to limit family size.

The accusation of 'ignorance' was at least partly directed at the issue of contraception. In the late 1970s and early 1980s many women were suspicious of the contraceptive pill. In a number of cases women explained they would not try the pill because their husbands would not allow them to do so. In some cases, husbands objected to the pill because of its possible consequences for their wives' health. To many, the pill appeared as an unnatural tampering with the body. Another explanation, suggested to me by a group of men, was that a woman using the pill would be free to engage in extramarital sexual relations, without too much remorse or fear of discovery. In the majority of cases, married and unmarried women discreetly stated that their husband or boyfriend 'was careful', and that was their method of contraception. Younger women were more likely to have an open mind about the pill, although they had not necessarily used it.[10] Some women knew about barrier methods and IUDs, but said these were not readily available in Italy. Clearly, many of these contraceptive methods involved consultation with a specialist doctor, which would be difficult for most women, in terms of financial considerations, time, contacts and finally shame at such intimate contact with a stranger, who, moreover, was often a man.[11]

The desire to educate one's children was seen as a priority by many of those interviewed in Naples. Many women who worked in factories or as outworkers wanted a better life for their children, male and female. Education was seen as a way of progressing to a better job. Women, who again were the ones most likely to discuss these matters with me, tended to talk more about their daughters' education and careers. This could be because the question of their sons' education appeared to be less problematic and more self-evident, or because their husbands were more inclined to think about sons' careers, or because they identified their daughters more immediately with their own experience. Since the majority of interviews concerned the women's lives and the history of their careers, this identification might be compounded by their view of my expectations. On the other hand, many fathers were equally concerned about improvement through education, whether their children were male or female. And then there were also those women who opposed their husband's wish to support the education of their children. In one, not entirely atypical, case a mother who was a full-time housewife refused to discuss the possibility of her daughter continuing her education after completion of primary school, in spite of the child's obvious achievements and the encouragement of her teachers. The girl's mother felt that this, her only daughter (she also had two sons), should stay at home and help her with the domestic chores. Indeed many daughters did end up giving up school and training in order to specialize in domestic work, while others worked part-time while attending school or left school very young to enter training and/or paid employment.

Although bookshelves were not frequently found in working-class homes in the old city, some families were careful to make available texts which they felt would assist their children with their studies. Thus encyclopedias, usually bought in instalments, were quite popular. In the homes of the families which were seen as being more 'progressive', a more varied selection of books was available, and reading books, but especially newspapers, was habitual.

A frequent theme in discussions regarding children's education and their future was the question of self-sacrifice or *sacrificio*. Parents often made the point that the choice in favour of keeping their children at school for longer, or even seeing them through higher education, was a more difficult one than sending them off to work. It required self-sacrifice for all concerned, as the parents would be the sole providers for a longer period of time. In the case of daughters, women would also sacrifice the help with household chores so often provided by daughters.

Although it was not common to come across open opposition to education, the number of young women and girls who had not completed their school education, or whose attendance was restricted because of their wage-work or apprenticeship, testified to a choice in favour of work at an early age, due either to family necessity, or a belief in the importance of having a saleable skill.[12] Only one case was encountered, in the outskirts of Naples, of a father who vehemently opposed schooling for his four daughters. None of the girls had ever attended school. The eldest was 15 at the time.[13]

In spite of the positive attitude towards education amongst so many of the families and individuals interviewed, Campania still falls short of national education trends. The average (of the population aged 6 and over) for Italy in 1981 was 11.5 graduates from upper secondary school, while Campania had an average of 10.3. But for Italy as a whole and for Campania as well, there has been a significant rise since 1971, from 6.9 for the national average and from 6.6 for the Campanian rate. Interestingly, Campania was on a par with the national average regarding university graduates in 1981, with a rate of 2.8, a statistic it shares with Lombardy, Tuscany, Umbria (2.9) and Sicily. But the figures from Campania for those graduating from vocational education are disappointing, accounting for only 6.3 per 1,000 employed versus a national average of 12.1 for 1981–2 (Nanetti 1988: 34).

In any case, providing a child or children with education is not incompatible with having a large family. We have already seen cases where a division of labour between children results in one child's subsidizing the education of another. So the drop in fertility no doubt responds to a number of different factors. One of these might be that parents are less willing to 'sacrifice' one of their children to benefit the others, and attempt a more democratic distribution of opportunities than was the case in their own families. Important changes have taken place; but the fact remains that Campania has the highest fertility rates in Italy and the largest family size. This would seem to indicate that change here has been more limited than elsewhere, and that childbirth and children are still highly valued.

In spite of changes in people's attitudes and behaviour, relative to the country as a whole, Campania is still pro-marriage and pro-natalist. For example, marriages in Italy have declined from 7.6 per 1,000 inhabitants in 1973 to 5.3 in 1983. In Campania they have also dropped, from 8.9 per 1,000 in 1973 to 6.7 in 1983, but Campania still has the highest rates of marriage of any Italian region. This is supported by the rate of birth of illegitimate children. There has been an increase for Italy from 22 per 1,000 in 1970 to 48 per 1,000 born in 1983; in Campania the rate has increased from 21 to only 35 in the same period.[14] The family has been changing, but familism remains an important feature of Southern Italian society.

Familism and Daily Life

As Ginsborg (1990) points out, familism in the South of Italy responds largely to the need for guaranteeing networks of support, or even creating a refuge from the hostile social and economic environment that characterizes much of the region. In the case of Naples, it is clear that the family remains an important institution, notwithstanding the significant changes that have taken place at local and supralocal levels. Not only has legislation changed, but there have also been significant changes in people's aspirations, and new or additional factors inform the process of planning and setting up a family. Couples are now more likely to compromise on what was considered by many to be the ideal family in order to improve their own standard of living and that of their children, by limiting the number of children so as to maximize the opportunities they can offer them, especially through education. However, as many informants pointed out, although they might 'be careful' and plan a certain number of children, it was not entirely in their hands to determine exactly how many children they would eventually have. This was especially so given the lack of reliable and safe contraception.

The family was important for many individuals because it could provide the framework for many petty entrepreneurial activities and, more generally, it still operates as a pooling device and as a means of redistributing income among a number of people. The advantages of this kind of familism have been exemplified in the earlier discussions of outwork, petty enterprise and more general household strategies. The costs of this are mainly shouldered by women, who are the principal agents in the creation and reproduction of kinship networks and who sustain the daily, routine actions which make for the perpetuation of the household. State interventions which have favoured subsidies rather than services have reinforced the importance of the family and strengthened the position and increased the responsibility of women within it.

Pro-natalist ideologies and practices, a heavy reliance on family relations and the continuing importance of household strategies mean that women's agency is heavily conditioned by the requirements of family life and by familistic ideologies. The scope of women's action and movement is delimited by the practical and emotional prominence of the family within Neapolitan social life.

Having children is an important and positive aspect of family life and indeed of adult experience. The practical implications are contradictory and of course variable, since in some households having a relatively large family can be advantageous, whilst these advantages are not realized in others. The most important consideration is the relative age of the children. Whereas older children, especially girls, frequently assisted in the household, younger children demanded attention. Very young children and babies were usually shown a lot of attention and affection, whilst older children were more rarely the centre of attention. But in many instances the intention of meeting the needs of even very young children was constrained by circumstances, particularly when mothers had to work at home. The contradiction between the importance of children and the relative lack of time available to spend on them was often resolved by the almost continuous presence of kin in a household, or by having children spend a lot of time in the home of grandparents or other kin, or having older children take care of them.

In spite of the many difficulties, most women seemed able to find a balance between the opposed responsibilities of motherhood and paid work. Some outworkers, for example, managed to work with a very large number of children around them. One such woman, Rosamaria, was capable of working whilst having a number of children in her care. On one occasion she had five toddlers playing around her sewing-machine, only two of which were her own. She carried on working cheerfully, with the occasional help of the slightly older children in her care. But for Rosamaria, as for so many other women, their roles as mothers and housewives were accentuated by the practical and ideological centrality of the family and of children. The effect was to force these women into perpetual compromises between conflicting demands, and to subordinate their own needs to those of others.

The Support of Kin

Women are the core of the family group and are also very much contained within the kinship network. This means that a woman's capacity for action is largely determined by the availability of her kin and their attitude towards her and her choices. The attitudes of family or husbands are therefore important in defining what women will be able to do. For women with children in particular it was important to be able to count on the assistance of older daughters, sisters or mothers to free them from child-care. Women factory workers in particular relied heavily on the help and support offered by kin. Given the lack of formal child-care, and where there were no children of the appropriate age to take over these duties from their mothers, a woman's own mother or her mother-in-law was the most likely person to take over caring for small children.

In some – though very few – cases, this support was extended to allow women to become involved in activities outside work and family, sometimes in areas that were defined as primarily 'male', such as political parties and trade unions or activities designed to further their careers. Carmela was a young and energetic woman who had been very successful at work. She was an active and experienced member of the trade union, and had been involved in a particularly protracted dispute which helped her build up her self-confidence. She was happy in her present employment, and her bosses were clearly satisfied with her. She had been promoted and sent on a training course for one week. Her husband had supported her throughout, as had her mother-in-law, who had taken care of her one-year-old child while she was away on the course. Her employers were now asking her to do further training. However, this involved her living in Torino for nearly one year. Again her husband supported her, and her mother-in-law, though somewhat bemused by both of them, agreed to help out with the little boy. She was concerned about being away from him for such a long time, but she had worked out ways in which she could travel down frequently to see her family.

Single women are also directly affected by the attitudes of close kin. Many young girls work with outworkers rather than in factories because of parental choice – usually the father's decision was quoted as the reason for not working in a factory. Those young, single women who did work in factories might have more autonomy than their outworking counterparts, and some were involved in trade union meetings and activities which occasionally took them out of Naples. During one such meeting, a group of women, some married and some single, discussed their involvement in activities outside the home or the factory.

Some of the young single women said their parents would never agree to them staying away from home even for a single night. Even though they might trust their daughters, parents were concerned about what the neighbours might say. It was already quite an achievement that they had been allowed to travel as far as Rome with the trade union – it had taken quite a lot of time for them to come round to this. Another woman pointed out that at marriage the problem does not alter: her husband would never agree to her spending a night away from home. Other married women agreed with this. Two very young sisters argued that there should be parity between fiancés, and that it was important to establish a trusting relationship, which meant that both should have the same freedoms. However, all these women and their partners and families were exceptional: in the majority of cases parents advised their daughters not to get involved in trade union affairs at all. Some were concerned about their daughters coming back late from meetings. Others were worried that they might be victimized by their employers if they were seen to support the trade union. In general the rule to be followed was to mind one's own business (*fare i fatti suoi*).

There were occasions, however, when workers did take action, and perhaps for the first time in their lives became involved in the politics of the workplace. A number of those interviewed had at some point in their careers participated in factory sit-ins. In one case the sit-in had been a protracted affair, and had involved men and women staying over and sleeping in the factory for many weeks. On these occasions anxieties, which were quite general, regarding contact between the sexes in the workplace seem to have been suspended. Families had been supportive, and there had been few recriminations concerning the fact that the men and the women were in the factory overnight. On the other hand, those involved also took precautions to ensure that there was little scope for gossip or scandal: meticulous care had been taken to segregate the men and the women and protect the privacy of both.

One sit-in had been started by a group of extremely young women workers – the only men employed by the firm worked in the administration – working in a small clothing factory. The young women had made known their wish to have trade union representation in the factory. They subsequently witnessed a decline in the volume of work and had reason to suspect that their boss was planning to take advantage of a long weekend holiday to close down the factory and transfer all machinery and materials to another unit he owned elsewhere in the city. This was not an unfounded suspicion, given their observation of management behaviour over the previous weeks and given that in Naples long weekends often provided the opportunity for 'disappearing' a factory without offering compensation to the workers. The young women locked the main gates to prevent machinery being removed, refused to leave the premises and summoned the trade union to come and represent them.

By the time the trade union representative arrived there was a crowd of people pressed against the main gate. These were parents, brothers and sisters who, on receiving the news about the sit-in, had come to find out what was going on and lend their support. As time went by, more families arrived. Since it was getting late and the young women had been in the factory since early morning, mothers arrived with parcels of food to hand over the gates to their daughters. Inside, while the union representative and the management discussed the situation, a festive and excited atmosphere prevailed. As food continued to arrive, sent by one girl's mother, then another's and another's, the girls offered around the abundant and substantial dishes that had been brought from home. Late into the night, the deliberations ended in an amicable agreement. The girls had succeeded, and with pride and satisfaction they left the factory for home, to the cheering and celebration of all the families reunited outside. This incident illustrates the extent of the involvement of families in the lives of their daughters. In this case, their support was unconditional. Any criticism of the young women's actions was immediately and forcefully rejected. Although the battle and the victory belonged to the girls, their mothers, fathers, husbands and other kin were happy to share in it and to contribute what they could: their presence, their verbal support and of course, their food.

Support of this kind was even more important for those women who worked on a more regular basis for the trade unions or for political parties. In general, women who were active in these organizations had supportive husbands who were usually also involved in politics in some way or other. Some of these women were anomalous because they were separated, and some were single. Some of the single women did face opposition at home, but were adamant that they would not give in to family disapproval.

Here again though, these women were the exceptions, and the trade unions faced many difficulties in drawing audiences to their meetings, or recruiting women representatives and activists even in those trades where women constituted the vast majority of workers. The reasons for these difficulties were manifold. Partly, those sectors which employed mainly women workers tended to operate in the precarious informal sector, where small firms prevailed and did their best to avoid a trade union presence amongst their workforce. But it was also the case that, even when that presence was established, the majority of women were unwilling to do much or say much. There was a problem of confidence and of engaging in a language that most of these women did not know and did not feel comfortable with. There was the problem of the pressures of running a household and having to rush off after work to do shopping and cook and take care of the family. There was also the problem of parents or husbands who opposed their staying behind for a meeting. Finally, the women themselves frequently felt alienated from the issues at stake. This was largely because for many, working in a factory was seen as a temporary step. Few had visions of a career or of a life-long dedication to their work. For most the hope was that this was a stop-gap and that at marriage they would give up factory work. For the majority of young women workers then, the ultimate and ideal objective was to marry and have children. This conditioned the way in which they experienced their present circumstances.

Conclusion

There is some suggestion in the accounts of informants, especially the younger ones, and in the demographic statistics, that changes are taking place in the way the family is conceptualized. The shift seems to be away from the emphasis on pooling resources and on generating divisions of labour which aim at improving the survival capabilities of the household, and towards increasing the potential of children to improve their social position. However, it is also likely that informants' statements reflect different moments in the developmental cycle of the households. A possible outcome, especially given the increasingly difficult circumstances which obtain in Naples, is a process of fragmentation of the working population whereby it is polarized into relatively upwardly mobile and 'respectable' families and those that just get by. However, the process of upward mobility is unlikely to be smooth, let alone guaranteed, as the availability of the more prestigious working-class jobs becomes increasingly restricted.

Whilst acknowledging the important changes affecting the family and the quality of family life, in Naples having children and creating a family remain important objectives for the majority of people, whether male or female. The importance of the family is explained by its centrality in strategies designed to help individuals and groups survive, or perhaps prosper. But in addition, the family provides the emotional context within which people experience their most important and intimate emotional relationships. Women as mothers play the central role here, forging and sustaining these relationships. Not surprisingly, women derive much of their self-esteem from their success in these tasks. This has important implications for women's agency, in that it is constrained by the practical and ideological conditions governing family life. But just as women uphold kinship and family and are limited by this responsibility, so too does the context of kinship offer different kinds of opportunities for women to exercise choice and control over their lives or push their potential to the limits of their circumstances.

But the centrality of the family does not arise from purely individual and local circumstances. On the contrary, these experiences and these attitudes have been shaped by the philosophy of the Church and the ideologies and policies of government. These have fomented familism, and have encouraged pro-natalist attitudes and practices; they have idealized motherhood, and have both idealized and supported the institutions of marriage and the family.

Familism is therefore a consequence of determinations from above, that is the Church and the State, and from below, in other words the practical and sentimental importance of family life. Of course these determinations can be contradictory. And people do not blindly follow the dictates of the Church or the government, as was exemplified by the results obtained on the issues of abortion and divorce. Indeed, government policies have themselves been contradictory, since they have responded to different claims and different interests. But overall, the heritage of Fascism and the particular orientations of the Catholic Church and of the Christian Democrat Party have placed the family not only at the centre of individual experience and subjectivity, but at the heart of political and social debate. Familism is thus not a product of backwardness and underdevelopment, as Banfield claimed. Nor does it necessarily reproduce backwardness or poverty. But it does seem accurate to say that official familism has found resonances at local levels; it has been internalized and interpreted, and it does inform people's views of themselves and their society. So in order to understand Italian familism, or the Neapolitan family, it is not enough to stop at individual or local identities. We are also forced to take into account the specific evolution of the State and of the relationships between the Church and the State, which have been, perhaps, the principal agents in the development and definition of familism.

Notes

1. Ginsborg cites as exceptional the case of the 'organized unemployed' of Naples in the second half of the 1970s (Ginsborg 1990: 413).

2. The coalition of the Christian Democrats with other parties resulted in the division of spheres of influence. Of particular importance was the alliance between the socialist PSI and the CD party. In Naples this alliance was present at all levels of local government. During the 1970s the Socialists were known for accepting bribes and for operating clientelistically. These rumours were confirmed officially in the early 1990s, when local government representatives from all parties were found guilty and condemned for accepting bribes.

3. The Amato and Ciampi administrations put through a number of unpopular measures aimed at curbing tax evasion and at cutting public expenditure. Their attack on welfare and services was met by widespread opposition in 1992 and 1993.

4. The figures are taken from a report by John Hooper in the *Guardian*, 15 October 1994, p.14.

5. The reaction against Pivetti's comments was forceful, coming from the centre as much as from the left of the political spectrum, from men and from women. Amongst the latter were figures such as Tina Anselmi, a long-term militant in the Christian Democrat party who had been a resistance fighter during the war. Others, such as a group of feminists named '*Controparola*' and including well-known figures such as Dacia Maraini, Elena Gianini Belotti, and Cristiana di San Marzano, reacted in the same way as Anselmi, pointing out Pivetti's ignorance of historical facts. They enumerate a number of decrees and interventions which severely limited women's freedoms. In addition to the legislation affecting women in the family, their restriction to family roles was further supported by laws which limited their employment. Starting in 1923, women were barred from the status of head in secondary schools; in 1926 women were barred from teaching in the final years of secondary schools; in 1927 women's wages were cut to one-half of male wages. In 1926 the national association of women, founded in 1897, was dissolved. (*Source*: Communique from '*Controparola*' to Irene Pivetti, published in *la Repubblica* 23 April 1994, p.2.

6. Pope Paul VI was clearly against divorce, but was also concerned to maintain good relations with the Italian state. Although the Council of Bishops expressed severe condemnation, individual bishops stated that the issue was a matter of individual conscience (Ginsborg 1990: 350).

7. The consequence of these different requirements and influences is reflected in legislation. Passerini points out that the law does not achieve what women's movements had striven for, i.e. a decriminalization of abortion. Instead, the law legalizes abortion 'as a concession to those "unable to take on a maternal role"' (Passerini 1994: 238). A crucial factor here was the need of the CD to obtain the approval of the Fascist MSI to pass the bill.

8. The statistics quoted are mainly taken from Nanetti (1988) and Ginsborg (1990).

9. In 1979 Campania was overtaken by Puglia, which had a rate of 9.2 (Nanetti 1988: 33).

10. Because this was a difficult topic for many women, it was only discussed where the relationship between myself and the woman allowed for it. Sometimes group discussions were more likely to bring up the topic, although of course the group context would affect what and how much each woman said. Some would be more modest than they might be in a one-to-one situation. Others were keen to show how progressive they were and might be encouraged to be more daring in their words than they actually were. Similarly, because the pill had such dramatic connotations, discussions and opinions tended to circle around whether or not to take the pill. Because of these problems I did not collect sufficient data to make useful generalizations, nor do I have data regarding the use of condoms and other methods.

11. Many women had never been seen completely naked by anybody except, perhaps, their husbands. The kind of close examination required for fitting a cap or IUD provoked a great deal of anxiety.

12. It would have been interesting to interview the fathers (given that most apprentice girls spoke of their father's decision to send them to an outworker, rather than their mother's) of the young girls encountered as assistants and apprentices. This would have been difficult, since fathers would be hostile to the questioning of their decisions and suspicious of outsiders inquiring into their daughters' business.

13. Many parents were concerned about leaving their children in school as they got older because of the sales of drugs which took place in many schools, which made them fear that their children would become drug-users.

14. The greatest increase in illegitimate births is registered in Sardinia (from 19 per 1,000 in 1970 to 50 per 1,000 in 1983), Puglia (from 15 to 45) and Val d'Aosta (from 31 to 100).

Motherhood and Identity

The early experiences of the child within the family have provided the focus for the development of psychoanalytic concepts, and have found their way into a number of anthropological approaches, most notably in the work of the 'culture and personality' school. Generally, however, sociologists and anthropologists have adhered faithfully to Durkheim's precept that a social fact can only be explained by another social fact, thus rejecting the usefulness of psychology or psychoanalysis within sociological explanation. Although attempts to marry psychological and sociological analyses have been fraught with difficulties and have, all too often, fallen into the traps of oversimplification and generalization (Morris 1985), the second, and dominant, trend has led to an equally problematic conception of social relations, whereby 'society' and 'culture' become discrete and homogeneous entities, confronting the individual and the environment (Hirst and Woolley 1982).

Yet it is important to recognize that, as Morris points out, culture (or society) 'does not pre-exist the human subject; they dialectically co-exist' (Morris 1985: 724). But the problem remains how to approach that dialectical co-existence. There is a danger that attempts to move from the particular experiences of individuals to the general will achieve little more than the definition of a 'personality type', or that the analysis of the relationship between society and the individual will reduce 'individual social agents to obedient social performers of required roles' (Hirst and Woolley 1982: 137). Nevertheless, if we recognize that different social contexts set different configurations and ranges of possible individual capacities and attributes, it becomes important to examine patterns of family relationships and of psychosexual development and explore the possible implications these might have for our understanding of the reproduction of particular sets of social relations and ideologies. This is especially so where the analysis of gender identities is concerned, so it is perhaps not surprising that feminist writers have been concerned to merge philosophical, sociological and psychoanalytical insights, as we shall see later in this chapter.

Because mothers play a central role in the construction of family life in Naples, both as bearers of a family ideal and as active members of the unit, the links between identity and motherhood will constitute the core of this chapter. The mother is at the centre of family activities and family reunions and celebrations. Through their nurturing role as mothers, wives and relatives, women fulfil important tasks in creating the conditions for binding relationships, even in the face of tensions and conflict. Women are also those who are primarily in charge of the family's relationships with kin and neighbours, for it is essentially a woman's network that is maintained and drawn upon either in moments of need or of celebration. This has implications for the organization of the household, as well as for the construction of male and female subjectivities.

Men, Women and Household Space

The division of labour in the household clearly demarcates the home as a female area. A majority of men did not participate in any aspect of housework and child-care – sometimes entirely as a result of their own attitudes, but frequently supported in this choice by their wives and mothers. The division of labour in the home, which defined it as a female space, tended to exclude men, who spent much of the day outside the home. Ideally men would be out of the house because they would spend most of the day at work, returning only to eat, rest and sleep. Men who were unemployed might spend more time in the home; but this was not considered desirable by husband or wife. The wife might complain that she had to get on with *'i servizi'* or the housework, and that her husband's presence got in her way. He might feel awkward and prefer to spend time in the cafés, or the *circolo* or the *sezione* of the party if he was a party member. During the daytime men might pop into the house, especially if it was a *basso* in the centre of the city. A woman's brothers, sons, and other male kin or close family acquaintance might visit. On one occasion a visitor who was calling on his sister who, as an outworker, could be relied upon to be at home, explained that his small book-binding enterprise, which relied primarily on the Universities for business, had been doing very badly in the last year and he now had no work at all. His wife, who, he explained, had remained 'affected' by the loss of a baby, got very angry with him for not bringing any money in. She pressed him to look for work, failing to understand that there was none available. So he spent much of his day out of the house and out of her way, visiting friends and family. On this particular day he had brought with him his very young daughter.

Parsons's research in Naples in the 1950s suggests that men's presence in the female sphere of the home is perceived as intrusive. From my own research it also seemed that the arrival of a man in a home did have an immediate impact. One of the reasons for this was the belief held by many men that they should dominate the conversation. Many felt that it was their responsibility to lead the conversation when it touched on matters such as politics, religion and even family and marital relations. There were few spheres of discourse for which they would claim incompetence and withdraw. Similarly, women often tended to cede the arena to the man. Thus, the arrival of a man altered the dynamic of a group conversation immediately.[1] However, the extent and form of the impact depended on the status of the man as well as on his personality. Sons, brothers, *parenti* might dominate the conversation, but allowed the women to converse, and the mood was little changed. Some men appeared to subvert expectations of authority: although they might still take over, they did this through joking, teasing and entering spheres of conversation which were not considered to be 'male', appealing more to the sympathy and humour of the women than the respect they might usually expect men to command from the situation. Generally such men were in some way anomalous, often deliberately so. Perhaps their relationship to the household did not fit any of the usual roles which defined household members and visitors. They might be young, single, and sometimes playing with ambiguities regarding their sexual identity; or be different because of a stated and recognized affiliation to a political view which was seen as subversive of tradition, such as communism.

Husbands and fathers on the other hand generally had an immediately inhibiting effect on their wives and daughters and their friends. The arrival of a woman's husband usually signalled the end of an interview, as he would either take over or his mere presence would inhibit his wife to the extent that conversation became extremely difficult. Even in informal social gatherings husbands and fathers had the same effect. In one household in the periphery of the city this inhibiting effect was witnessed on innumerable occasions. It was usual for this household to have a large number of visitors. The atmosphere was jovial, with loud discussion, and a lot of teasing and joking, occasional use of vulgar language, especially by the eldest daughter, and playful teasing between the youngest daughter and her fiancé. The father's imminent arrival was generally pre-announced. This unleashed a flurry of activity, as the eldest daughter (who was married and no longer lived with her parents, but ate at her parents' home on a daily basis) put out her cigarette and attempted to dispel the remaining cloud of smoke, the radio was turned down, the youngest daughter sat slightly further away from her fiancé and everybody assumed a posture of decorum and concentrated on whatever tasks they were engaged in. For the duration of the father's presence in the room everyone's behaviour was contained, reserved and polite. The man's wife was a cheerful accomplice of her children in allowing what was prohibited behaviour – smoking, swearing, physical familiarity between the sexes; and she was equally happy to participate in the cover-up. This household was perhaps extreme in the extent of the joviality and the contrasting formality that ensued with the arrival of the father. However, to some extent, this transformation was witnessed in many households throughout the city.

Whereas women as mothers were always conceded a central place and were seen as caring and loving, fathers were frequently perceived as being rather distant. Relations with fathers were often formal, and communication was maintained at a minimal level. This was not universal, however, and some fathers were relaxed and warm with their children. And even the gruffest of fathers was likely to indulge in what were often rather rough caresses and tussles with small children.

The division of labour and space, the importance of women's networks, the centrality of children in the family and of food in defining membership within the household, contributed to making women and especially mothers central to household organization and family life. This had significant implications for women, for whom the successful performance of the role of mother constituted a central axis of their ideas about themselves and their identity in relation to the world.

The Importance of Children

'A woman is not complete until she has had a child.' Neapolitan women would emphasize this even after acknowledging that women could and sometimes did achieve a lot in their work, in the media, in politics. But regardless of a woman's qualities and accomplishments, motherhood was regarded as making her a full and proper woman. Not surprisingly, few women were willing to envisage a future without children. Indeed, children were often considered to be the natural product of all sexual relationships, but were also seen as the cement that kept a couple together. Marital problems could, it was frequently suggested, be resolved by the arrival of children.

Children were seen to bring joy and satisfaction and were centres of attention. Adults doted on children – parents, kin and visitors always recognized a child, especially a small child, with teasing and humorous admiration. Babies were shown a great deal of physical affection. A baby might be passed round a room, especially amongst the women; but men too would hold the small child playfully. The penis of the baby boy was often singled out for teasing or caressing. It was not unusual for a boy's penis to be taken into the mouth of the mother during nappy-changing. As they grew older such intimacy was curtailed, but teasing continued.

The sexual and gender identity of the child was emphasized from an early age, and was often the focus of teasing behaviour between adults and young children and toddlers. For example, adults paid a lot of attention to the boy's penis as a focus for verbal teasing, and boys might also be provoked into displaying what was considered to be appropriately 'masculine' behaviour, for example in defending themselves or their families, verbally or physically. On the other hand, little girls were often praised for their prettiness and were not usually expected to display the same extent of aggression as boys. However, they too could be teased, and they were expected to respond appropriately.

For example, when a young girl aged about seven or eight dropped by a neighbour's home wearing a pretty dress, she became the centre of attention. Her dress had a tie attached to it, which prompted a young woman to ask whether she was a boy, since she was wearing a tie and ties were worn by men. The child responded rather shyly that she was a girl. But the teasing persisted, so she made all the men leave the room, after which she raised her skirt to prove to the women that she was a girl. Another guest pointed out that she could see nothing, so perhaps she did have a hidden penis and was a boy after all. She retorted by challenging the woman's own status, accusing her of being a man. But the woman pointed to her breasts and then indicated every other woman in the room, observing that all had breasts. Since they had breasts they were women, while the men who had left the room did not, precisely because they were men. Therefore, she who did not have breasts was a boy.

The girl was confused by this discussion, which had rendered her anomalous, and finally appealed to them by crying out: 'I'm only little, what do you expect from me?' While the joke was making clear statements about being a woman or a man, and was enforcing conformity to certain gender-defined codes of dress, she was also being prompted to defend herself and to work out what it was that made her like the other women, whilst still being different from them. Although the girl may well have left feeling that she was being defined entirely by absence or lack, her perseverance in the face of a formidable opponent and the ingenuity with which she faced the adults was admired. In one sense, the incident was communicating a fairly Freudian orthodoxy: that femininity is defined by lack of a penis. However, there was an alternative and more positive definition offered when breasts were used to define women. A corollary of this definition is that femininity or womanhood are defined primarily in relation to the nurturing role of the mother.

The uninhibited display of physical affection that characterizes the relationship with babies gradually declines. As children grow they are expected to be modest, and neither boys nor girls would show themselves naked in public. Extreme modesty seemed to be the rule between brothers and sisters. Even when lack of space forced brothers and sisters of different ages to share a single bedroom, it was uncommon for siblings to see each other naked. Instead, each would retire into another room to change, and substantial nightwear was considered appropriate, and it seemed usual for several layers to be used at night, enhancing a sense of personal boundaries. For some women at least, this degree of modesty was carried over into their marital relationship.

In spite of the very positive value placed on children, women emphasized that motherhood was a status inextricably linked to pain and suffering. As one woman explained: 'One child is a constant worry; ten children are ten worries.' Children were a source of concern because they were vulnerable. There was also the worry about their future as adults, having to make a living in a difficult world. In order to bring up children and help them secure a good future parents had to make many sacrifices. Women tended to subordinate their own needs to those of their family and especially their children. This was not limited to when their children were young, for mothers were equally concerned about their adult children. For example, despite their poverty mothers might be unwilling to take money from their children, in order to allow them to save up for their own marriage and set up a home of their own one day.

Childbirth was the event which signified entry into full womanhood. And this entry was marked by pain. Older women spared few details about the agonies of childbirth when enlightening the younger and as yet uninitiated women. There was a complicity between those who had had a child and knew what the experience entailed. In such discussions attention usually focused on the young woman who was pregnant for the first time or on other non-initiated women, who would react with appropriate awe and discomfort. From my very limited experience as a witness to the process of childbirth, it was clear that in this case at least there was little emphasis on pain control. In a maternity clinic serving a local working-class population, women at different stages of labour were packed into a small ward. Some had already had their babies, others were in the advanced stages of labour. The ward was buzzing with people and activity, mainly from parents and kin, bringing and fetching, chatting and encouraging the women. No pain relief was offered and no physical contact or movement was encouraged. The midwife made regular visits to the ward, admonishing women for complaining and pointing out that pain was what motherhood was about. The pain of childbirth was a necessary component of becoming a mother, and with it, becoming a woman in the full sense of the word.

Women and the Madonna

The relationship of women with religion was closely associated with the experience of motherhood. Many Neapolitans, both men and women, distinguished between the church as a place of worship and Catholicism as a practice and an identity on the one hand, and the officers of the Church on the other. Thus a fairly uncompromising belief in the tenets of the Church was sustained while harbouring deep suspicions towards priests and nuns. At the same time, regular church attendance was difficult for many women, given the pressures of domestic and paid work. This was especially so with women who had small children and for outworkers who rarely left their homes.

However, religious practice was widely decentralized from the church and was maintained in the home and in the neighbourhood. A typical *basso* would have a shrine set up in a corner or some other suitable space. A figure of a Madonna or a portrait of the *Volto Santo di Gesu* (sacred face of Jesus) were the most frequent centre-pieces of the shrine. Sometimes these figures were adorned with small coloured light-bulbs. Almost always there would be, included in the glass case or propped up near the figure or portrait, photos of family members, especially children. Other significant objects might be included. For example, in one home the shrine, which was a small statuette of the Virgin and Child in a wooden case with a glass door and small star-like light-bulbs around the edge, contained photos of the children of the home and a necklace which had been given to one of the sons for his First Communion. This son had lost a leg in an accident, and the communion necklace had been placed next to the Virgin to ask for grace.

The old quarters of Naples are dotted with small shrines which are built into the walls and are generally dedicated to the Virgin. No matter how dark, damp and poor the alleyway, the shrines were almost invariably well cared for. Some of these shrines were very beautiful, and many were adorned with flowers and light-bulbs. These shrines were a matter of pride and affection. Respect was shown as people walked by, by making the sign of the cross. One woman, explaining her anger at the disdain shown by a Protestant sister-in-law towards the shrines, made a passionate appeal in favour of cultural relativism. She explained that different people had different beliefs. She, as a Neapolitan, grew up with the shrines and with the Madonna – this was part of her heritage, part of her identity as a Neapolitan. This, she felt, was no longer a matter of doctrines: it was an issue that went beyond what was right or wrong, correct or erroneous.

The shrines were not generally maintained either by the *comune* or the Church. Instead, residents of the alleyways where the shrines were located took responsibility for cleaning them, for repairs, for placing flowers and generally maintaining them. Margherita was an outworker who lived opposite a shrine built in 1889 and restored in the 1940s, dedicated to the beautiful dark-skinned *Madonna di Constantinopoli*. Margherita was not a happy woman. Most of her children were grown up and she had had a long and unhappy marriage. To make matters worse, life had always been a struggle from a financial point of view. She had been working for twenty years or so, whilst bringing up a family and enduring a selfish husband and a loveless marriage. Although Margherita had to count every single penny she spent, she took responsibility for the Madonna's shrine. She saw to it that it was clean and in good repair and she paid the bill for the neon lighting, which was left on night and day. The cost was significant for someone with her income level. But she did after all have an income from her own work, she never went anywhere and, as far as she was concerned, the Madonna was worth every penny spent. During the time that she had worked in a factory she had made some extra money by selling things at work, in order to maintain the shrine. Now that she relied exclusively on her earnings as an outworker and her husband's small pension, she made extra savings, shopping around for reduced items in the market, finding bargains and using her ingenuity to cook cheap meals, all in order to keep up payment of the electricity bills and other costs emerging from the upkeep of the shrine.

Margherita's sewing-machine was placed near the glass door which looked on to the street, and from where she sat she could see the Madonna. This, she said, brought her great comfort. When things got her down and she felt tired and sad, she would look up at the Madonna and would find renewed hope there. She explained that the Madonna was 'the only thing in her life'.

When, for my benefit, a comparison was made by another informant between Neapolitan Catholic beliefs and Protestant beliefs,[2] it was explained to me that Protestants were against the figures and the statues and didn't have the Madonna or the Saints. It was not however the case that Catholics didn't believe in God – they believed in God just as much as the Protestants did. The point was that the Madonna and the saints were intermediaries, since they were closer to humans than God. But saints and virgins had their own important status within Neapolitan cosmology. Naples has a miraculous patron saint, San Gennaro, who is able to pre-announce significant events affecting the city, and Neapolitans can count on the special protection offered by the Madonna dell'Arco. Other saints and other aspects of the deity, such as the *Volto Santo*, are especially treasured for their miraculous capacities. Indeed, the miracle is a feature of Neapolitan discourse. Amidst a fairly generalized discourse of scepticism and mistrust, of a refusal of authority and discipline and of humorous self-mockery,[3] nevertheless love and miracles can find spaces and opportunities for expression. Thus prayers, *voti*,[4] and pilgrimages to sacred places were conducted in moments of need, to bring about the intervention of the sacred and miraculously bring the problem to a happy end – or at least provide comfort and fortitude. Margherita, who asked her Madonna for *grazie*, favours or blessings, felt that the Virgin did concede these. The Virgin's concessions seemed to be more to do with providing emotional and psychological support than material solutions to Margherita's problems.

For women such as Margherita, the Madonna was more than an intermediary. The Madonna's capacity to inspire and to elicit deep emotions derived not so much from her place in the sacred hierarchy, as from the potential for identification between woman and Madonna. This identification was particularly generative of emotion because it took place on two axes, both of which revolve around the Madonna as mother. On the one hand, the Madonna is mother of all; all who worship her, whether male or female, young or old, can find in her the solace of the mother's love and embrace. The Madonna loves all her children, just as a mother is supposed to do, forgiving and understanding frailties and shortcomings. This was exemplified during a pilgrimage to a shrine which had opened quite recently on one of the hills of the city, because an image of the *Volto Santo di Gesù* in a woman's home had proved to be miraculous. The home was converted into a shrine and queues of devotees lined up to take the holy sacraments, offered by men who, though attired in robes that were appropriately priestly in appearance, had a ruddy complexion and robustness more reminiscent of farmers or butchers than priests.[5] Behind me in the queue two working-class housewives, probably in their early fifties, encouraged a third who, on closer observation, turned out to be a transvestite. The women assured their companion that all were the same in the sight of God and that the Madonna welcomed all her children as equals.

Love and Pain

The Madonna, like the mother, offers love in spite of disappointment and in spite of failure. And because she is the supreme mother, her capacity to do this goes far beyond that of any mortal mother, no matter how 'saintly' she may be considered to be by her children. This offers adults who have to bear a heavy burden of responsibility, who have to be strong and supportive of others, who take on the principal caring roles in their families and constantly subordinate their own needs to those of their families and especially their children, the opportunity to be dependent themselves, to have spaces within which they can be children. For once they can plead, they can cry, they can show weakness, doubts and fear. For once it is they who can seek the solace of another, who can feel the love and forgiveness of one who is superior, as the mother is to the child.

On the other hand, women like Margherita, for whom life is primarily to do with her children, who while being her source of joy are also the source of her anxiety and pain, are themselves mothers who can recognize and understand the pain of the Madonna. The full identification of women with the Madonna comes from this shared experience of pain and sacrifice which is integral to motherhood. Just as Mary suffered because her son suffered, so Margherita and all mothers suffer because of their children. There is thus a mutual understanding coming from the overlapping experiences of the Madonna and the mortal woman. Furthermore, this shared emotional area is experienced as deep and essential, and indelibly marks the identities of women. Few women thought there could be many human experiences that could match that of the Virgin, seeing her son ridiculed, taunted, tortured and crucified. This slow death and total humiliation was not something that most women, for all the suffering in their own lives, expected to experience. The Madonna therefore offered them an example, a lesson for life. The lesson was that motherhood, for all the pain, is a worthy role and that the suffering associated with it can be accepted. The serenity of the beautiful figures of the Neapolitan Madonnas only partially hid the sadness beneath, either as a premonition of what was to come while Jesus was still a baby, or with the full realization of his destiny in later life. But the serenity was there, to be admired and possibly emulated. This was the enormous source of inspiration of the Madonna: that human pain was inevitable and in spite of all the hurt, it was bearable. Indeed, to carry it well resulted in the serenity, wisdom and composure that characterized the Madonna herself.

The theme of pain is significant within Christianity, and it is experienced as gender-bound and gender-specific. For Cavarero (1993) the fact that the body of Christ is a male body means that the identification of men with Christ is immediate and direct. But according to Christian doctrine Christ is a symbol of universal redemption, which must encompass male and female believers. However, the maleness of the image does not allow women to relate directly to the figure of Christ. Instead, women come to identify with the agony of the crucifixion. It is with the suffering body of a defenceless man that women identify, and, although this man is different from others (is it, Cavarero asks, because of his defencelessness, because of his agony?), he is nevertheless a man. So while on the one hand women identify primarily with the pain, their experience of redemption from it requires a denial of their own specificity, of their own sexual difference. What remains for women of their encapsulation by this divine male figure, is the agony itself (Cavarero, ibid.).

The close identification of women with Catholic values and/or practices and the centrality of motherhood as the ultimate fulfilment within women's lives are ritually conveyed to girls and the community through their First Communions. This takes place well before puberty, and is a special day for most girls. For the time up to their Communion, and certainly on the day itself, girls become the centre of attention. They will wear long white dresses and a light veil. It may be pointed out to them that the next time they enter a church dressed in this way will be on their wedding day. The white dress clearly emphasizes the virginity of the girl and the ritual presentation of her in this way expresses her approximation to adulthood as a virgin girl, preparing for womanhood, marriage and the sacrifice of her virginity to become a mother.

For Parsons (1967), a Neapolitan girl's First Communion represents a resolution of Oedipal affects, and the ritual communicates to her the importance of delaying and redirecting wish-fulfilment. Another, alternative or complementary, view is that the ritual expresses a recognition of liminality, from the time when a girl is no longer a child but is not yet a wife and mother. This liminal period is embodied in the state of virginity. The First Communion signals entry into the virginal liminal state, which ideally is not abandoned until the ritual of marriage ends liminality, and the girl becomes a woman as a wife and an expectant mother.

Parsons considers that the First Communion is far less important for the boy, who does not experience the 'cultural elaboration of the Oedipus crisis' that girls undergo (Parsons 1967: 378). However, for the boy the First Communion is also a rite of passage, and he too enters a liminal stage which is only resolved at marriage when he sets up his own household and achieves full adult identity. On their First Communion boys dress in dark, sober and elegant suits. They, like the girls, are expected to behave with restraint and humility. Their role is also being defined, in that they too resemble miniature grooms to the girls' miniature brides. But their experience is not elaborated to the same extent, and it is less clear what is expected of them between their First Communion and their marriage, beyond adhering to sober and responsible behaviour. It is true that, as Parsons points out, the steps taken by the boy are not so clearly marked and that in particular virginity does not operate as a symbol of their liminality, a fact that implies greater ambiguities but allows boys greater freedom and flexibility.

The strength of Neapolitan attachment to Catholicism as an integral aspect of identity – in spite of the scepticism directed towards the Church hierarchy – may be a reflection of the capability of the Church to address simultaneously two separate spheres which provide the poles for the dynamics of the development of subjectivities. On the one hand Catholicism offers an external 'other', representing the Law, embodying strictures and recommendations, morality and punishment. But it also offers the maternal 'other', standing for the intimate relationship with the mother, the reciprocity and affectivity felt to characterize close social relationships.

Catholicism is also significant because it provides a rather specific model for motherhood. The archetypal mother–son relation is represented in the imagery of the Virgin and child, even though that child is male and the Catholic (or more generally the Christian) pantheon offers no model for mother–daughter relations. So both within family structures and religious iconography and practice the ideal of motherhood is powerful and ubiquitous, and informs the construction of women's sentiments and aspirations. It also creates very specific spaces within which women can be recognized and feel fulfilled and valuable. Belmonte goes further, suggesting that marriage and mothering represent the only spaces available to women, for 'women as wives are extolled and women as mothers are deified but women as women do not count for much in Southern Italy' (1979: 93).

Motherhood and the Construction of Subjectivity

In the 1950s Anne Parsons combined anthropological and psychological methodologies to analyse the family structure of the poor working classes of Naples. In this work she identified a 'nuclear complex' which she saw as existing at both the collective and intrapsychic levels. Representations of this 'nuclear complex' are passed on from one generation to the next. This complex differs from the patriarchal structure analysed by Freud because of the relatively weak position of the father in the Southern Italian families she studied. This weakness is reflected in the greater respect for the mother than for the father and, in psychodynamic terms, in the greater continuity of the boy's (and man's) relationship with his mother than with his father. The centrality of the mother does not mean that the Southern Italian complex is matriarchal, since there is strong evidence of strict limitations to the influence and authority of women. The main difference between the Freudian model and the Neapolitan case is that the mother–son relationship, which she characterizes as being 'an oral dependent tie' (A. Parsons 1967: 381), is extended into adulthood, which means there is a continuation of the sons' expectations of receiving maternal comfort and support. Feeding and eating are central to the relationship between mother and child, but it is also expressed more widely in the importance of exchanges of gifts and food within Neapolitan culture. Yet she refuses to characterize Neapolitan culture as an 'oral' culture because such exchanges take on very complex forms that cannot simply be deduced from early childhood experience. Furthermore, although the boy maintains oral dependence he also undergoes the Oedipal crisis, and thus enters a 'phallic phase'. From here comes an underlying fantasy of an exclusive maternal object which is frustrated in real life.

Oedipal repression in men finds expression in the imagery of asexual maternality attaching to the Madonna, who fulfils the maternal role for her son and all believers without being a wife. But men also internalize the Madonna as a superego figure, dictating the man's conscience. This means that, unlike the patriarchal model discussed by Freud, the superego is feminine, involving male identification with feminine values or 'as very concretely perceived according to a feminine body image' (Parsons 1967: 382). For Parsons virginity plays a key role here, linking men and women, the Madonna and courtship taboos, for 'the infantile wishes underlying the image of the pure woman are also seen in a sometimes extreme degree of defensiveness concerning the issue of whether or not the purity is real and to be believed' (Parsons 1967: 383). On the other hand, the male peer group provides the context within which men can rebel against these values and identifications and can express the aggressive impulses arising from them, which men are prohibited from expressing within the mother–son relationship.[6]

Parsons argues that the continuities in the mother–son relationship would tend to preserve existing family arrangements and act against the formation of new families. The father–daughter relationship, however, which she sees as being complementary to the mother–son tie, has the opposite effect. The relationship between father and daughter is quite different, for the father's interest in his daughter is less continuous, arising at two points in the girl's life: the Oedipal phase and the courtship phase. The incest prohibition is less contained in this relationship, to the extent that father–daughter incest is not unheard of, particularly when the wife/mother dies. Incestuous impulses can be expressed quite openly, as when daughters explain that their fathers are 'jealous' of their contact with other men. The tensions emerging when the girl is in courtship place the man in a more active role than the one he fulfils as husband. The space allocated to the man is that of protector of his daughter's and his family's honour. Furthermore, the father is active in managing the daughter's courtship, and must relinquish her to her suitor. For Parsons it is the strength of the incestuous wishes which accounts for the dramatic and explosive quality of the courtship situation; and the father–daughter relation, by accentuating incestuous tension and at the same time by imposing a taboo, acts as a kind of spring mechanism which running counter to the strong centripetal forces inherent in the mother–son tie has sufficient force as to cause the family unit to fly apart, resulting in the creation of a new one. (ibid., 387)

Thus, the Madonna complex which is internalized by both male and female children provides girls with a quite specific source of positive symbols of femininity, while the courtship complex provides spaces for the positive expression of masculinity. This, however, occurs principally with the sublimation of incestuous desires in the father–daughter relationship through the authority of the father in the courtship triangle. This would seem to indicate that the spaces defined by control over female sexuality and, perhaps, quite specific emotional fields involving sentiments such as jealousy, are particularly important in defining male subjectivity.

Parsons argues that cross-sex relations in the Neapolitan family are more significant than same-sex relations, and that this has implications for Neapolitan culture, such as generating an emphasis on values associated with romanticism on the one hand and conservatism on the other. The weaker repression of Oedipal impulses within the father–daughter relationship than in the classical Freudian model means that in spite of a theoretical emphasis on the purity and control of girls, girls are in fact quite knowing about sexual relations and sexual dynamics, a claim which is borne out by my own experience in Naples. She also insinuates that the weak internalization of paternal authority by boys results in a generalized disrespect for authority and a rebelliousness against it. Individual restraint does not emanate from interaction with and the internalization of a male authority figure, but comes instead from a feminine superego (the Madonna) and is operative principally in connection with the sphere of family and gender relations. In any case, the purpose here is not to derive a specific 'Neapolitan' or 'Southern Italian' personality type from the experience of the family, but rather to determine the dominant dynamics within the family which predispose individuals towards specific ideals and patterns of behaviour.

After Freud

Modifications to Freud's model have been suggested by a number of theorists of psychoanalysis (e.g. Klein, Winnicott) for whom the nurturing role of the mother takes precedence in the formation of the child over the authority of the father. Chodorow (1978) explores the importance of the mother for the formation of male and female identities, in the context of contemporary United States society. Chodorow is critical of socialization theories as explanations of gender difference and points to the importance of the intrapsychic developments that take place, differentially, within the family. It is here rather than in 'taught' behaviour that we can find the roots of the characteristics of men and women and of fathers and mothers, as well as the relationships that might exist between these two pairs.

Chodorow argues that in contemporary Western societies the mother is the central figure within the process of family care, whilst fathers are relatively absent from it. The centrality of mothering means that daughters are produced with mothering capacities and the desire to mother. Sons on the other hand have their nurturing capacities, inclinations and needs systematically limited. Because of the particular object-relational experiences of girls, their Oedipal resolution is only partial. This means that their relationship to heterosexuality and to themselves is quite different from that of boys, who undergo full resolution of the Oedipal crisis. Ultimately, women want to be mothers because of their Oedipal experience and because they attempt, through motherhood, to express and resolve the contradictions and limitations they encounter in heterosexual love experiences. These limitations are in turn the result of the particular dynamics affecting boy children and girl children, which give rise to incompatible needs and capacities to satisfy these: men suffer from a lack of emotional availability, whereas women's heterosexuality is less exclusive and less focused than that of men. Ultimately, then, women must seek fulfilment through mothering. However, this resolution of internal and relational conflicts through mothering means that women '. . . contribute to the perpetuation of their own social roles and position in the hierarchy of gender' (1978: 209).

For Chodorow the specific emotional and behavioural characteristics that result from the centrality of mothering are functional to capitalism. Women are produced who are primarily concerned with reproduction, and are equipped to nurture and provide emotional support. Men are produced who are less affective, and this supports their role both in the family and in the extra-familial spheres of social life. With the erosion of the material basis of fatherly authority, the position of fathers has declined, and mothers assume even more space in the family context. Exclusive maternal involvement in the emotional development of the boy results in the extension of his dependence. Because of this, the boy grows up with a generalized need to please and to be successful, and is unable to challenge the structures within which success is sought.

For Chodorow, then, mothering reproduces itself and serves to reproduce differential places in society and in the labour-market. Mothering is thus located within specific family structures, and more broadly within capitalist and patriarchal structures. Parsons also locates the importance of mothers within a social context within which women's power is limited versus that of men. The question of the reproduction of gender inequalities is not directly addressed by her, but her research does feed into the work of a number of contemporary feminist writers. Irigaray (1977) for one argues that the privileging of motherhood underwrites all of Western thought, denying women any conceptual spaces beyond those attaching to their reproductive role, as mothers.

Irigaray suggests that male domination of discourse (as well as male control over the material base) denies women the capacity fully to become subjects. Women's identity is an imposed identity, and their attempts at self-definition are limited by their being restricted to male language and values. So for Irigaray, femininity is 'a role, an image, a value, imposed upon women by male systems of representation. In this masquerade of femininity, the woman is lost, and she is lost because she plays the game' (Irigaray 1977: 80, my translation). This restriction of the spaces available to women to motherhood therefore has very specific implications for women. Irigaray argues that the only desirable relationship for men is that with the mother, a desire that will be disappointed when they search for the body of the mother-nurturer in real women. Real women, on the other hand, deprived of their selves, will only be fulfilled through their children.

Virginity is a reflection of the power relations that underpin discourses of femininity. Irigaray argues that for women being or not being a virgin does not represent a significant change in itself: losing virginity does not in itself make a woman. What virginity signifies is the lack of marking by men. The virgin is unmarked, unpenetrated, unpossessed: 'Not yet a woman by and for them. Not yet imprinted by their sex, their language' (1977: 211).

This is relevant to Parsons's argument that virginity provides the link between what she calls 'the Madonna complex' and 'the courtship complex', and the female and male spheres. Perhaps the respect of men for virginity which Parsons describes can be attributed to this anomalous position of virgins in the discourse of gender and sexuality, a recognition of their untouched and non-incorporated selves. This would go some way in explaining male jealousy of girlfriends' and wives' earlier sexual experiences, which is particularly strong when the woman has 'lost her virginity to another'. If the loss of virginity can be seen as an initiation of women into male-centred discourses, relations and exchanges, if the first penetration is what 'makes a woman' for men and this in turn is associated with becoming a mother, it might be important for a man to control the initiation of 'his' woman. This would mark her simultaneously as a woman and as his woman, and would involve her in his specific set of relationships. Alternatively, a woman who has 'lost her virginity' to another man has entered the sphere of male discourse and circulation, if not as a free agent, certainly autonomously of her husband. This would have important implications in a context which, according to Parsons, defines men in relation to women very much in terms of control over female sexuality. It might also provide some insight into the interest shown by many men (in contrast to the respect that Parsons describes) in seducing virgin women, because by so doing they exercise their power to mark women and initiate their entry into womanhood. However, a more straightforward explanation, and one that is compatible with 'folk' accounts, is that where virginity is socially valued, there is an enhanced achievement and satisfaction for the man in being bestowed the gift of a girl's virginity and the honour of being her 'first man'. But in any case, all of these observations reflect the importance *for men* of women's virginity.

From a Jungian perspective, Montefoschi (1993) comes to conclusions which in their substance are close to those of Chodorow. She argues that the centrality of motherhood is limiting for the creation of subjects, whether male or female. The domination of family groups by the figure of the mother blocks the development of the child: the dedication with which the mother protects the child from tensions and dangers impedes the child from developing his or her own sense of possessing the capability to deal with such tensions and become self-sufficient. The centrality of the mother also curtails the influence of the father in much the same way that Parsons describes for the Southern Italian complex. The father's dependent position prevents him from communicating the affective content of his relationship with his children, and he is reduced to becoming a vehicle for symbols of normative authority. This also means that the father's ability to influence the development of his children is limited, so that mothers constitute the single most important presence here.

In order to fulfil her role as a mother, a woman must deny her own needs. The maternal role precludes self-affirmation and creativity in women, who compensate by investing fully in the maternal role, which is the only model they have. The man, because he is a man, cannot legitimately follow this path, but remains dependent on the mother and all women to satisfy his affective needs. Both man and woman are incomplete and dependent, trapped by the maternal role. Women as mothers transmit the affective bases of relations of dependence between those who have power and those who do not, those who can satisfy affective needs and those who cannot. A model of dependency which is rooted in the mother–child relationship reproduces an affective structure and a relational model which finds expression in all forms of exploitation and alienation. Indeed, Montefoschi argues that because of the dominance of the mother, dependency is the only affective model available to the individual in his or her struggle to construct his/her identity within a given social system. Woman is thus 'the mediator of a relational model of needy interdependency upon which a whole social system was built. By giving in to the needs of others, she aids in the repression of the self-reflective and critical side of the human subject' (Montefoschi 1993: 114).

The Neapolitan material thus shows important continuities with 'Western' or 'European' family structures. It can best be understood as a variant of these structures, which because of the specific history and socio-economic characteristics of the area, finds some features magnified. The continuities are clear: the importance of mothering, the distance and absence of the father, and the continuing dependence of the child. In the Neapolitan case these features appear accentuated or are expressed more openly in conscious actions and discourses. The difficult economic circumstances which afflict working-class households undermine the material role of fathers, although as Belmonte (1979) indicates, Neapolitans were rarely unemployed in the strict sense of the word, most being involved in a number of activities which brought in small and irregular incomes. However, in many cases it was the wife/mother who through her work (particularly in the case of outworkers) brought in a steady income.

Parsons stresses the importance of cross-sex relations in the family, as opposed to Chodorow, who focuses on the mother–daughter relationship. In Parsons's analysis the mother–son relationship is privileged, and the continuing dependence of the son on the mother is not, as Chodorow and Montefoschi imply, merely internalized. It is also acted out in the mother–son relationship in concrete ways. The marital conflicts that ensue are not only the consequence of a subjective lack of autonomy or a tendency towards dependence; they are also the result of the continuing importance of the mother in the lived-in experience of men. The Oedipal experiences of men and women are conducive to marital conflicts and predispose to particular patterns of behaviour in both men and women.

For Chodorow and Montefoschi the centrality of mothering and the relative marginality of the father predisposes individuals towards exploitative relationships. For Chodorow the man produced by these familial relations will strive to comply with authority and submit to external authority. Parsons on the contrary hints that Neapolitan men respond to the strong authority of the mother and the weak father with a lack of respect for external or public authority. It is possible that the male sphere she identifies as offering peer-group support for men provides the opportunities for acting out anger and rebellion and that this translates into diffidence and distrust of authority. In Naples this is reflected in ambivalence: on the one hand the tendency expressed at various times in the history of the city, as well as in the statements of contemporary informants, to put faith in 'a strong man'. On the other hand, a generalized pessimism and distrust with regard to governments and politicians has also been discernible. On a more intimate level, although a lot of men had experienced constraining relationships with older male kin, as for example in the institution of the apprenticeship, where many had learnt a trade with a male kinsman, the desire to become independent had been overwhelming. On the whole, Neapolitan men expressed dissatisfaction with the obedience and subservience required in the wage-labour relation. Thus, a greater degree of rebellion against authority was evident than Chodorow's model would predict.

Conclusion

The family is the locus for the formation of differentiated subjects. In the case of Naples the figure of the mother plays a particularly important role. This she does through nurturing and in particular through providing food, a 'gift' that extends beyond childhood and, through hospitality, beyond the household as well.

Women's identities are enmeshed in ideals of the family and in their sense of fulfilment through family life. Although marriage might not be all that was expected, having a child was generally considered to be the most important event in a woman's life. Here and only here could a woman find true fulfilment. At the same time, motherhood provided women with a shared language, the language of suffering and sacrifice. This language carried them over into the realm of the sacred, reinforcing the acceptance and resignation that women often acquired with age. An acceptance that life, their life, was hard and that the joys of life brought with them pain as well, reinforced women's ability to be anchors within families which underwent insecurity and crisis fairly continuously.

The theme of sacrifice runs through the experience of being a mother. Typically mothers were totally giving, putting their children before themselves, indeed neglecting their own well-being in order to ensure that their children were as well off as could be expected. So mothers would often refuse a contribution from their children to give them a chance to save up for their own futures.

Yet conflicts within the household were not infrequent, and sibling rivalry often resulted in a mother's taking sides. Although material wealth was limited, there were many cases where disputes had emerged within a family in relation to property, in particular access to houses. Because of the shortage of homes in Naples, this was an important issue. Decisions often had to be made without offering compensation to those who lost out. Often a woman would remain in her home and would favour one child who would stay on to live with her. This automatically excluded other children. Another source of friction was the division of labour within the household, which favoured some children's upward mobility at the expense of others. In spite of frequent accounts of such experiences, loyalty to the ideal of motherhood was usually held on to tenaciously by the disaffected parties. Even where real disappointments had been experienced with regard to their mothers, most agreed: *la mamma è sempre la mamma* (mother is always mother). So although human frailty might be all too evident in the experience of individuals, the idea of the mother, and the loyalty that this demanded, remained intact.

Psychoanalytical writings on the family and on mothering, and, in particular, Parsons's combination of psychological and anthropological research techniques, provide important insights. In particular, they clarify the mechanisms through which specific spaces are produced and reproduced through the family which condition the subjectivity and behaviour of men and women. The home as a place of safety, associated with the nurturing and protective role of mothers, shapes both men's and women's understanding of their world and their relation to it. The psychoanalytic approach provides insights into why areas of female sexuality and male jealousy are significant in specific contexts, and why women are drawn so strongly to motherhood and men feel so compelled to concern themselves with the sexual reputations of their mothers, wives and sisters.

But although important insights are provided into the formation of personal identities, there are many difficulties involved in jumping from individual developmental patterns and family forms to the social and cultural characteristics of a society. A number of important works have dealt with this issue and provided very significant insights (Freud 1930; Horkheimer 1936; T. Parsons 1964; Todd 1985). The emphasis in these works has generally been on the formative role of repression and/or authority, embodied in the father figure and its structuring effects on relationships within the family unit. Underlying these works is the opposition of authority or the Law personified in the father to the nurturing role personified in the mother. Parsons is arguing for a specific configuration of these two elements in the Southern Italian family complex, which in her opinion makes for significant differences.

A danger of approaches based on the psychosexual development of individuals is that they might lose sight of the impact of society and its repressive effects on individual fulfilments – outside the family as well as within it (Marcuse 1969). A further danger is that the links between individual, family and society will frequently be conceptualized as functional relations. This is apparent in Chodorow's work and more so in Gilmore's idiosyncratic use of her theory. For Gilmore

(1990), ideologies of masculinity are socially adaptive. They represent the attempt to avoid male regression into dependence. Such a regression would be damaging to society as a whole, since it is men's courage, action and self-sacrifice which guarantees social reproduction. In the Mediterranean, masculinity is pushed to an extreme of exhibitionism, given the importance of male active roles and the lack of clear institutional markers of separation from the mother. Whereas on the one hand his argument is supported by Parsons's research in Naples, she stresses the fact that dependence within the mother–son relationship is not superseded, but merely finds an outlet of rebellion in the male peer-group.[7]

Women face enormous difficulties in breaking away from the models they internalize as members of a family and as members of the wider collectivity. The majority accept these models, and many attempt to juggle with them while at the same time fulfilling other needs, whether these are material or subjective. Those who do accept the learned models inevitably, as Chodorow has pointed out, reproduce and perpetuate their own social roles and the gender hierarchy (Chodorow 1978: 209).

The point is that, for both women and men, motherhood is a determining point of reference in their development and their daily lives, both in practical and in psychological terms. Gender models which derive substantially from parental ones and which involve an ideological elaboration of motherhood, are effective on the one hand as collective discourses and on the other are formative at the level of the intimate and unconscious dynamics involved in the process of creation of the self.

Notes

1. My presence would aggravate this tendency, since for many it was a cue for 'public discourse', which men (along with a majority of women) felt belonged to them.
2. Discussion on these matters was prompted by the phenomenon of conversion to Protestantism amongst people's kin and neighbours. A number of Protestant groups, amongst which the Mormons were perhaps the most prominent, were proselytizing in Naples.
3. Anne Parsons (1967) refers to a male culture based on scepticism as a style and on negative attitudes towards authority. Although male scepticism is more encompassing, women too were not inclined to naïveté, and in my experience working-class Neapolitans were never worried about expressing disbelief.

4. *Voti* were promises of offerings or personal sacrifices made to sacred figures in exchange for their intervention in difficult matters. If the favour was granted, the supplicant had to fulfil his or her part of the bargain. Commonly, silver objects or *voti* representing the miracle would be given to the shrine of the sacred figure and appended nearby. So, a leg might be hung near the Madonna if a family member had been able to walk again, an eye would be given if somebody had regained her sight, and so on.

5. In fact these were not ordained priests and the shrine was not recognized by the Catholic Church.

6. Male anger is indicated by Parsons as an important feature of the Neapolitan family. She argues that generally this is expressed by the man's exiting from the home and by the importance of swearing in Neapolitan culture. This is often based on the reversal of the positive images of womanhood and the Madonna (383–4).

7. For further discussion of masculinity in the Mediterranean see Brandes (1980), Herzfeld (1985). Also relevant is Gilsenan (1989).

ten

Food, Family and Community Memory

I t is difficult to generalize about Neapolitan culture or Neapolitan society. Naples is a complex and contradictory city. Its population is heterogeneous and its landscape is fragmented. Whilst aware of this, and in spite of it, Neapolitans frequently express a strong sense of identity and recognize themselves as members of a collectivity which shares a number of characteristics. This collective identity is expressed, and realized, through various channels, most notably Neapolitan theatre and song. The enormous appeal of these can be explained by the fact that they draw directly from daily experience, and they reflect social life as experienced by individual Neapolitans, who recognize themselves, and their collectivity, in the lyrics and in the scripts (De Matteis 1991: 21). However, there is much about daily life itself which also simultaneously expresses the condition of being a person and being a Neapolitan.

In this chapter we will consider some of the practices and ideas which constitute and express the collectivity in the experience of individuals. These practices and ideas can be seen as intersections of individual subjective experience and family life with the sense of recognition of and of belonging to a collectivity. The discussion includes a wide range of features such as food and festivities, as well as the experience of family life. Indeed, the family plays a dominant role here, as the principal context where these experiences are realized.

For De Matteis, Neapolitan identity has a highly performative character, and its daily performance is an assertion of a collective history. This history, of conquest and rebellion, of survival in the face of the exploitation or neglect of the rest of the world, has encouraged a strong sense of self in opposition to the 'other', whilst also feeding on, and deriving strength from, the 'other' (De Matteis 1991). The sense of boundedness has implications for the way in which family and society are perceived and the ways in which individual men and women are located within them.

Food and the Family

The regional differences that characterized the Italian peninsula prior to Unification have changed in substance and intensity. Nevertheless, regionalism persists in a number of features. Amongst these are the differences in food consumption patterns, which, according to a survey carried out by ISTAT in 1994, indicate that there are interesting contrasts and continuities in these regional patterns. For example, although Naples, the former coffee capital of Italy, has lost its place as the most important consumer of this item to Calabria, the people of Naples and Campania are still the main consumers of pasta in the country. Regional culinary and dietary conservatism may not only be explained in ecological terms, in terms, in other words, of the relative availability of foods, which no doubt is in many cases an important factor, but may also be attributed to the fact that the family remains the central context for the preparation and consumption of food, and the mother is the principal provider. It is mainly in the home that women learn to cook. They learn from their mothers or their mothers-in-law. This, coupled with the strong emotional attachment to certain foods as experienced within the context of the family, discourages major dietary changes from taking place. Food that is emotionally as well as physically satisfying is the kind of food that mother prepared. And this food is Neapolitan food. So food becomes one of the links between individuals, their families and their place of birth.

Whether the family is primarily a means towards a survival strategy or not, it remains a central concern for Neapolitans. For Bell, referring to the Italian family in general, 'Family may be a strategy, a way of maximizing resources or of providing the bare requirements of nutrition. Family may be a vehicle to accumulation of wealth, retention of land, a job opportunity, or a chance to migrate. What one means by *la famiglia* varies with the context' (Bell 1979: 75). For Belmonte the family in Naples was primarily intended for sharing, pooling and distributing, for 'the family is an organizational innovation to facilitate feeding' (1979: 59). He argues that the giving and receiving of food is crucial here, and the mother's central role as the emotional linchpin of the family unit is attributed to her role as nurturer. She is the unconditional giver of food and love, expecting no recognition for her generosity.

Indeed, Neapolitans' perceptions of the family and of mothers were imbued with the experiences of commensality and the preparation and giving of food. These experiences are at once individual and collective, for Neapolitan identity is impregnated with images and sensations derived from family life. In fact food provides the nexus between these two areas of experience and sentiment: it is at one and the same time the focus for family life and one of the central themes in expressions of Neapolitan identity.

Neapolitans abroad remember with nostalgia the beauties of the city, its music, the charm and humour of its people. Their nostalgic itinerary might follow closely that chosen by a tour operator, selecting the beauty spots of the city and its surroundings: Marecchiaro, Posillipo, Capri. For some Neapolitans nostalgia and longing follow very rapidly upon departure from the city. An example of this was provided by an expedition to Reggio Calabria organized by the trade unions. Travelling with a coach-load of burly *metalmeccanici*, it was not long before one of them started hankering for *'o ccafè*, a cup of Neapolitan coffee which is not comparable to that obtained elsewhere in the country, especially as you travel north. He was soon joined by a chorus of apparently desperate men. With time, anxieties focused on the need for a plate of *maccheroni* with *ragu*, or *salsicce e friarielli*.[1] The chorus responded sympathetically, listing alternative favourites. There was a surprising degree of consensus concerning this list of key dishes, closely linked to ideas of 'home'.

For many Neapolitans food provides an important emotional focus, and like Proust's *madeleines*, it is evocative of specific times and places. The remembrance triggered by the smell of tomatoes cooking with basil fills one with nostalgia and longing for an experience, a time and place stretching back into the past. And the dishes that have this power are felt to be, essentially, Neapolitan. Neapolitans have developed an impressive cuisine, comprising both the creations invented by the ingenuity of the very poor, intent upon producing a pleasurable experience out of meagre resources, and the creations developed by grand chefs, intending to delight the royalty and nobility of Naples and the whole of Europe. The cuisine of Naples reflects the history of the city, incorporates the influences of those who have at different times passed through it or dominated it, and talks of the city's past glories and its hardships. Food can mark history and create a sense of history, as is the case of the Christmas *struffoli*,[2] said to have originated with the Greek founders of the city. Other dishes are more recently associated with the *haute cuisine* introduced by the Anjou and the Bourbons. But in spite of their ability to incorporate different influences and different cuisines, working-class Neapolitans were very conservative about food, and usually rejected the dishes they considered to be 'exotic' from the Centre or North of the country.

Yet many of the most basic ingredients of popular dishes are, ironically, imported: the tomato was only fully adopted in the nineteenth century. However since then it has become an essential ingredient, or even more, a symbol of the place. In the words of Petravalle:

'... per noi napoletani è e rimane sempre la nostra più verace e clamorosa espressione geografica; un fervido sole, un bellissimo cielo; la calda gioia d'una razza prolifica, fantasiosa e impetuosa; ed è il chiasso, il prodigio d'una vita patetica e spensierata, che piange e ride nello stesso tempo e che ha per simbolo questo frutto modesto e orgoglioso, paesano e mondiale.'[3]

'... for us Neapolitans it is and will always be the most clear and true expression of our geography; an ardent sun, a most beautiful sky; the warm joy of a prolific race, imaginative and impetuous; and it is the chaos, the prodigy of a simple and thoughtless life, which laughs and cries at once and which has as its symbol this fruit which is modest and proud, local and international.'[4]

Tomatoes are combined in a number of ways with pasta, rice, bread and pizza doughs and other ingredients in relatively cheap and nutritious dishes. Beans, chick-peas, lentils were combined with pasta, broccoli and other greens to make substantial soups, to which pork meat or fat was added for flavour and substance. *Maccheroni* and *pasta* generally was widely used in the Italian peninsula, especially in Sicily and Calabria. But with the invention of machinery for the mass production of pasta a number of factories were established in the area surrounding Naples at the end of the eighteenth and the beginning of the nineteenth century, notably in Gragnano, Torre del Greco and Torre Annunziata, names which are to this day associated with the production of pasta products. In combination with the tomato, with vegetables, with seafood, beef, and pulses, *maccheroni, vermicelli, spaghetti* and other forms of pasta are part of the daily diet of Neapolitans. Some dishes can be prepared very rapidly and require very few ingredients. Others are laborious or expensive.

Food is an important marker of special events and special days. Sundays are distinguished by a midday meal where everybody meets at the table to enjoy *maccheroni al ragù*, a dish which requires long and careful cooking so that the meat cooked in the tomato flavours the sauce and serves as main course as well. Special days are also marked by special dishes, such as the *lasagna di carnevale*, a labour-intensive and expensive dish traditionally consumed during Carnival. Easter, Christmas Eve, Christmas Day and New Year all have their special menus, which again often involve not only a large quantity of dishes, but some expensive and laborious items which sometimes require preparation weeks in advance.

In contrast to the Sunday meal and the meals marking celebrations, on ordinary days cooking and eating is more flexible, each household adapting to its particular circumstances. Where household members worked some distance from home they were likely to take in lunch. This could be a sandwich or the equivalent of a three-course meal which involved considerable planning and preparation in the early hours of the morning. In other households, residents and other family or friends gathered at the lunch-table. In yet other cases different household members trickled in at different times expecting a hot meal. This meant that for several hours (sometimes from midday to 4 o'clock in the afternoon) the kitchen and the cook were constantly on alert, ready to provide a meal.

In all cases, women were central to the provision of these meals. The different arrangements households made for food had different implications for the women who were in charge of the cooking, particularly on a routine, day-to-day, basis. Resources had to be carefully calculated, menus meticulously arranged to match financial circumstances with the different needs of household members, while ensuring that all felt they had had 'a proper meal'.

Women, particularly mothers, took a great deal of pride in the preparation of food. Although invitations to dinner appeared to be rare amongst the working-class families I frequented, invitations to join the family for Sunday lunch were not uncommon. On these occasions a woman would display her art with care. Typically she would spend most of her time in the kitchen or hovering over the table to ensure that everyone was taken care of. Younger women were more likely to sit at the table and organize the meal in such a way that they could participate in the conversation to a greater extent than their mothers did. Offering large helpings and multiple helpings was a way of offering hospitality. And accepting more than one helping of every dish was a way of expressing satisfaction at the hospitality offered. And it confirmed the woman's skills as a cook. The woman head of household would therefore spend most of her time preoccupied with the meal, and would eat intermittently, frequently doing so in the kitchen while she completed the next stage of the meal.

A number of sweet dishes are prepared for specific festivities, such as Christmas or Easter. Some, like the *pastiera*, are labour-intensive and require that preparation starts several weeks before the dish is to be consumed. Raw wheat must be soaked for approximately 15 days, changing the water frequently. The night before the preparation of the cake the wheat is boiled in milk with other ingredients. The following day the pastry is made and the ricotta and wheat filling are prepared. Each family is reputed to have its own version, or rather each mother's *pastiera* is special as far as her children and her family are concerned. Many adults remembered its preparation with affection, and the *pastiera* was a significant personal and family mnemonic and a topic of conversation with other family members as Easter approached. However, aside from the very special sweet dishes, it was rare for housewives to prepare desserts, even when guests were expected. On the contrary, a typical contribution made by guests when invited to share a family meal was a tray of sweet pastries bought from the patisserie.[5]

Daughters or daughters-in-law might help at different moments of the meal, but men would rarely get up from the table. Towards the end of the meal the women, guests included, might retire to the kitchen to prepare coffee together and wash the dishes. This was also an opportunity for chatting, commenting on the meal, exchanging recipes and hints for the preparation of the food and more general conversation. Men were usually excluded from these conversations. It was generally considered inappropriate for men to assist with these tasks, and families which broke tradition could cause bewilderment. On one occasion where the host and hostess and a male guest arose together to take the dishes to the kitchen, the women present exploded into laughter. Although some men did wash up and others, attempting to appear to be 'modern' and 'progressive', protested that they did occasionally do so, their wives would delight in putting them to the test, asking them in which order plates, pots, glasses and cutlery should be washed and how. Inevitably the men made mistakes, again causing a hilarity which was not free from satisfaction. There seemed to be absolute consensus amongst the women as to the order and procedures involved in washing up, and this consensus playfully marked the women off from the men.

There is also a long tradition of street food in Naples, ranging from pizzas to fried savories or sweet pastries. These might be consumed 'on the run', and at any time of the day. Street hospitality, which tended to be male, might involve some of these items; but coffee was almost universally the focus of this form of hospitality. Naples has innumerable bars, which pride themselves on their good coffee and quick service. A chance meeting with a friend will generally lead to an invitation to take 'o ccafè'. This is usually taken standing up and rather quickly, almost as a punctuation to the conversation. It is generally men who invite other men for a coffee, although women colleagues and friends would also be in a situation in which they would be invited (i.e. outside the home). Men would insist on 'inviting', that is to say, offering the coffee. One friend refused my attempts to treat him, or failing that, to pay my share. While the woman at the cash desk took his money rather than mine, declaring that it was wrong for a woman to pay, he spent some time elaborating his argument on the ethics of sharing, and expressed disdain for what he called the 'Roman' style, which involved dividing the bill. He found this to be rigid and formal. Instead, a more relaxed and spontaneous (and more Neapolitan) approach was preferable, since we should be mature enough and have a sense of responsibility, which would even things out in the end. This time he paid, next time I could pay, and so on. In other words, a greater sense of trust and therefore friendship was involved in the 'Neapolitan' way.

Coffee is also central to home hospitality, when this takes place outside mealtimes. Usually a large pot is made, the sugar is added to the freshly brewed coffee while it is still in the pot, and it is served very hot. Sometimes whisky, or another *liquore* is offered in the afternoons. Given that coffee was an expensive item, I was reluctant to accept this every time I visited or interviewed someone. I was advised that indeed coffee was an expensive item for most households, but that if I was to refuse the coffee I should ask instead for a glass of water. This would prove that I was not refusing because I considered the family to be 'dirty'. I was frequently moved by the generosity of women who kept a careful account of every expense, for whom every item in the home and every ingredient in the family's menu was priced or accounted for, but who nevertheless offered drink, food and fruit that they could ill afford to a complete stranger.

Food and drink, especially coffee, are thus important elements in social relationships. They are central to expressions of hospitality and friendship. Although men operate circuits of exchanges of coffees and other drinks out of the home, the responsibility for the hospitality offered within the home falls to women. This is a responsibility which most women assume with gusto. On the other hand, not to comply with the rules of hospitality would reflect on them, either as being too poor to offer hospitality, which few would be willing to admit to even though they might admit to financial hardship, or as being inadequate home-makers and representatives of their household. Women struggled against all odds – insufficient means, lack of time, inadequate housing – to display their expertise in home-keeping. Everything that was done and offered was worthy of praise and the achievement of praise was a constant element in the exchanges of hospitality with non-kin.

The exchange of praise for hospitality was not expected of family members, who would take a mother's skills for granted. However, here too, most adults seemed to harbour fond memories of the special ways in which their mothers prepared particular dishes. At the same time, a mother's expression of love frequently finds its vehicle in food. This was shown in the emphasis placed on the quality as well as the quantity of food provided and consumed.

The importance of children was frequently expressed through food, and food was one of the most important ways of communicating with small children. Babies were preferably breast-fed, although modesty, the pressures of work, and ideas of what constituted 'modern' approaches to child-care meant that many of the younger women preferred bottle-feeding their babies. But Maria, who was in her fifties, was proud that her youngest daughter had been breast-fed until she was nearly three years of age. Her other children had breast-fed for a much shorter period, but this was because they had refused the breast early on and not because she was unwilling or unable to feed them herself. Many women stressed with pride that when they had infant children they had large breasts full of good milk.

It was also a matter of pride for Maria to be able to say that her children had grown tall and strong, and her grandchild was following in their footsteps. As far as she was concerned, this was largely to do with the 'natural' qualities of the food they were fed: *tutta roba buona*, which was grown locally and prepared carefully. The relative absence of commercially prepared foods was seen as positive: 'You know what you get this way, you can trust it.' And indeed with very limited resources and few ingredients, she fed a large table of people twice a day, every day.

She pointed out that although some of her children had stopped breast-feeding while still young, they had had the advantage of the milk freshly milked from the cows belonging to the little farm across the road from them. Still warm, this was mixed with biscuit to make a nutritious substitute for breast milk. However, the opportunity for taking and desire to take advantage of freshly milked cow's milk were not universal. To some of those who had grown up in the densely urbanized centre as opposed to the semi-rural periphery of Naples, the thought of fresh milk, straight from the cow, was repulsive. During one conversation on the topic, a city-bred woman reacted with disgust to Maria's enthusiastic description of the local cow's merits and argued that she preferred the milk from the *'centrale'*, which had the advantage of being far removed from its original source – which incidentally got completely suppressed by both parties to the argument that ensued, as though the milk from the *'centrale'* did in fact have a quite different origin – and was diluted with water and perhaps other things as well.

The link between good food, love and well-being was expressed frequently – usually by women who had children. Mothers, and adults in general, would often appease a small child with offers of food. Food in different combinations was also a means of curing ailments, for example boiled lettuce and garlic for stomach upsets. And food was the key to the well-being of adults as well. On every occasion that I returned to Naples from London I was inevitably greeted by some of the women with the horrified lament: *'Ma come sei sciupata!'* This referred to my thin and haggard appearance. Their anxiety over my condition would only subside when I accepted a large plate of pasta or soup, whichever was to hand. Similarly, children who were 'good eaters' were seen as healthy and their 'good eating' met with widespread approval. On the other hand, children whose appetites were limited were a cause for concern. Generally speaking, appreciation through consumption was a source of gratification and satisfaction for the woman, whose role was primarily that of nurturer at that moment – whether the consumers were her children, grandchildren or other guests. It is hardly surprising that nurturing is then identified with food. And specific foods are especially associated with the nurturing role of the mother and the comforting aspects of family life. Thus, many memories centred around food, and food was a catalyst for remembrances.

If identity is constructed through memory, the memories of time and place linked to food, eating and nurturing play a key part in retrieving significant memories. Food could be seen as the sensory point of entry into a web of sentiments, memories and fantasies which largely constituted a sense of identity, as a person and as a member of Neapolitan society. This has implications for family life and how it is perceived and remembered and for women, whose role as nurturers provides a thread of continuity within these identities.

Celebrations and Identity

Neapolitan and family traditions undoubtedly play a role in the construction of identity and sentiment. Celebrations which are seen as family celebrations but involve the entire city are governed by a great deal of consensus in relation to the appropriate activities and consumption that should mark that particular celebration. Christmas was one of the most important celebrations. It was seen as a big family affair. The time up to Christmas was a busy time. Some families would have bought a piglet, which they would fatten up and have slaughtered before Christmas. Others bought the pig already grown and had it killed. Subsequently they would all busy themselves with preparing sausages, cuts of meat, and lard. From early December the pastry shops gave up their free time and worked non-stop on the preparation of the special Christmas pastries and sweet almond paste delicacies, for which there was a massive demand in spite of their cost. Along San Gregorio Armeno stall after stall sells pieces for the manger, Christmas trees, decorations. Artisans carry on the work of painting plaster angels and figures of the baby Jesus. In churches and homes people prepare elaborate mangers, which are displayed and judged in yearly competitions. One small *basso* which was usually a shop had been completely taken over by an enormous manger.

Outside one *basso* I had to stop to look at the display of a very large and elaborate *presepio*. It consisted of about six levels. Every detail had been taken care of. At the higher levels of the mount there were houses and shops, washing on the line, chickens, animals, trees, balconies, and statuettes of people busy about their business. Down the hill walked a band of shepherds, each carrying a musical instrument: flutes, drums, bagpipes. The shepherds were very beautiful and old terracotta figures. At the base of the hill and placed at the centre of the display was the 'manger' proper: Mary, Joseph and a straw cradle. The child Jesus was placed in the cradle on the night of 24 December. Above it some rather baroque versions of angels hung. On either side were a shepherd with a flute and one with a bagpipe. Above it all was a star made from metal paper, which guided the three wise men, who approached by camel from the left. At the extreme right of the display was a miniature group of shops, an *osteria* with salames and carafes of wine hanging outside the door, people eating at table and drinking outside.

The author of this construction was Mr Esposito, an old-age pensioner who had been designing a new *presepio* every year for the last thirty years. He argued that it was easy to do, and that principally it required imagination and patience as well as time. It had taken him seven days to make the framework from wood and cork and complete the details. He had been collecting pieces over the years so that some were very old. The *pièce de résistance* was a very beautiful, delicate 40-year-old baby Jesus. He also invested a considerable amount of money in the *presepio*, since every year he bought new figures to add to his collection. He was extremely proud of his achievement, and saw this work as an integral aspect of celebrating Christmas. Children may be involved in the purchase of figures, or placing them, or are simply taken to view the different *presepio* exhibits in the churches. Mr Esposito was keen to transmit his skills and enthusiasm to his children. He showed me a small manger with miniature pieces which had been made by his 14-year-old son.

The appearance of *presepios* indicates the approach of Christmas and is intimately associated with it. However, the theme of the birth of Christ represents only a fraction of what the home *presepio* communicates. Here the *presepio* mimics Neapolitan life, with its busy shops, homes, people. The stalls which sell the figurines offer an enormous variety of sizes and styles of figures representing the street vendors of Naples, many of whom are no longer seen on the streets of the city. Nevertheless the water vendor and the lemon saleswoman are found side by side with the fishmonger, the fruit and vegetable saleswoman, and the tripe salesman. Many of these figures therefore belong to a Naples of a time now gone by, but which is passed on in family memory through the *presepio* figurines.

The musician-shepherds of the *presepe* also mimic Neapolitan life and its Christmas traditions. While I chatted with Mr Esposito, we were interrupted by a loud sound outside his *basso* door. There were four men, *zampognari*, shepherds playing pipes, flutes, bagpipes and drums as a Christmas serenade. These same men had been coming to his house for the last fifteen years, so they and Mr Esposito knew each other well. They came down from Avellino and stayed in the city for eight or nine days, playing their music and collecting people's contributions.

On Christmas Eve, many attend the midnight mass. But for all, whether practising or lapsed Catholics, atheists, Protestants, Christmas is celebrated with a large meal starting after midnight. Ideally this should be attended by a large family group, although some said they would be happy to spend the evening with friends. This was unlikely, however, amongst the people I frequented, since all spent the evening with their families. It was important that the food be very abundant in such a meal, which would consist of a number of dishes, starting with broccoli or other green vegetables cooked with pine nuts and currants, then *vermicelli* with clams, followed by *insalata di rinforzo*,[6] *capitone*,[7] lamb, nuts, dried fruits, fresh fruit, Christmas cakes, *panettone* and *cassatta*. The meal is taken slowly, dish by dish, and goes on for several hours. At the end of the meal champagne and *spumante* are served and the family will indulge in games of tombola until weariness has the better of them. Next day, the procedure starts all over again, in preparation for Christmas Day. As a concession to the large meal consumed the evening before the first dish is relatively light: a soup or *tortellini*. But a similar sequence of dishes follow one another, from 3 or 4 o'clock in the afternoon until late. New Year's Eve involves similar preparations and consumption, but the younger members of the family are likely to celebrate independently of their families.

Christmas provides many opportunities for family reunions. There are a number of activities which focus on the home and the family, and for a considerable period up until Christmas, many activities focus attention on one's family, relatives and friends. At the same time, given the consensus that existed surrounding these matters, there was also a sense in which this celebration was accomplished in a particularly Neapolitan style. The experience of Christmas was therefore both a family and a Neapolitan experience. Food provided the focus for many, many hours around a table, when, perhaps for the only day of the year, all relatives would be reunited. The predetermined sequence of dishes generated consensus and a perceived continuity of years of family gatherings which summed up years of family life. The mother takes a central role, which, however, is usually performed with modesty. She would not fail the expectations that her children and perhaps her children's children have of her special rendering of the *capitone* or the *strufoli*.

So food, whether the special food of celebrations or the food of daily life, can be the conductor within an emotional triangle linking the self to the mother and to one's place. Thus, certain things are done because 'we are Neapolitans'. This makes Neapolitans different from others: different kinds of Catholics, different kinds of Communists, different kinds of Italians. These three elements are in constant dialogue, expressing both who one is and explaining why this should be so.

The Neapolitan socio-religious calendar offers many other opportunities for the expression of family unity. The celebration of '*i morti*' is another important occasion, where the family looks further back into its history and pays homage to its dead. On All Soul's Day, the family will visit the cemetery and in turn leave flowers and offer their remembrance to dead parents and grandparents.[8] The cemetery buzzes with activity on that day; crowds fill the aisles to reach the niches of their kin. Outside the cemeteries, in the main streets of the neighbourhoods of Naples, stalls offer toys, candy-floss, different varieties of *torrone*. The atmosphere is one of a happy family outings, a celebration. The city also offers more profane and more local opportunities for family enjoyment, such as the festival of Piedigrotta and its carnival atmosphere, which is looked forward to by all, and adds another layer to the experience of being Neapolitan.

Kinship and Social Memory

The family provides the context for experiences which constitute subjects as gendered individuals, whereby rights, duties, roles and expectations are expressed and internalized consciously and unconsciously; and, as an integral aspect of the same process, these subjects also internalize a sense of belonging and acquire a sense of place. Family life generates experiences which are constitutive of wider identities that largely rely on the emotional potency of intimate relationships. Kinship can then be seen to define individual places in a society and at the same time provide the language for the construction of a sense of community. These themes are explored within recent work in the study of kinship which links family and society by looking at social memory and identity. Zonabend's collaborative and extended study of a village in Burgundy, for example, stresses the importance of kinship for the construction of individual identities, for 'social man, a man who is first and foremost a member of a kin group. It is kinship that is at the base of society' (1984: 202). This is because:

> All discussion of a person is first of all made up of proper names and indications of relationship. One is above all a father, son, spouse or brother of such and such an individual mentioned by name. Absence of such guide marks indicates 'the stranger' . . . Family names, the real tools of memory, place an individual in his descent and situate him in a known time and space. (ibid., 142)

This means that every individual is fixed in space and time through genealogical knowledge. Past and present, kindred and community are intermingled, and kinship and family history provide the principal channels through which social identity is constructed. So the family is also important in structuring the identities of groups, as family history intertwines with the history of the village and as social memory draws on genealogies to recall and recreate events from the past. This family time is independent of History, and can in fact structure the events of History, anchoring them to genealogies and to past generations of kin. These forms of recall are important for forging group identities, as each group invents and creates its own history; but they also forge a village identity and a sense of unity, based on the idea that in the past the village was one large family. The village is identified with a family and a group of relatives, 'as if living there implied an ideology of blood relationship and family feeling' (ibid., 202). Because kinship is seen as generative of solidarity, identities constructed from kinship are also perceived as being solidary.

Similarly, Bestard incorporates oral history into his account of change in Formentera. Here too genealogies provided the means of representing social continuity. Family histories, retold through genealogies, represented very particular accounts of the past and provided a framework for understanding the social world. Kinship also provided symbols which were relevant beyond the domestic sphere and were to do with local models of hierarchy, status and identity (Bestard 1986: 10).

For Zonabend, family and community time create a sense of unity in the village, whilst also creating a sense of the Other, since 'the collective memory conceives the notion of otherness, where possession of a history that is not shared gives the group its identity' (Zonabend 1984: 203). In these recollections, some memories were highlighted, whereas others were forgotten. Amnesia surrounded events from the World Wars, which had created rifts within the village. Collard too found that the social memory recounted in a Greek village spoke in detail of the experiences under Ottoman domination, whilst it remembered nothing of the Civil War. Again, the point was to avoid those events which would exacerbate internal divisions, privileging instead those events which represented the village as a unified whole (Collard 1989).

In the process of constructing community history, History is itself concealed and its duration reduced and controlled. So as Chapman, McDonald and Tonkin point out, an individual or group 'has no one identity, but a variety (a potentially very large variety) of possibilities, that only incompletely or partially overlap in social time and social space' (Chapman et al. 1989). Identities are therefore fluid, fragmented and even contradictory.

The sense of identification with a locality has been discussed at some length in Italy, where it is known as *campanilismo* (Silverman 1955).

This refers to a strong attachment to one's village or the area near the *campanile* or church spire, and a corresponding sense of rivalry towards other localities. However, these very localized loyalties can be extended. Bell shows there is a tendency in the villages he studied for marriages with 'outsiders' to increase, but rather than dilute the phenomenon of *campanilismo* as might be expected, this has led instead to 'an extension of its scope over more space and new space. Village attachments gave way to regionalism . . .' (Bell 1979: 162). He suggests that there is some continuity between these very localized attachments and wider identities, in that nationalism contains all the elements of *campanilismo*, most clearly expressed within fascist nationalism. Pratt too argues that 'the ideology of nationalism shares many of the characteristics of *campanilismo*, and in its structure and imagery is often a simple transposition of the ideology of local sub-national identities' (Pratt 1980: 43). At the same time we have seen how family history provides the elements and structure for village histories and identities. There are thus cross-cutting themes, symbols and sentiments between family and kinship and local and supralocal identities.

Urban Identity and Civic Awareness

In Naples there was a simultaneous recognition of differences in wealth, status and power and of belonging to a common and rather specific social reality. Indeed, Belmonte writes of the 'urban patriotism of lower-class Neapolitans', which he found to be the 'only meaningful collective sentiment, regularly expressed, that transcended class boundaries' (Belmonte 1979: 40). This sense of 'urban patriotism' finds its roots in the history of Naples, which, as we have seen in earlier chapters, has repeatedly involved domination by powers which were, or were perceived to be, foreign. Furthermore, these rulers were unable to break down the localism and fragmentation that characterized their realm.[9]

The urban nature of Neapolitan identity is important here. As Gramsci points out, Naples has been a 'city of silence', meaning a city which rather than being based on industrialization is instead based on a relationship of dependence with the countryside. It was in Naples that most of the landed classes, whether aristocratic or commoner, lived and spent the income they derived from the countryside. The economy of such a city is parasitic, reminding Gramsci of the proverb: 'Where a horse shits a hundred sparrows feed' (Gramsci 1973: 283). The dependence on the countryside translates into an attitude of disdain towards rural populations, creating divisions between the city and the rural areas which have been activated at different times in the political history of the South, as in the defeat of the Parthenopean

Republic in 1799.

In Naples, as in other cities of this kind, there is what Gramsci calls an 'urban ideological unity' against the rural areas. The opposition between the styles and values associated with urban living and those thought to attach to rural populations was expressed by many of those who had been born and bred in the city of Naples and who disliked the *'cafoni'* (country bumpkins) of the suburbs and the hinterland. These were seen as being physically different: darker-skinned, harsher in features and heavier in body. They were also perceived as being different culturally: more backward, less refined and less educated than the urban folk. However, these same stereotypes were extensible to urban categories, and Neapolitans often used these same terms to describe themselves and/or their neighbours, especially in comparisons with foreigners, whether Italian or otherwise. This reversal of the content of the us/them distinction which was applied against rural dwellers, now places Neapolitans in an ambiguous position, an aspect, perhaps, of Gramsci's observation that the contradictions between the city and the countryside are reproduced on a national level, in the divisions between the North and the South. Here, the North would be the structural equivalent of the city and the South would be the enslaved countryside, subordinate to the demands of the North (Macciocchi 1974: 142), a subordination which is recognized in Neapolitan self-identity.

The population of Naples has a reputation for lacking in civic consciousness, a lack which has frequently been attributed to the external character of government and the weakness of the local dominant classes.[10] The nobility was concentrated in Naples and lived largely off the abusive use of its powers in the countryside; it dominated rather than ruled and 'was never able to become an organ for the expression of a national conscience' (Croce 1944: 167). A sense of identity and patriotism did evolve, but without this implying an identification with government or a strong sense of civic duty (Croce 1944: 188). In fact Croce quotes Laurenze, writing in 1804, as saying:

> Se lealtà, onore, fermezza, fedeltà alle istituzioni, devozione alla patria, decoro dei costumi, virtù sociali e grandi memorie sono ciò che costituisce veramente un carattere nazionale, i napoletani non hanno carattere nazionale e sembrano possedere invece le qualità a esso opposte (1944:224).

> (If loyalty, honour, steadfastness, fidelity to their institutions, devotion to their country, decorousness in their customs, civic virtues and memories of great events are what truly constitute a national character, Neapolitans do not have a national character, and seem in its place to possess the opposite qualities.)

He also quotes a contemporary English general, Moore, as saying: 'There is nowhere else in the world so lacking in public spirit as Naples' (ibid., 225).

One of the obstacles to the development of a more positive identification with 'a common good' that would encompass public authority and the State was the way in which the struggles and objectives of the Risorgimento were compromised in the South, ending in the suppression of peasant demands and in the upholding of the privileges of the landed classes, which did little to allay distrust towards central authority in general and the new Italian state in particular. There have been times when the Neapolitan populace did identify with authority, to the extent that it rose several times in support of the Bourbon monarchy.[11] Furthermore, the *lazzaroni* or lumpen-proletariat supported the claimants to the Bourbon throne for long after the unification of Italy.[12] The support gained by the powerful from the poorest and weakest has at different moments been a factor in the failure of more 'progressive' movements. For example, Pisacane, a Neapolitan noble, attempted to raise a 'national army' of liberation against the Austrian army. But Pisacane was killed after the failure of a landing which took place near Naples in 1857, at the hands of peasants who were led by the landowners and the leaders of the Church, in circumstances which reminded Macciocchi of Che Guevara's defeat in Bolivia (Macciocchi 1974: 145).

The question of Neapolitan identity, and more generally Southern identity and its relationship to public authority and to the Italian state has been a contested one,[13] both in intellectual and political writings and debates and also in the history and attitudes of the people of Naples. Here the attitude to government and the outside world has been ambivalent, coupling a sense of pride with one of inferiority, a strong sense of place with a distrust of the powers that be, a fervent religiosity with a cynical opinion of the clergy. The history of Naples has fostered such a sense of distance, lack of control and non-participation in government. Distrust has found expression in the perception of a discontinuity between government and locality, and between private life and public life. An ideological opposition has associated the private sphere with the values of the family and kinship, or in other words, with the morality of reciprocity and generosity, contrasting it with the amorality associated with the public sphere.

The Public, the Private and the Transmission of Identity

The opposition between the public and the private also underlies many analyses of gender relations. For Chodorow, for example, the private sphere is associated with women and has had the effect of restricting female subjectivity. And although Parsons does not utilize the public–private dichotomy in her analysis she does argue that the home represents a safe place, opposed to what is seen as a hostile and dangerous world. The street is the male sphere and is particularly dangerous to women, whereas the safe area of the home is essentially female.

Women, then, are closely associated with the private sphere of the home in these works, and are seen to play a key role in the reproduction of social relations of kinship and neighbourhood. Because of this, they are also central to the reproduction of local identities and the transmission of social memory. For example, in the village of Minot described by Zonabend, the transmission of the oral tradition of the group took place according to a well-established process: 'At the *veillée*, one approached the grandmothers and talked of past times . . .' (1984: 4). In Minot, then, it was the older generation of women who bore most of the responsibility for passing on memories to future generations. Where women play central roles in the family and in reproducing relations with kin and neighbours, they will also play a crucial role in the formation of memory.

This raises important considerations for Buttafuoco (1993), who asks whether we are talking about *female* remembrance or whether instead it is *the task of remembering* which is female. Women are the bearers of group memories which are transmitted through women, so that women are the keepers of memories which are not their own. However, she also postulates the existence of a 'gender' memory which mainly takes place through physical experiences, intimately linked to those aspects of the body which are specific to women. These are experiences such as menstruation, pregnancy, childbirth.

But if women remember by their bodies, societies too remember through the bodies of women. The specific experiences of women are appropriated by wider discourses, taking on other, more general and disembodied meanings. Indeed, Irigaray argues that the very discourses which define women are male discourses. In any case gender, sexuality and kinship can generate symbols that can be mobilized within 'collective representations' and in the construction of group identities and ideologies. And it is precisely such cultural markers of women as virginity and motherhood that are privileged symbols in the expression of group identity (Anthias and Yuval-Davis 1989). There are two levels to be considered here: on the one hand, the deployment of symbols anchored in the family and in gender ideals by states and dominant groups in order to legitimate their position (Caldwell 1978; Kandiyoti 1989) and on the other the ways in which women, because of their structural position, are active in reproducing ethnic identities, whether directly, through their nurturing role (Anthias and Yuval-Davis 1989; O'Brien 1994) or indirectly, because of their mediating role.

Mediation is a theme that emerges repeatedly in these discussions, where women are seen as mediating between men, between families and groups, between the past and the present, the local and the national. Central here are the sexuality and the reproductive capacity of women, which become a focus of these relations of mediation. Bodies, in particular women's bodies, can become a symbol and a means of conceptualizing social and cultural boundaries (Douglas 1966), and the mediating role of women makes them outsiders who nevertheless carry much of the responsibility for social reproduction. Women are simultaneously insiders and outsiders, and are therefore potentially dangerous, because, while being at the margins of the group, they are crucial to the group's survival and integrity.

The pronounced social responsibility of women in defining and maintaining group boundaries means that their own individual 'integrity' must be safeguarded. By the very process of their control by men and their relegation to and identification with the domestic sphere, women are in a unique position to provoke a crisis within the group. Their identification with the intimate and the nurturing spheres of life mean that they are capable of undermining the boundaries of the private and intimate life of a group.

This was illustrated when a scandal was provoked by the revelations of a woman fruit-picker who lived in the suburbs of Naples. She had told a television crew how, while at work in a field, she had had a miscarriage (*aborto bianco*). She told her story in her own words, in her own dialect, and used a gesture to indicate the size of the lost fetus. When the interview was shown on national television, her town reacted angrily, especially her husband and the other women fruit-pickers. At a meeting held to try to resolve the crisis, the women admitted that miscarriages in the fields were frequent. Most of the women had experienced miscarriages as a result of the heavy work in the fields or because they had deliberately provoked them. The woman had spoken the truth about their hardships, but she had unwittingly revealed much more than they wished the world to know about themselves. She had exposed something very private about themselves as a group, and this exposure would encourage the world to label them as backward and ignorant. Their sense of dignity would have been protected had she explained these things in Italian. Instead, she had used their language and their gestures, which had opened a door into their most intimate experiences as women, but also as women belonging to a particular group and a particular town and region.

Language is an important element in the definition of identity, but the relationship between identity and language is complex. In her discussion of St Llorenç de Cerdans, a small town in French Catalunya, O'Brien points out the importance of women in the transmission of language and identity (O'Brien 1994). Here there is an interesting inversion of the relations which represent and reproduce identities related to the State and to the locality. Considerations of social status favour the use of French, especially amongst young women. Catalan, on the other hand, is associated with men and the male sphere of the café, of drinking groups, or hunting and a number of other activities which exclude young women. Catalan is seen as a rough and masculine language, whilst French is considered genteel and more appropriate for young women. As women grow older they enter another cultural world, which, although almost exclusively female, is Catalan. However, women as mothers are under pressure to educate their children in French, in order to offer them as many opportunities as possible of becoming successful French citizens.

As in Minot, grandparents are important in St Llorenç as 'reservoirs of Catalan culture and customs' (O'Brien 1994: 205). Grandmothers speak mainly in Catalan, and are the principal source of knowledge about Catalan culture and about family history. The shift in language use during different stages of the life-cycle is exclusively a female phenomenon. This is because women, unlike men, 'play a central role in the ideological reproduction of the collective identity of the community' (ibid., 206). In St Llorenç the contradictory nature of identity is revealed, expressing the hegemonizing strategies of the French state and the responsive strategies of the Catalan community, at once attempting to ensure success in the national society whilst preserving cultural identity.

In the Neapolitan case Italian was also perceived as the 'official' language. This was considered to be the appropriate language for use in a public arena such as the media or political speeches. Neapolitan, on the other hand, was expressive of the intimate and the private. But Neapolitan was often seen as an inferior language. Men, and especially older women, would struggle with Italian when speaking to outsiders, partly as a concession to the advantages of speaking in a shared language but also because Italian was considered a more polite and refined medium. For many the use of Italian was difficult, and they were frequently apologetic about this. As is the case with French in St Llorenç, speaking 'proper Italian' was important in getting work as a state functionary, a job that many aspired to for themselves or for their children. However, the reality was such that the majority found a number of more or less precarious work arrangements in which the use of Italian was irrelevant. There was some sense in which older women, the poorer sections of the population, and those living in the outskirts were less confident and more apologetic about their use of Italian. Only a few of the younger and more politically aware men and women were assertive and positive about the use of Neapolitan.

The incident in the Neapolitan agrotown illustrates the link between language and disclosure. It also reveals the association felt to exist between group identity as perceived by women and those intimate experiences of women as they are predominantly defined, that is experiences related to their sexuality and their reproductive capacities, those gender-specific memories referred to by Buttafuoco. These experiences should not be disclosed, for disclosure makes one vulnerable. Because these memories do not belong entirely or exclusively to women, revelation renders the entire group vulnerable.

In Naples the private domain, which was associated with women, was also seen as a place of safety and of acceptable morality. The sense of safety is heightened by and embodied in the mother's role, both within ideological discourses and in everyday practices and experiences. Food was part of the formation of relationships and the evolution of a sense of personhood, and what food did was to provide a medium for the expression of statuses and the values attached to them. In particular, one's place in the family was expressed through the giving and receiving of food. Nurturing was seen as characterizing the relationship with the mother, which in turn represented the relationship of the individual with the family. These ideas of home and place feed into identities ranging beyond the family, to the neighbourhood and the city itself.[14]

Motherhood and Social Boundaries

The centrality of motherhood provides important sources of symbols for Neapolitan identity. The attributes of motherhood come to represent the integrity of the group – whether this be the family or the community – against the negative effects of systems which operate according to different moralities. Both capitalism and the State are seen to be based on principles deprived of personal content, where personal considerations are irrelevant. Here, calculation and gain overrule reciprocity and self-sacrifice. Profit is seen as the aim of capitalist production, and this is seen as being accomplished through exploitation, through patterns of work which are disadvantageous to the weaker parties. The capitalist work context implies inequality and exploitation. Similarly, the State is perceived as distant, unwieldy, misusing those it is supposed to protect or inadequate when it does attempt to protect them. Women, on the other hand, when located in the context of the family, stand for self-negation and generosity. Women as kin stand for the positive identity of the poor of the city and for an opposition to the amorality of work and State.

It is women's sexuality which is at the centre of social discourses relating to identity. It is precisely through their sexuality that women assume their symbolic role, whether as virgins or, more importantly, as mothers. The embodiment of positive morality in the mother-figure has significant implications for women. It reinforces the role of motherhood as a positive model for women's fulfilment and self-realization. It also informs the ways in which men perceive women. If their point of departure is the mother, and all positive images derive from here, all other women, women who do not constitute part of the universe of family, kin and neighbours, are a negative reflection of this. A corollary of the centrality of motherhood is the split in the male perception of women, whereby some women are good and some, the outsiders, are bad. Women of the group, who stand for the group, deserve respect and protection. On the other hand, 'other' women are not conceded this respect, and instead become victims of male predatory interest or are potentially disruptive of the existing social order.

If motherhood is the desired goal and represents the true fulfilment of women, other activities that remove or distance a woman from the tasks of nurturing and caring for her family endanger her ability to fulfil her role. This was generally accepted by men and women in Naples, who were concerned both with the practicalities involved in women's performing several roles at once and with the subjective problems relating to their reputation.

The fact that women's participation in wage work elicited strong emotions can be attributed to the perceived contradiction in their ideal status and in the ways in which the work situation is defined. For 'good' women, their participation and performance within what were seen as the amoral relations of the public sphere, of capitalist work, of the politics and the State, is in contradiction to their status. This means that women, as mothers, wives, sisters and daughters, are at risk when placed in the context of impersonal, exploitative relations such as those that prevail in the factory. There were a number of concerns expressed by informants on this, but all were to do with anxieties concerning the 'corruption' of the women. A woman in such a context would be in contact with 'other' women, women who are not kin, who do not belong to the social world of her family. Women workers were themselves preoccupied by this, and often said that they did not like the 'atmosphere' of the factory. Generally these were women who did not work, but also women with factory experience expressed concern about their daughters' working in such an 'ambiente'. Men sometimes explained that these 'other' women 'had funny ideas in their heads', which could be dangerous.

Another anxiety, more openly expressed by non-working women than by men, was that women would be sexually corrupted. Women who had been housewives all their lives might accuse those who worked in the factories or fields of being 'whores'. Yet contact between workers in a factory situation was in fact limited. The pace of work was such that little conversation was possible, except during rather brief lunch-breaks. Furthermore, contact between male and female workers was generally reduced to a minimum. In most factories the division of labour was such that there were separate male and female departments. Often these were physically segregated, being on separate floors, for example.

Although very few cases of workplace sexual liaisons were encountered during fieldwork and these always involved single women, the stereotyped anxiety of seduction at work seemed to persist. This might result from the recognition of the relations of inequality which govern the work relationship. A woman in a factory is doubly vulnerable: as a worker and as a woman. Her subjection to factory discipline and to the authority of her (in most cases) male employer, was seen as creating the opportunity for abuse of the employer–employee relationship. This means that, far from accepting the capitalist work context as clearly impersonal and formalized, there was instead a recognition that in fact there were continuities between the personal and the public, the subjective and the material. There was an awareness that sexuality and sentiment cannot in fact be limited to one area of life and experience. The woman, the mother, takes her qualities with her when she becomes a worker. There is therefore a danger that these qualities can be used or abused in the public sphere. This is in contrast with official representations of capitalist work and of the public arena, which are seen ideally as being expurgated of the personal, of the sentimental and of the sensual, and where sexual contact is interpreted as a quite different phenomenon from sexual contact elsewhere in life. Instead, the workplace and work relations are constructed through ideas of gender and sexuality which constitute an integral aspect of the vertical nature of work relations. Neapolitan men and women recognize this, and anticipate the possibility and potential of sexual abuse as a corollary of economic abuse.

The sphere of political action is similarly seen as amoral and as essentially male, or more precisely, as unsuitable for women. Women themselves tended to recoil from politics and all discussion of politics. They claimed ignorance or explained that 'they didn't have the head for politics'. A large number of women interviewed voted according to their husbands' preferences. Some women had abandoned family tradition by voting as their husbands instructed. Others disapproved of their husband's allegiance, but complied anyway. Generally women were able to discuss a wide range of issues which could be defined as political. However, they approached them from a different perspective, one which defined the issues in other than political terms. For instance, women could talk about the cost of living, changes in the availability of goods and services, and about laws concerning the family, whilst refusing to talk 'politics'.

Whereas the opposition between the different moralities of capitalism and the family suggests a differential involvement of women and men in these, it is important to recognize that the dichotomy between private and public is neither spontaneous nor concrete. In fact, persons and activities, forms and institutions straddle the public and the private, move between these conceptual fields, operate in both, as both, simultaneously. Furthermore, the distinction does not emerge naturally from Neapolitan culture or the Neapolitan family. Instead, historical processes have been active. Whereas history has shaped Neapolitan conscience and family strategies, in the post-war period the State has acted quite deliberately in the sense of promoting familism in the South (see Chapter 8). It is therefore important to stress that the opposition expressed at various points and the differences described between the public and the private are not the result of natural differences but are instead the consequence of historical processes and of State policies which have found it convenient to underwrite familial ideologies in their deployment of Catholic ideologies and their economic and political projects for the South and for Italy as a whole (Gribaudi 1980).

Conclusion

Neapolitan identity is firmly grounded in what are seen as the positive attributes of family life. Kinship solidarity provides a template for wider sets of relationships and identities which, while mobilized under particular circumstances, may not always be realized in everyday life. Nevertheless reciprocity persists as an ideal, and is seen as characterizing the private sphere, which is the area of safety. Because women are central both to concrete household and family strategies and to the idealization of the family and its morality, they take on special responsibility for the integrity of the family unit. As Schneider (1971) pointed out, women are a convenient metaphor for expressing the boundaries of the group. But whereas Schneider sees virgins as occupying the primary symbolic space here, in Naples this space is dominated by the figure of the mother.

Food provides a most important medium for the exchanges that take place within the family and for the construction and expression of family relations and sentiments. At the same time, these experiences are seen as belonging simultaneously to the realm of family and to the realm of local identity. Family experiences, objectified in the consumption of certain foods, contribute in important ways to creating a sense of belonging and of a specific, Neapolitan, identity.

Motherhood is the dominant idea behind these relations, and it is the point where positive experiences and relations meet. The mother personifies reciprocity and abnegation. The two complexes identified by Parsons – the courtship and the Madonna complexes – are resolved through motherhood. The contradictions she identifies between male and female spheres and between individual men and women are also resolved through motherhood or more broadly through parenting. Children are the desired outcome of all marriages, and to some extent male, but more especially female, identity is constructed around this. But while motherhood determines male and female subjects, defines their universe and conditions their options, it also becomes a central element in the construction of wider identities. This happens concretely through the experience of nurturing, the memory of the past that underlines the mother's position in the family, and through the idealization of the mother within Neapolitan culture. Women become the bearers of identity, and they do so especially as mothers and potential mothers, in other words, as 'good women'. The corollary here is that the possibility that their potential might be undermined, through undesirable sexual contact or through association with 'bad women', generates anxieties and constrains women's space and agency.

Women's sexuality is intertwined with these different levels of meaning and identity, and at the same time women have difficulty in establishing a space for themselves which can be empty of sexual content. On the contrary, women's reputations are largely judged or expressed in sexual terms, so that being a poor housewife is tantamount to being dirty, which is, in turn, tantamount to being promiscuous. On the other hand, there are some indications that even where what might be considered to be immoral sexual behaviour is engaged in, a woman may not be condemned, so long as this behaviour was forced on her by circumstances and it could be seen as an act of self-sacrifice.[15]

The burden of identity is carried by women. They are expected, and they themselves expect, to be guided by a spirit of self-sacrifice. This is seen as an integral aspect of mothering, but might under extraordinary circumstances call upon women to go beyond nurturing, to do extraordinary things, whether to sell their bodies, or to sell their labour. The important point is that a woman should not be guided by self-interest, for the needs of others are her main inspiration. Ultimately, it is her capacity to sublimate her own needs and to subordinate her own desires that makes 'a good woman'.

In spite of the discontinuities that are felt to obtain between the family and the external world, the experiences of individuals, as family members and as members of communities, constitute a web which involves the different fields of action within which they participate. The family is far from constituting a separate field of relations, actions and feelings. Nor does family structure reflect ideologies of egalitarianism and reciprocity. Instead, the family is an integral part of social and political processes and is integral to issues of power, authority and economic rationality. The family experience does not determine individuals, who they are and what they become, in any simple way, but kinship does ground people by constituting subjectivities differentially. It provides the elements with which the individual subject grapples as part of the process of living. They can, in dealing with their lives, subvert, confirm, reproduce or alter the meanings and the contents of these subjectivities and ideals.

Notes

1. *Maccheroni al ragu* refers to pasta served with a meat sauce and *salsicce e friarielli* refers to Neapolitan sausages cooked with fried greens.
2. *Strufoli* are small balls of dough which are fried, piled high and served covered with honey, almonds and small multicoloured confetti.
3. Lina Pietravale was a Barese who lived and died in Naples in 1956. She was a well-known writer during the 1920s and 1930s. She is quoted by J. Caròla Francesconi (1977).
4. Tomatoes are used raw and cooked, for salads and sauces. They are used fresh during the season or as canned tomatoes or as concentrate during other times of the year. Conserve can also be produced at home to be used on its own or in conjunction with the commercial product to add flavour. Boxes of San Marzano tomatoes are purchased at the height of the season (preferably in August) and prepared in a number of different ways to cater for the massive use of tomatoes in everyday cooking. The home-made product was considered to be cheaper and infinitely superior to the commercial variety.
5. The art of pastry- and sweet-making was a predominantly female art, but not one primarily attached to the home. According to Caròla Francesconi (1977), from approximately 1500 onwards there are references to the convent as a place where sweet pastries were made. Some of these became famous for their delicacies, which sometimes took their names from the nunneries that had created them. After 1860 many convents were confiscated, and following that the art declined. However, commercial producers and outlets took over. Those sweets which are generally prepared at home for special occasions seem to derive not from the convents but from 'profane' society, and some have their roots in Roman and Greek times.
6. *Insalata di rinforzo* is a salad made from cauliflower and pickled vegetables, traditionally eaten at Christmas
7. *Capitone* is an eel-like fish. Because it is traditionally prepared for Christmas, the price of this fish climbs dramatically as the season approaches. This has induced some families to forsake the *capitone* and replace it with lamb.
8. There is a long tradition of visiting the dead in Naples. The visitors are usually women, and they may visit people who are long dead and who are not relatives but with whom they strike up a special relationship. They will visit the catacombs, stroke the stone and talk at length to the dead. This is

seen as a further manifestation of women's close relationship to the religious and the supernatural. For a discussion of religious practice in Naples see Pardo (1989).

9. Sometimes these rulers might come to be seen as 'belonging' to the people, although usually only in contrast to other, more recent rulers. Croce suggests there was nostalgia for the French Anjou rulers during the period of Spanish rule; and more recently, after 1860, there was nostalgia for the Normans. Yet the Norman monarchy, while putting an end to the autonomy of the maritime states in the South of Italy, was not successful in forging a nation. Sicilians remained Sicilians, Neapolitans Neapolitan, Pugliesi were always Pugliesi, and so on (Croce 1944: 13). Local identities remained especially strong in the South. Furthermore, as we have seen, as a capital Naples occupied a special place in the South prior to Unification. This contributed to Naples' particular character and to a strong sense of identity, as from the early fifteenth century a Neapolitan culture and literature developed and slowly the interests of the Kingdom came to be identified with the interests of Naples.

10. The sense of political autonomy and integrity has varied during the history of Naples. When the South became a Spanish viceroyalty autonomy was completely lost and the area was left without any political life of its own. Attempts to rebel met with harsh repression. On the other hand, the city prospered by the concentration of the nobility living in the centre and the Spanish, Catalan or Genoese families that were brought into the city to service the needs of the Spanish Crown. The expansion of a wealthy class offered enormous opportunities for merchants, artisans and servants. The hinterland on the contrary obtained few if any benefits, and continued to suffer the abuse of barons and the invasion of outsiders. Whereas the Spanish Crown offered some protection from outside invasions, especially to the cities, and in the later period of the viceroyalty also contained baronial abuse in the countryside to a greater extent, it is also true that the population of Naples was directly affected by the ups and downs of Spanish foreign policy. Thus, taxes increased as the Spanish Crown attempted to support its growth. Rebellions were not infrequent responses to the increasing tax burden. On the other hand, according to Croce the Spanish controlled and disciplined their soldiers and imposed respect towards women. Croce warns against the idea that the Spaniards were regarded with the hatred that has characterized the view of other outsiders who have conquered and ruled other Italians (Croce 1944: 150).

11. The *lazzaroni* of Naples supported the monarchy against the experiment of the bourgeois Parthenopean Republic in 1799, in the *Sanfedista* rising. The Republic was founded by a 'Jacobin' bourgeoisie with support from a large proportion of the Neapolitan aristocracy. French influence prevented implementation of their revolutionary aims, particularly in the countryside. This facilitated the intervention of Cardinal Ruffo who, supported by the British who were keen to limit French influence in the area, raised the rural population against the Republic. With the withdrawal of French support the Republic was doomed and external pressures together with the struggle of the *Sanfedisti* brought the government down. Ruffo had promised leniency towards the followers of the Jacobins, but once reinstated the Bourbons reneged and instead they were brutally repressed. The bloodbath and the mass exile that followed the defeat had long-term effects, because they both decimated the intellectual population of the city and created long-lasting disdain towards the monarchy amongst many sectors of the population.

12. There was also support for the Bourbons amongst the upper classes and the intellectuals, most notably from Errico Malatesta, who was rumoured to

have a 'special relationship' with Maria Sophia, last Bourbon queen of the Kingdom of the Two Sicilies, who never ceased to intervene in the affairs of the new Italian Republic after her exile in 1861.

13. The question of identity has been discussed, debated, and fought over, not only at the level of 'popular' discourse but also amongst intellectuals. Here too there have been contradictory trends, ranging from the work of Niceforo to that of Guido Dorso. Niceforo, a sociologist and criminologist who taught in Naples in the latter years of the nineteenth century, proposed the natural inferiority of Southern Italians. He was not alone in supporting this position. There were also those whose understanding of the political and economic conditions of the South inspired radical proposals. Dorso, in *La Rivoluzione Meridionale*, called for the overthrow of the centralized Italian State and the downfall of the Southern land-owning classes. The South produced great thinkers who grappled with the problems of the Italian state and the social, cultural and political characteristics of the South, such as Croce, and especially Salvemini and of course Gramsci.

14. The emotional focus on mothers is not merely a private affair; it is stated in public expressions of Neapolitan culture, such as songs. One of the songs most frequently associated with Naples is Bixio's *Mamma*, where love for the mother seems to encompass all other sentiments and attachments: to the family, to home, to Naples. The son speaks of his love and longing for his mother and of the pain of separation. The idea is to return, never to leave again. He remembers his mother's hand in his hair, her voice singing cradle songs. There is the longing for reunion and the sense that he returns to take care of her in her old age. He asks what could possibly justify living far from home. We should not neglect the impact of the long history of emigration which characterizes Naples and its surrounding area. Mothers were usually the focus for memories and communication, and at their death contact was often interrupted or weakened. The experience of exile has enhanced both a sense of belonging and a sense of loss in respect of the city, the family and most potently, the mother. Emigration and nostalgia are thus important aspects of popular culture, which has in various ways attempted to capture and express these experiences, which inform the sense of identity both of those who leave and those who stay.

15. This seemed to be the case of a woman who had been a prostitute. At that time she had had no alternative but to survive as a sex-worker, and she had 'sacrificed' herself for the well-being of her family. Her husband appeared to accept this situation, as did the women who were her neighbours, who under different circumstances would have been likely to be critical of this type of behaviour.

For an interesting discussion of these issues in relation to Cairo and Oman, see Wikan (1984).

eleven

Conclusions

Naples welcomed the 1990s with renewed hope. Bassolino's new administration has been energetic and innovative in its drive to bring about a renaissance of the once-great city, which over the years has gained more of a reputation for crime and decay than for its beauty. There are many daunting obstacles in the way of change, not least the problems involved in trying to generate employment and solve the dramatic effects of unemployment and underemployment that besiege the city. Furthermore, reforms and innovations have to be carried out in the face of reduced funding from central government: one of the first steps taken by Berlusconi's government in 1994 was to cut the flow of funds to local governments.

The problems of the city have not diminished during the 1980s. Research carried out by the Department of Sociology of the University of Naples indicates that, in 1995, in some areas of the city, 33 per cent of families are living below the poverty line, and 25 per cent of young people are unemployed.[1] At the same time, the informal economy has been dislocated by the effects of the 1981 earthquake. As families have been rehoused in the outskirts of Naples, their networks, and the well-established flow of goods and services, as well as the links between outworkers, artisans and enterprises, have been interrupted. New networks are emerging in the Neapolitan hinterland, as factories relocate in these areas. Experienced outworkers from the centre of the city may resume their contacts with employers, although entrepreneurs are also drawing on the inexperienced – and cheaper – residents of the Neapolitan hinterland.

The shoe industry has suffered a serious decline. Hundreds of firms have closed down, some of them small, some larger and established, but all of them starved of the funds needed to turn their firms around and meet the challenge of an increasingly difficult market. To the competition from Third World producers which emerged in the 1970s is now added the far more damaging impact of the European Union, which has meant that Southern Italian goods are being displaced by their cheaper Spanish and Greek counterparts.[2] The situation of the Neapolitan shoe trade contrasts with national trends: during the first nine months of 1994, the Italian shoe industry increased its output by 3 per cent and exports increased by more than 12 per cent. The majority of firms involved in this success started off as small artisan units, and have developed into large, computerized firms. In the Centre and North of the country, the shoe industry is becoming a highly technical trade, requiring suitable training and investments in computerized machinery. The emphasis on education is important here, and many enterprises have invested in the creation of Institutes to supply the trade with trained personnel.[3]

In 1991, 42.7 per cent of the population was unemployed, while the figure for unemployed youth was as high as 74.7 per cent (1991 Census, ISTAT). The problem of unemployment is not only reflected in the statistics. The Neapolitan invention of the 1970s, the *disoccupati organizzati*, has not disappeared after years of the Christian Democrat 'politics of welfare'. In 1994 a section of the unemployed who call themselves the 'historical' group to emphasize the antiquity of their claims, occupied the Duomo and only left the cathedral after long negotiations, which included the intervention of a cardinal. On 23 January 1995 two men and one woman were hospitalized as a result of a massive demonstration held by the unemployed from several lists, including the *'storici'*. Protesting outside the Palazzo San Giacomo where local government meets, they blocked the traffic by sitting in the road, burning wooden boxes and throwing traffic signs into the road. Violent skirmishes with the police ensued, in which clubs, stones and bottles were resorted to. The immediate cause of the demonstration was a meeting held by the leaders of the local government to set up the next Council meeting. The unemployed wanted to have placed on the agenda the issue of government-sponsored training. The expectation was that one thousand posts would be offered and the organized unemployed argued that in the selection process they should be given precedence over other candidates such as the those who were on the official unemployment lists produced by the labour exchange. They felt they had done the fighting to obtain these concessions and they should be the first to reap the benefits of these victories. 'It was we who obtained them, with our struggle on the streets. And now they want to assign them to people who are at home: when people don't come out on the street to demonstrate, it means that they don't have a real need.' This was the explanation offered to Di Vincenzo, the correspondent from *Il Corriere della Sera,* on the day of the demonstration.

The closures of large plants like Italsider have had dramatic consequences, owing both to the direct loss of jobs and to the effect this can be expected to have on satellite firms. At the same time, there are indications that there is a trend for small enterprises to decline in the South as a whole: numerically, in terms of employment figures and in terms of productivity.

The causes of this decline are no doubt many and complex, but some insights emerge from the discussions included in this book. The first point to emerge is that the failure of small business in Naples and the South cannot simply be attributed to a lack of entrepreneurship within the local culture. There was no lack of inventiveness, resourcefulness or entrepreneurship amongst those interviewed. It has been suggested that in some small-scale units the relations of production impose limits to the expansion of the units.[4] In the majority of very small units a high percentage of workers are family, kin or neighbours of the head of the unit. Although there is no contradiction between exploitation and kinship, there is some indication that, while some forms of family relations and ideologies constitute an excellent basis for the creation of small businesses, enterprises benefit from opening up recruitment of staff to non-kin at certain points of their development. The cases of Central and North-eastern Italy tend to confirm this. As Capecchi (1989) and others have pointed out, the success of the small family enterprise on a regional basis here has been accompanied by a shift towards a lower dependence on family labour.

It is worth pointing out that much of this non-family labour recruited into the successful Emilian enterprises is technical staff. This means that the availability of highly trained technical workers constitutes an important resource for firms wishing to expand and/or to keep abreast of the market. In Central Italy expansion has in most cases meant transformation and greater investment in technology. As we have seen, technical training in Naples is scarce. Similarly, credit facilities are not readily available to the very small entrepreneur, who is therefore limited to operating on a limited scale, often with old and inefficient machinery.

As we have also seen, Neapolitans are resourceful and energetic. Many men and women in the interview sample expressed the wish to be autonomous, a wish which, in the case of men in particular, was very much oriented towards the experience of work. Giannola (n.d.) also suggests that it is not a lack of entrepreneurial spirit or ability that can explain the decline in productivity which is widening the gap between enterprises in the South and those in the Centre–North. As he and others (especially Nanetti 1988) have emphasized, we must take into account a number of factors related to the local environment. The question of availability of capital for investment is central here, and Southern enterprises are at a disadvantage. This was recognized by Ciampi, governor of the Bank of Italy in 1985, who argued that credit institutions in the South of Italy were less efficient and offered fewer advantages to their customers than did their equivalents in the Centre and North (Graziani, n.d.: 30). In addition, access to these institutions is limited. This means that some categories of would-be entrepreneurs may never have access to credit facilities. This is especially so in the case of women.

Given the significance of local conditions, the kinds of developments that have favoured enterprises elsewhere in the country, such as technological or organizational innovations or functional relationships between enterprises, have not been possible in the South. The same cost–benefit analyses and consequent strategies pursued by entrepreneurs in the Centre or North could be pursued in the South, but the impact of these would be quite different in the two cases. In the South there is little potential for the territorial integration of enterprises, little scope for innovations or for searching for and targeting new markets. The dictates of necessity, of keeping going, whether as individuals or as enterprises – the need to survive, in fact – impose a narrow and direct adaptation to the economic conditions of the areas, which precludes innovation and change in a positive direction (Giannola, n.d.).

Although the welfare-oriented interventions of the State in the South have resulted in improved consumption levels, the structural problems, such as unemployment, remain. In spite of higher incomes, the differences between the South and the North persist. Welfare policies are seen as offering at best a stagnant and at worst a declining future for the South. In any case, international pressures on government from the European Community in particular are likely to result in dramatic cuts in this field.

A number of responses have been put forward. For many leaders in the Confindustria (the union of entrepreneurs), the fact that Italy was still rated fifth economic power in the world at the beginning of 1995, in spite of unemployment, devaluations of the currency and the public debt crisis, is of little comfort. They are unsure of the country's future and attribute this uncertainty to the conduct of Italian politicians. For them it is imperative that Italy sort out its political affairs, which in the period between 1993 and 1995 have been particularly unstable, so as to prevent capital flight from the country and instead make Italy a more attractive investment option for international firms.[5]

Academics are also concerned with the situation, particularly in relation to the South. Some suggest that those measures taken by government to promote industrialization have, for all their limitations, had a growth-inducing effect. A historical review of government policy since the Second World War shows that the rate of creation of new enterprises of all sizes is positively correlated to industrialization programmes. The first category of enterprises to show signs of numerical growth were the large units (which peaked in the period from 1961 and 1965). But they were followed by increases in the medium and small categories (that is, units employing between 50 and 199 workers), which peaked in the period from 1971 to 1975. The very small units, consisting of 10–49 employees, also underwent a process of increase, which was sustained until 1975. After 1980 there was a reduction in the number of new firms in all categories. On the basis of this review, Giannola suggests that there is a positive connection between industrialization policies and local development (Giannola, n.d.). Graziani's analysis supports this, and he suggests that positive State intervention is a necessary prerequisite of growth in the South (Graziani, n.d.).

The fragility of small enterprises and the mobility and capacity for manoeuvre of enterprises in some trades were clearly a concern for the trade unions. Although their brief was to unionize workers employed throughout the range of different unit sizes and types, and their aim was to ensure that wages and work conditions complied with national regulations and trade agreements, they tended to proceed with a great deal of caution. They were aware that many enterprises operated on the basis of a very fine margin of profit, that they were in a weak position within national and international markets, and that for many, meeting trade union and government requirements would signify the end of their operations. Generally, the unions opted for a gradual improvement of conditions and for negotiations which were based on flexibility in these respects. Tipping the balance too far could result in the closure of the unit and the loss of jobs for those people whom the union was supposed to represent. A similar problem existed with the outworkers, for whom illegality was a major condition of existence. Payment of taxes and contributions was rarely in the interests of the employer, with the exception of the outworker teams, which, as we have seen, were able to secure proper contractual conditions. For the trade unions, organizing the outworkers was a near-to-impossible task given the difficulties involved in tracing outworkers and, once this is accomplished, of convincing them that it might be in their interest to become union members or join a league of outworkers. As we have seen, the majority were fearful that they would lose their jobs if they gave information or took any action which might be construed by the entrepreneur as conducive to providing outsiders with knowledge of and the ability to intervene in the enterprise's operations.[6]

In Italy there is a significant link between the family and the enterprise. For instance, a high percentage of male heads of family are entrepreneurs and a significant percentage of enterprises are constituted by family members. In the case of Naples we have also seen how family and kinship are indeed important to the formation of income-generating units, some of which can be defined as enterprises. Family and kinship structures provide important resources for the operation of these units, and family ideologies can help to mobilize support and labour. Yet research in other areas of Italy, coupled with the current trend towards the declining productivity of enterprises in the South, suggests a hypothesis that local and regional support structures are required to assist small enterprises, and indeed outworker units and teams, to move operations and recruitment beyond the networks created by family, kinship and neighbourhood.

Small-scale industries often relied heavily on the use of outworkers. This strategy was not restricted to small enterprises, however, for indeed the system of subcontracting also involved medium and large units. There can be little doubt that the use of outworkers benefited the parent-enterprise. Costs were avoided in connection with overheads and machinery, and some enterprises operated entirely or partially in the informal sector, thus avoiding tax and the application of legislation concerning health and safety, the employment of child labour and so on. Entrepreneurs also saved on labour costs, both by paying outworkers lower wages (which however was not a universal occurrence) and avoiding payment of contributions, holiday and sickness pay and maternity leave. This relates to arguments put forward by labour-market researchers such as Padoa-Scioppa (1977), who argued that legislation intended to protect women as mothers rendered their labour particularly costly, a fact that would encourage informal patterns of employment for women. Furthermore, Livraghi (1976), writing in the same period, argued that the rigidity of women's labour resulted from the rate of absenteeism of women workers. This rate was primarily a result of women's exclusive responsibility for family affairs and of the lack of adequate State provision to cover matters such as health, education and child-care. That there are links between household and family types and the patterns of women's participation in the labour-market has been demonstrated for many contemporary economies (Braidotti 1994). And although the material realities of households, such as divisions of labour, kinship networks, etc., are crucial here, we must also take into account the impact of ideological factors, particularly those pertaining to gender, sexuality and the family (Beneria and Roldán, 1991). And these are related to women's decisions, priorities, choices and perceptions of themselves and their reality.

Similar issues emerge in connection with small-scale industries. Households and family relations are an important focus for the activities of individuals and groups. Yet we have seen that although the household division of labour and family ideology are important for the survival and sometimes the success of a particular initiative, the benefits of kin-based strategies are not equally distributed. The result of these strategies is frequently that some children are privileged at the expense of others; girls are usually more constrained by the demands of the household, and often enjoy fewer opportunities to develop alternative lives and careers. Younger married couples often expressed a different approach to planning the future for themselves and their children. They hoped to have fewer children and offer equal educational opportunities for all, which meant relying on the continuation of parental support over a considerable period of time. So opportunities and alternatives are not only dictated by the concrete relations within which men and women live. In this book we have tentatively examined some of the social factors that condition the choice and action of individuals. The case of women is particularly significant because their actions are especially over-determined: by the household division of labour, by the labour-market, by ideologies of gender and familism. These conditions inform the construction of the subjectivity of women and men, which again shapes their aspirations, their choices and their capacities to deal with the challenges of everyday life. These are important because they help explain how and why men and women accept, reject or modify the ideals and expectations defined for them, and how they act upon them and reproduce them. In recognition of the importance of subjective factors in the reproduction of gender roles and ideals, which then feed into and construct the material relations of the household, as well as the work situation, or the experience of government, we have discussed Anne Parsons's important work on the relations which she saw as characterizing poor Neapolitan families, and have considered the implications of psychoanalytical and philosophical analyses of gender and family.

These issues are significant when understanding what processes are involved in the formation of gender identities and what are their implications. But the issue of gender identity is also relevant to the construction of wider, more encompassing identities. Neapolitan identity, in particular, derives much of its symbolic repertoire from the domestic sphere, and especially from the intimate relationships generated by love – and especially the nurturing love of the mother. Here too, as in the survival strategies of the poor and the struggle to improve the conditions of at least some of the members of the family, too much of the burden has been placed on the family. Within this, women, particularly as mothers and wives, have had to carry a disproportionate responsibility. Women have been constrained by these responsibilities, yet they have risen to the challenge admirably.

But while recognizing the resourcefulness of the Neapolitan people, one has to acknowledge that there are limitations to these material and ideological strategies. There are high costs to pay, in terms of the opportunities denied individual women and men, reflected both in the ideological and emotional boundaries which to varying degrees constrain them, and in the persistence of poverty and marked inequalities between Naples and cities of the Centre and North of the country. Growth and development that reaches the majority of the population cannot take place through individual effort and self-sacrifice alone. These men and women, these families and households must be supported by an environment which sustains their efforts and shifts the burden of responsibility from the family, from women, to 'the society'. Individual and group initiative has to be met with credit, with efficient infrastructures, with marketing support. One of the striking differences between Naples and areas in the Centre where small enterprises have been successful is the local provision of technical training. Making available appropriate training and technology, both to men and women workers, as well as recuperating the advantages offered by the holistic approach to training of the artisan system, would go some way to preparing them for a more positive and flexible economic strategy.

Neapolitan identity might be seen as atavistic, perhaps even as potentially dangerous and divisive. But it might also be seen as a compelling force which could be mobilized in the interests of the city. A critical review of Neapolitan identity and its history could be the point of departure for the development of that sense of civic society which historians and politicians have yearned for and which seems to have eluded this dynamic and inspired city for so long.

Notes

1. In contrast to the Neapolitan figures, in Bologna the percentage of those living below the poverty line is equal to 0.2 - 0.3%. The outcome of the research carried out by the University of Naples was commented upon by Maria Fortuna Incostante, adviser on Social Policy to the Bassolino administration. She suggested that the administration could promote, organize and coordinate the 'spontaneous', grass-roots activities that have sustained the urban poor in Naples for so long. This would involve, amongst other things, providing support and adequate services for the individuals and households in need (Pasquale Esposito, 'Disoccupazione e povertà', *Il Mattino*, 16 June 1995, p.13).

2. Interview with Maria Giuliano, Federazione Italiane Lavoratori Tessili e Abbigliamento (FILTEA), Naples, 1995.

3. However, in spite of the success of the shoe trade in these areas, and the promotion of training schemes, the trade is unable to recruit young people, who shun the possibility of a future in the shoe industry (*la Repubblica*, 20 February 1995, p.33).

4. Kahn (1980) is discussing petty-commodity producing units, and suggests that there are limits to the exploitation of labour in these units because of the nature of the relationships which constitute these units.

5. Although in terms of gross domestic product Italy is ahead of the UK, the UK leads when it comes to foreign investments. Britain absorbed 26% of foreign investments in Europe in 1993, whereas Italy only accounted for 6% of these, which in fact represented a fall from the 7% obtained in 1990 (G. Lonardi, 'Il prezzo dell'instabilità', *La Repubblica* 1 February 1995).

6. Mr Pavone, who had been a trade unionist in the immediate post-war period, remembered his numerous visits to Naples when he and some colleagues had succeeded in arranging meetings with outworkers and a league had been created.

Appendix I: Naples: A Brief Statistical Profile

1. Population

Number of residents:
1991: 3,016,026 (Province of Naples)

      1,067,365 (commune)
        513,860 (male)
        553,505 (female)

Population density:

1991: 7,433 persons per square km. (province)
      9,102 persons per square km. (commune)

Average family size (province):

1971: 4.5
1991: 3.5

Percentage of families with more than 5 members (province)

1971: 35.9%
1991: 25.5%

2. Labour Market

Rate of employment 1991 (commune)
Male: 55.4%
Female: 24.4%
Total: 39.3%

Rate of unemployment 1991 (commune)
Male: 39.9%
Female: 48.8%
Total: 42.7%

Rate of youth unemployment 1991 (commune)
Male: 72.6%
Female: 78.1%
Total: 74.7%

Source: *Censimento Generale della Popolazione e delle Abitazioni*, ISTAT, 20 October 1991.

Appendix II: Labour Force: Comparisons Between Northern and Southern Europe

	1	2	3	4	5
GREECE	48	66	39	12.9	34.0
ITALY	60	77	56	14.7	43.2
PORTUGAL	47	68	54	18.3	41.7
SPAIN	50	75	52	19.2	35.6
W. GERMANY	65	91	56	55.3	38.5
JAPAN	72	78	56	35.3	39.5
G. BRITAIN	74	93	57	45.3	?
USA	75	92	61	61.2	43.0
SWEDEN	83	95	62	65.4	46.5

Where:
1 = % active in total population over 15 years of age, 1981.
2 = wage earners as % of non-agricultural active population, 1981.
3 = % salaries in GDP 1983.
4 = industrial labour cost as % of Gross Industrial Product, 1980.
5 = women as % of total active population, 1983.

(From Hadjimichalis and Vaiou 1990, p. 91)

Bibliography

Allum, P. (1975). *Potere e Società a Napoli nel Dopoguerra*, Turin: Einaudi.
Anderson, B. (1983). *Imagined Communities. Reflections on the Origin and Spread of Nationalism*, London: Verso.
Anthias, F. and N. Yuval-Davis (1989). 'Introduction'. In *Woman–Nation–State* (ed. N. Yuval-Davis and F. Anthias), London: Macmillan.
Ascoli, U. (1987). 'Il sistema italiano di Welfare tra ridimensionamento e riforma'. In *La Società Italiana degli Anni Ottanta* (ed. U. Ascoli and R. Catanzaro), Rome/Bari: Laterza.
Ascoli, U. and R. Catanzaro (eds) (1987). *La Società Italiana degli Anni Ottanta*, Rome/Bari: Laterza.
Bagnasco, A. (1977). *Tre Italie. La Problematica Territoriale dello Sviluppo Italiano*, Bologna: il Mulino.
Balbo, L. (1976). *Stato di Famiglia*, Milan: Etas.
Banfield, E. (1958). *The Moral Basis of a Backward Society*, New York: Free Press.
Barbagallo, F. and M. D'Antonio (1976). 'Meridionalismo, Capitalismo, Socialismo', *La Voce*, Anno IV: 14.
Bell, R.M. (1979). *Fate and Honor, Family and Village – Demographic and Cultural Change in Rural Italy since 1800*, Chicago: University of Chicago Press.
Belmonte, T. (1979). *The Broken Fountain*, New York: Columbia University Press.
Beneria, L. and M. Roldán (1991). *The Crossroads of Class and Gender. Industrial Homework, Subcontracting and Household Dynamics in Mexico City*, Chicago and London: University of Chicago Press.
Berlinguer, G., L. Cecchini and F. Terranova (1977). *Gli infortuni sul lavoro dei minori*, Rome: il Pensiero Scientifico.
Bestard Camps, J. (1986). *Casa y Familia. Parentesco y Reproducción Doméstica en Formentera*, Palma de Mallorca: Institut D'Estudis Balearics. (English translation, 1991: *What's in a Relative? Household and Family in Formentera*, Oxford: Berg.)
Bettio, F. (1988). 'Women, the state and the family in Italy: problems of female participation in historical perspective'. In *Women and*

Recession (ed. J. Rubery), London: Routledge and Kegan Paul.

Bimbi, F. (1985). 'La doppia presenza: diffusione di un modello e trasformazioni'. In *Profili Sovrapposti* (ed. F. Bimbi and F. Pristinger), Milan: Franco Angeli.

Blok, A. (1975). *The Mafia of a Sicilian Village: a Study in Violent Peasant Entrepreneurs*, Oxford: Basil Blackwell.

Blok, A. (1981). 'Rams and billy-goats: a key to the Mediterranean code of honour', *Man*, 16(3), 427–40.

Boccella, N. (1987). 'Uno sviluppo eterogeneo'. In *La Società Italiana degli Anni Ottanta* (ed. U. Ascoli and R. Catanzaro), Rome/Bari: Laterza.

Boccella, N. (1989). 'Sussidi e disoccupazione'. In *L'Economia Italiana dal 1945 a Oggi* (ed. A. Graziani), Bologna: il Mulino.

Botta, P., M. Fonte, L. Improta, E. Pugliese and F. Ruggiero (1976). *Ristrutturazione e decentramento produttivo nel settore calzaturiero: il caso di Napoli*. Portici: Centro di Specializzazione e Ricerche Economico-Agrarie per il Mezzogiorno.

Braidotti, R. (ed.) (1994). *Women, the Environment and Sustainable Development: Towards a Theoretical Synthesis*, London: Zed Press.

Brandes, S. (1980). *Metaphors of Masculinity: Sex and Status in Andalusian Folklore*, University of Pennsylvania Press.

Brusco, S. (1975). 'Relazione al Convegno FLM di Bergamo sull'organizzazione del lavoro e decentramento', *Inchiesta*, 17.

Brusco, S. (1982). 'The Emilian model: productive decentralisation and social integration', *Cambridge Journal of Economics*, 2.

Buttafuoco, A. (1993). 'On "mothers" and "sisters": fragments on women/feminism/historiography'. In *The Lonely Mirror. Italian Perspectives on Feminist Theory* (ed. S. Kemp and P. Bono), London and New York: Routledge.

Cafagna, C. (1973). 'Italy 1830–1914'. In *The Emergence of Industrial Societies (I)*, The Fontana History of Europe, London and Glasgow: Collins/Fontana.

Caldwell, L. (1978). 'Church, state and family: the women's movement in Italy'. In *Feminism and Materialism* (ed. A. Kuhn and A.M. Wolpe), London: Routledge and Kegan Paul.

Caldwell, L. (1989). 'Women as the family: the foundation of a new Italy?' In *Woman–Nation–State* (ed. N. Yuval-Davis and F. Anthias), London: Macmillan.

Capecchi, V. (1989). 'The informal economy and the development of flexible specialization in Emilia-Romagna'. In *The Informal Economy: Studies in Advanced and Less Developed Countries* (ed. A. Portes, M. Castells and L.A. Benton), Baltimore and London: Johns Hopkins University Press.

Caracciolo, C. (1973). 'La storia economica'. In *Storia d'Italia*, Vol.3, Turin: Einaudi.

Carocci, G. (1975). *Italian Fascism*, London: Pelican.

Castronovo, C. (1973). 'La storia economica. Dall'Unità ad oggi'. In *Storia d'Italia*, Vol. 4, Turin: Einaudi.

Cavarero, A. (1993). 'Towards a theory of sexual difference'. In *The Lonely Mirror. Italian Perspectives on Feminist Theory* (ed. S. Kemp and P. Bono), London and New York: Routledge.

Centro Studi Federlibro (1974). *Piccola Azienda Grande Sfruttamento*, Fim, Sism-Cisl di Verona, Verona: Bertani.

Chapman, M., M. McDonald and E. Tonkin (1989). 'Introduction – History and Social Anthropology'. In *History and Ethnicity* (ed. E. Tonkin, M. McDonald and M. Chapman), ASA Monographs 27, London: Routledge.

Chodorow, N. (1978). *The Reproduction of Mothering. Psychoanalysis and the Sociology of Gender*, Berkeley, Los Angeles, London: University of California Press.

Chubb, J. (1982). *Patronage, Power and Poverty in Southern Italy*, Cambridge: Cambridge University Press.

Clough, S.B. (1964). *The Economic History of Modern Italy*, New York and London: Columbia.

Collard A. (1989). 'Investigating "Social Memory" in a Greek Context'. In *History and Ethnicity* (ed. E. Tonkin *et al.*), London: Routledge.

Crespi, F. *et al.* (1975). *Lavoro a Domicilio: il Caso dell'Umbria*, Bari: De Donato.

Croce, B. (1944). *Storia del Regno di Napoli*, Bari: Laterza.

Cutrufelli, M.R. (1975). *Disoccupata con Onore. Lavoro e Condizione della Donna*, Milan: Gabriele Mazzotta.

Cutrufelli, M.R. (1977). *Operaie senza Fabbrica*, Rome: Editori Riuniti.

D'Antonio, M. (1973). *Sviluppo e Crisi del Capitalismo Italiano 1951–1972*, Rome: De Donato.

Davis, J. (1973). *Land and Family in Pisticci*, London: Athlone Press.

Davis, J. (1977). *People of the Mediterranean: An Essay in Comparative Social Anthropology*, London: Routledge and Kegan Paul.

De Cecco, M. (1972). 'Una interpretazione ricardiana della forza lavoro in Italia nel decennio 1959–1968', *Note Economiche*, 1.

De Marco, C. and M. Talamo (1976). *Lavoro Nero, Decentramento Produttivo e Lavoro a Domicilio*, Milan: Mazzotta.

De Martino, E. (1949). 'Intorno a una storia del mondo popolare subalterno'. Reproduced in *Cultura Popolare e Marxismo* (1976, ed. R. Rauty), Rome: Editori Riuniti.

De Matteis, S. (1991). *Lo Specchio della Vita. Napoli: Antropologia della Città del Teatro*, Bologna: il Mulino.

De Meo, G. (1970). *Evoluzione e Prospettive della Forza Lavoro in Italia*, Milan: De Angeli.

Donolo, C. (1972). 'Sviluppo ineguale e disgregazione sociale in Meridione', *Quaderni Piacentini*, **47**.

Douglas, M. (1966). *Purity and Danger*, London: Routledge and Kegan Paul.

Elson, D. and R. Pearson (1981). 'The subordination of women and the internationalisation of factory production'. In *Of Marriage and the Market*, (ed. K. Young, C. Wolkowitz and R. McCullagh), London: CSE Books.

Elson, D. and R. Pearson (eds.) (1988). *Women's Employment and Multinationals in Europe*, Basingstoke: Macmillan.

Esposito, L. and P. Persico (1978). *Artigianato e Lavoro a Domicilio in Campania*, Milan: Franco Angeli.

Feagin, M.P. and J.R. Smith (1987). *The Capitalist City: Global Restructuring and Community Politics*, Oxford: Basil Blackwell.

Foster, G. (1965). 'Peasant society and the image of limited good', *American Anthropologist*, **67**: 293–315.

Francesconi, J.C. (1977). *La Cucina Napoletana*, Naples: Edizioni del Delfino.

Freud, S. (1930). *Civilization and its Discontents*, London: Hogarth.

Frey, L. (1973). 'Dal lavoro a domicilio al decentramento dell'attività produttiva', *Quaderni di Rassegna Sindacale*, Anno XI:44–5.

Frey, L., R. Livraghi, G. Mottura and M. Salvati (1976). *Occupazione e Sottoccupazione Femminile in Italia*, Milan: Franco Angeli.

Galasso, G. (1978). *Intervista sulla Storia di Napoli*, Bari: Laterza.

Geertz, C. (1963). *Peddlers and Princes: Social Development and Economic Change in two Indonesian Towns*, Chicago: University of Chicago Press.

Geremicca, A. (1977). *Dentro la Città. Napoli Angoscia e Speranza*, Naples: Guida.

Germani, G. (1962). *Política y Sociedad en una Epoca de Transición*, Buenos Aires: Editorial Paidós.

Giannola, A. (1972). 'La nuova industria nel Mezzogiorno'. In *L'Economia Italiana dal 1945 a Oggi* (ed. A. Graziani), Bologna: il Mulino.

Giannola, A. (ed.) (n.d.). *L'Economia ed il Mezzogiorno*, Milan: Franco Angeli.

Gilmore, D. (1990). *Manhood in the Making. Cultural Concepts of Masculinity*, New Haven and London: Yale University Press.

Gilsenan, M. (1989). 'Word of honour'. In *Social Anthropology and the Politics of Language* (ed. R. Grillo), London: Routledge.

Ginsborg, P. (1990). *A History of Contemporary Italy. Society and Politics 1943–1988*, London: Penguin.

Giovannini, M. (1981). 'Woman: a dominant symbol within the cultural system of a Sicilian town', *Man*, **16**, 409–26.

Goody, J. and S. Tambiah (1973). *Bridewealth and Dowry*, Cambridge: Cambridge University Press.

Gramsci, A. (1973). *The Prison Notebooks*, London: Lawrence and

Wishart.

Graziani, A. (ed.) (1989). *L'Economia Italiana dal 1945 a Oggi*, Bologna: il Mulino.

Graziani, A. (n.d.). 'Il Mezzogiorno e l'economia Italiana'. In *L'Economia e il Mezzogiorno* (ed. A. Giannola), Milan: Franco Angeli.

Gribaudi, G. (1980). *Mediatori. Antropologia del Potere Democristiano nel Mezzogiorno*, Turin: Rosenberg and Sellier.

Hadjimichalis, C. and D. Vaiou (1990). 'Whose flexibility? The politics of informalization in Southern Europe'. In *Capital and Class*, 42.

Harris, O. (1981). 'Households as natural units'. In *Of Marriage and the Market* (ed. K. Young, C. Wolkovitz and R. McCullagh), London: CSE Books.

Hart, K. (1973). 'Informal income opportunities and urban employment in Ghana', *Journal of Modern African Studies*, 2.

Harvey, D. (1989). *The Condition of Postmodernity. An Enquiry into the Origins of Cultural Change*, Cambridge, Mass. and Oxford: Blackwell.

Herzfeld, M. (1985). *The Poetics of Manhood. Contest and Identity in a Cretan Mountain Village*, Princeton: Princeton University Press.

Herzfeld, M. (1987). '"As in your own house": hospitality, ethnography, and the stereotype of Mediterranean Society'. In *Honor and Shame and the Unity of the Mediterranean* (ed. D. Gilmore), Washington: Special Publication of the American Anthropological Association No. 22, 75–89.

Hirschon, R. (1978). 'Open body/closed space: the transformation of female sexuality'. In *Defining Females* (ed. S. Ardener), London: Croom Helm.

Hirst, P. and P. Woolley (1982). *Social Relations and Human Attributes*, London and New York: Tavistock.

Horkheimer, M. (1936). 'Authority and the family'. In *Critical Theory*, New York: Herder and Herder, 1972.

IDS (1981). 'Women and the Informal Sector' (ed. K. Young and C. Moser), *Bulletin of the Institute of Development Studies*, July, 12 (3).

Imbruglia, R. (n.d.). 'Divari territoriali nell'economia meridionale'. In *L'Economia ed il Mezzogiorno* (ed. A. Giannola), Milano: Franco Angeli.

Irigaray, L. (1977). *Ce Sexe qui n'en est pas un*, Paris: les Editions de Minuit.

Kahn, J. (1980). *Minangkabau Social Formations: Indonesian Peasants and the World Economy*, Cambridge: Cambridge University Press.

Kandiyoti, D. (1989). 'Women and the Turkish State: political actors or symbolic pawns?' In *Woman–Nation–State* (ed. N. Yuval-Davis and F. Anthias), London: Macmillan.

Kemp, S. and P. Bono (eds) (1993). *The Lonely Mirror. Italian Perspectives on Feminist Theory*, London and New York: Routledge.

Kenny, M. (1963). 'Europe: the Atlantic fringe', *Anthropological*

Quarterly, **36**(3), 100–19.
Kenny, M. and D. Kertzer (eds) (1983). *Urban Life in Mediterranean Europe*,Urbana, Ill.: University of Illinois Press.
Kertzer, D.I. and R. P. Saller (1991). *The Family in Italy from Antiquity to the Present*, New Haven: Yale University Press.
La Malfa, G. and S. Vinci (1970). 'Il saggio di partecipazione della forza-lavoro in Italia', *L'Industria*, October–December.
Lash, S. and J. Urry (1987). *The End of Organized Capitalism*, Cambridge: Polity Press.
Levi, C. (1982). *Christ Stopped at Eboli*, transl. F. Frenaye, Bungay, Suffolk: Penguin.
Lewis, O. (1968). *La Vida: a Puerto Rican Family in the Culture of Poverty – San Juan and New York*, New York: Random House.
Livraghi, R. (1976). 'Differenziali salariali, flessibilità del lavoro e occupazione femminile'. In *Occupazione e Sottoccupazione in Italia* (ed. L. Frey, R. Livraghi, G. Mottura and M. Salvati), Milan: Franco Angeli.
Loizos, P. (1975). *The Greek Gift: Politics in a Cyprus Village*, Oxford: Basil Blackwell.
Lutz, V. (1962). *Italy: A Study in Economic Development*, London: Oxford University Press.
Macciocchi, M.A. (1973). *Letters from within the Communist Party*, London: New Left Books.
Macciocchi, M.A. (1974). *Per Gramsci*, Bologna: il Mulino.
Mandel, E. (1975). *Late Capitalism*, London: New Left Books.
Marcuse, H. (1969). *Eros and Civilization*, London: Sphere Books [1955].
Martinez-Alier, V. (1972). 'Elopement and seduction in 19th century Cuba', *Past and Present*, **55**.
May, M. (1977). 'Il mercato del lavoro femminile in Italia', *Inchiesta*, **25**.
Mingione, E. (1983). 'Informalization, restructuring and the survival strategies of the working class', *International Journal of Urban and Regional Research*, **7**(3).
Mingione, E. (1985). 'Social Reproduction of the Surplus Labour Force: the Case of Southern Italy'. In *Beyond Employment* (ed. N. Redclift and E. Mingione), Oxford: Blackwell.
Mitter, S. (1994). *Dignity and Daily Bread: New Forms of Economic Organising among Poor Women in the Third World and the First*, London: Routledge.
Montefoschi, S. (1993). 'Maternal role and personal identity: on the women's movement and psychoanalysis'. In *The Lonely Mirror. Italian Perspectives on Feminist Theory* (ed. S. Kemp and P. Bono), London and New York: Routledge.
Morris, B. (1985). 'The rise and fall of the human subject', *Man*, **20**, 722–42.

Moser, C. (1978). 'Informal sector or petty commodity production: dualism or dependence in urban development', *World Development*, **6**, 1041–61.

Mottura, S. (1973). 'Le classi sociali nel Sud'. In *Mezzogiorno e Classe Operaia* (ed. various), Rome.

Nanetti, R.Y. (1988). *Growth and Territorial Policies: the Italian Model of Social Capitalism*, London and New York: Pinter.

O'Brien, O. (1994). 'Ethnic identity, gender and life cycle in north Catalonia'. In *The Anthropology of Europe. Identity and Boundaries in Conflict* (ed. V. Goddard, C. Shore and J.R. Llobera), Oxford and Providence, Rhode Island: Berg.

Offe, C. (1985). *Disorganized Capitalism*, Cambridge: Polity.

Paci, M. (1973). *Mercato del Lavoro e Classi Sociali in Italia*, Bologna: il Mulino.

Paci, M. (1976). 'Crisi, ristrutturazione e piccola impresa', *Inchiesta*, **20**.

Paci, M. (ed.) (1980). *Famiglia e Mercato del Lavoro in una Economia Periferica*, Milan: Franco Angeli.

Paci, M. (1982). *La Struttura Sociale Italiana*, Universale Paperbacks, Bologna: il Mulino.

Padoa-Schioppa, F. (1977). *La Forza Lavoro Femminile*, Universale Paperbacks, Bologna: il Mulino.

Pahl, R.E. (1984). *Divisions of Labour*, Oxford: Basil Blackwell.

Pardo, I. (1989). 'Life, death and ambiguity in the social dynamics of inner-Naples', *Man*, **24**, 103–23.

Pardo, I. (1992). '"Living" the house, "feeling" the house: Neapolitan issues in thought, organization and structure', *European Journal of Sociology*, **33**, 251–79.

Pardo, I. (1993). 'Socialist visions, Naples and the Neapolitans: value, control and representation in the agency/structure relationship', *Journal of Mediterranean Studies*, **3**(1),77–98.

Parsons, A. (1967). Is the Oedipus complex universal? A South Italian "nuclear complex". In *Personalities and Culture* (ed. R. Hunt), Austin: Texas University Press.

Parsons, T. (1964). *Social Structure and Personality*, London: Free Press of Glencoe.

Passerini, L. (1994). 'The interpretation of democracy in the Italian women's movement of the 1970s and 1980s', *Women's Studies International Forum*, **17**(2/3), 235–40.

Perlman, J.E. (1976). *The Myth of Marginality*, Berkeley, Los Angeles, London: University of California Press.

Piore, M. and C. Sabel. (1984). *The Second Industrial Divide*, New York: Basic Books.

Piselli, F. (1975). *La Donna che Lavora. La Condizione Femminile fra Arretratezza e Società Industriale*, Bari: De Donato.

Piselli, F. (1987). 'Famiglia e parentela nel Mezzogiorno'. In *La Società Italiana degli Anni Ottanta* (ed. U. Ascoli and R. Catanzaro), Rome/Bari: Laterza.

Pitkin, D.S. (1963). 'Mediterranean Europe', *Anthropological Quarterly*, 36(3), 120–9.

Pitkin, D.S. (1985). *The House that Giacomo Built: History of an Italian Family, 1898–1978*, Cambridge: Cambridge University Press.

Pitt-Rivers J. (1974). 'Honour and social status'. In *Honour and Shame. The Values of Mediterranean Society* (ed. J. Peristiany), Chicago: University of Chicago Press.

Pratt, J. (1980). 'A Sense of Place'. In *'Nation' and 'State' in Europe: Anthropological Perspectives* (ed. R. Grillo), London: Academic Press.

Procacci, G. (1968). *History of the Italian People*, London: Penguin.

Pugliese, E. (1993). *Sociologia della Disoccupazione*, Bologna: il Mulino.

Pugliese, E. and G. Pinnarò (1985). 'Informalization and social resistance: the case of Naples'. In *Beyond Employment* (ed. N. Redclift and E. Mingione), Oxford: Blackwell.

Quijano, A. (1974). The marginal pole of the economy and the marginalized labour-force. *Economy and Society*, 3 (4).

Roberts, B. (1978). *Cities of Peasants*, London: Edward Arnold.

Romeo, R. (1961). *Breve Storia della Grande Industria in Italia*, Turin: Einaudi.

Sales, I. (1993). *La Camorra Le Camorre*, Rome: Editori Riuniti.

Saraceno, C. (1976). *Anatomia della Famiglia*, Bari: De Donato.

Schneider, J. (1971). 'Of vigilance and virgins: honor, shame and access to resources in Mediterranean societies', *Ethnology* 10 (1), 1–24.

Schneider, J. and P. Schneider (1976). *Culture and Political Economy in Western Sicily*, New York: Academic Press.

Serao, M. (1988). *Il Ventre di Napoli*, Naples: Adriano Gallina Editore.

Seroni, A. (1977). *La Questione Femminile in Italia, 1970–1977*, (ed. E. Rava), Rome: Editori Riuniti.

Silverblatt, I. (1981). '" The universe has turned inside out . . . There is no justice for us here." Andean women under Spanish rule.' In *Women and Colonization* (ed. M. Etienne and E. Leacock), New York: Praeger.

Silverman, S. (1955). *Three Bells of Civilization: the Life of an Italian Hill Town*, New York: Columbia University Press.

Silverman, S. (1975). 'The life crisis as a clue to social function: the case of Italy'. In *Toward an Anthropology of Women* (ed. R. Reiter), New York and London: MRP.

Stivens, M. (1978). 'Women and their kin'. In *Women United, Women Divided* (ed. P. Caplan and J. Bujra), London: Tavistock.

Tentori, T. (1976). 'Social classes and family in Matera'. In *Mediterranean Family Structures* (ed. J.G. Peristiany), London: Cambridge University Press.

Todd, E. (1985). *The Explanation of Ideology. Family Structures and Social Systems*, Oxford: Blackwell.

Togliatti, P. (1973). *L'emancipazione Femminile*, Rome: Editori Riuniti.

Tonkin, E., M. McDonald and M. Chapman (1989). *History and Ethnicity*, London and New York: Routledge.

Trigilia, C. (1987). 'La regolazione localistica: economia e politica nelle aree di piccola impresa.' In *La Società Italiana degli Anni Ottanta* (ed. U. Ascoli and R. Catanzaro), Rome/Bari: Laterza.

Vicarelli, G. (1987). 'Famiglia e sviluppo economico nell'Italia centro-settentrionale.' In *La Società Italiana degli Anni Ottanta* (ed. U. Ascoli and R. Catanzaro), Rome/Bari: Laterza.

Wikan, U. (1984). 'Shame and honour: a contestable pair', *Man*, **29**, 635–52.

Yalman, N. (1967). *Under the Bo Tree: Studies in Caste, Kinship and Marriage in the Interior of Ceylon*, Berkeley, Los Angeles: University of California Press.

Yuval-Davis, N. and F. Anthias (eds) (1989). *Woman–Nation–State*, London: Macmillan.

Zonabend, F. (1984). *The Enduring Memory. Time and History in a French Village*, Manchester: Manchester University Press.

Index

De Martino, E. 9
De Matteis, S. 205
De Meo, G. 10
decentralization, of production
    35–41, 81
    and women 38
    of local government 41
deindustrialization 37, 39, 49
democracy 58 *passim*
di San Marzano, Cristiana
    181n5
Di Donato 61
Di Vincenzo 234
Di Vittorio 32
Di Lorenzo 61
Dini, L. 62
disoccupati organizzati 95, 113,
    234; *see* organized
    unemployed
divorce 153, law 168–9
Donolo, C. *borghesia dello*
    sottosviluppo 67
Dorso, Guido 231n13
dote (dowry) 103, 130
Douglas, Mary, 16, 222
Duchy of Milan 24
Durkheim, E. 183

earthquake 60, 233
economic dualism 30
economic miracle 34, 35
education, 172–4
EEC 4, 33, 34, 41
Einaudi 31
emigration 25, 34
    transoceanic 26
    migrants' remittances 25
Emilia-Romagna 41
    Emilian model 42, 43
ENI 31
enterprise 97 *passim*
    and family 237;
        entrepreneurial families 13
    entrepreneurial camorra 61
    entrepreneurial spirit 128

micro-enterprise 139, 142n3
mushroom 44, 76; phantom
    44
small 5, 11, 14, 35, 38, 41, 42,
    43, 76, 120 *passim*, 234
    passim, 238
entrepreneur, 129 *passim*
    138, petty 136; in South 44;
    in small firms 37, 238,
    political patronage 33
entrepreneurship, petty 17,
    41
Esposito and Persico 111
ethnicity, work on 16
Europe, unification 167, 169,
    220
    impact of unification 233
European markets 34
European Monetary System 36
European Community 34, 236
European Common Market 33

factories 97 *passim* factories,
    mushroom factories 76
    women workers 172, 176
    workers 135 *passim*
familism 18, 164 *passim*, 180,
    227
    amoral familism, 163
family 11–8, 206
    enterprise: 12–3, 237;
        distribution 19
    labour 93 *passim*
    Ministry for the Family 167
    solidarity, strategies 163
        passim
Fanfani Plan 31
fasci, Sicilian 24, 45
Fascism 12–3, 24, 27 *passim*, 54
    passim
    and corporativism 28
    squads 28, *squadrismo* 5
    views on gender 168
Fascist government,
    interventions 167